ADVANCE PRAISE FOR *STATELET OF SURVIVORS*

"For almost a decade, Washington has battled the extremist Islamic State along with Syrian Kurds. Holmes, through her on the ground meticulous research, sheds a unique light on the complex history, organization and successes of this hitherto misconstrued 'nation.' She brings to life the women and men who have sacrificed to protect, against all odds, a diverse set of populations and themselves from powerful states and terror groups. This is a must-read guide to them."
—Henri J. Barkey, Cohen Professor of International Relations, Lehigh University, and adjunct senior fellow for Middle East studies, Council of Foreign Relations.

"In this fascinating and timely book, Amy Austin Holmes puts a different spin on the Kurdish-led social experiment in north and east Syria. Insightful and provocative, the book highlights a secular/democratic alternative that carries the potential to counter the rising tide of religious movements in the Middle East."
—Mehmet Gurses, Professor of Political Science, Florida Atlantic University

"In this book, Amy Austin Holmes combines the keen gaze of an academic with the very relatable first-person narrative of a travel writer. Anyone who ever wanted to see past the headlines and better understand what has really been happening in northeast Syria since 2011 should read this. Dr Holmes has crisscrossed the region back and forth during the past decade, speaking extensively with and surveying Kurds, Arabs, Christians, Yezidis, Turkmen and the leadership of a wide array of autonomous bodies in northeast Syria. Whether layperson or expert on the region, no one will be able to put this book down without having learned a good deal they did not know before."
—David Romano, Thomas G. Strong Professor of Middle East Politics, Missouri State University

Statelet of Survivors

Statelet of Survivors

The Making of a Semi-Autonomous Region in Northeast Syria

AMY AUSTIN HOLMES

OXFORD
UNIVERSITY PRESS

OXFORD
UNIVERSITY PRESS

Oxford University Press is a department of the University of Oxford. It furthers
the University's objective of excellence in research, scholarship, and education
by publishing worldwide. Oxford is a registered trade mark of Oxford University
Press in the UK and certain other countries.

Published in the United States of America by Oxford University Press
198 Madison Avenue, New York, NY 10016, United States of America.

Library of Congress Cataloging-in-Publication Data
Names: Holmes, Amy Austin, 1973– author.
Title: Statelet of survivors : the making of a semi-autonomous region
in Northeast Syria / Amy Austin Holmes.
Description: [New York] : Oxford University Press, [2024]. |
Includes bibliographical references and index. |
Contents: Statelet of Survivors—A Genealogy of Rojava: Kurds and Armenians declare
the Republic of Mount Ararat 1926–1932—The SDF: The evolution of the YPG into
Syria's second largest armed force—Life Under ISIS: A War of Women Against
Women—The Women's Revolution in Rojava and Beyond—Delinking from Damascus:
The Economic Underpinnings of Political Autonomy—The School of Revolution:
The Autonomous Administration creates a new Education System—Yezidis and the
Statelet of Survivors: Recognition, Representation, Religious Freedom, and Protection.
Identifiers: LCCN 2023006283 (print) | LCCN 2023006284 (ebook) |
ISBN 9780197621042 (paperback) | ISBN 9780197621035 (hardback) |
ISBN 9780197621066 (epub) | ISBN 9780197621073
Subjects: LCSH: Autonomous Administration of North and East Syria (Syria)—History. |
Syria—Politics and government—2000– | Autonomous Administration
of North and East Syria—History.
Classification: LCC DS99.A43 H65 2023 (print) | LCC DS99.A43 (ebook) |
DDC 956.9104/23—dc23/eng/20230322
LC record available at https://lccn.loc.gov/2023006283
LC ebook record available at https://lccn.loc.gov/2023006284

DOI: 10.1093/oso/9780197621035.001.0001

Paperback printed by Marquis Book Printing, Canada
Hardback printed by Bridgeport National Bindery, Inc., United States of America

To the survivors, and those who gave their lives to defend them

ܠܘܡܐ ܕܦܠܝܛ ܠܘܡܐ ܣܝܡܝ ܗ ܡܝܢ ܠܘܡܝܐ ܦܠܠܝܟ̈ܐ
ܗܝ̈ܝܠܐ ܟܗܐ ܠܘܐ

Dîyarî rizgarbûyîyan û ewên ku ji bo berevanîya di ber wan de xwe
kirin qurban

Ձօն՝ վերապրողներուն, եւ անոնց պահապան կանգնելու ի
խնդիր իրենց կեանքը զոհողներուն

مهداة إلى الناجين وإلى أولئك الذين ضحوا بحياتهم للدفاع عنهم

CONTENTS

ACKNOWLEDGMENTS

Conducting research in an active conflict zone is never easy, especially one that features the Islamic State, Russia, Iran, the Syrian regime, Turkish proxies, and no shortage of other nonstate actors. But this book was also difficult to write because my own life took an unexpected turn. When I began fieldwork in 2015, I had just been tenured and promoted to Associate Professor of Sociology at the American University in Cairo. As the first woman in my extended family to have received a PhD, it was an accomplishment I had spent my entire adult life working to achieve. Instead of being able to enjoy the exceedingly rare privilege of job security and academic freedom that comes with tenure, I found myself having to resign from my position because Egypt became increasingly repressive and AUC's commitment to academic freedom was more rhetorical than real. By the time I finished this book some eight years later, I had lost the salary, pension, health insurance (during the pandemic), and job security of tenure. I often thought I would never finish this book. Without the support of friends and family, I never would have.

I thank my parents, Ann and Bert Holmes, for their unwavering support—even though they were not keen on me traveling repeatedly to Syria. My maternal grandmother was one of 13 children and received an eighth-grade education. Six of her siblings and both parents died of unclean water in rural Pennsylvania. She married a carpenter and World War II veteran, Austin Reber. My mother dreamed of becoming an architect, but was discouraged from pursuing what was considered a male profession. Instead, she became a self-taught artist whose stained glass and quilts have been displayed across the country. My father was born to a family of small farmers living under the poverty line. They lost the little they had when their farmhouse burned to the ground, and the local fire department would not help because they lived in the countryside. He went on to become a chemistry professor whose research was supported by grants from the National Science Foundation for 27 consecutive years. My parents' journey taught me to persevere.

I would like to thank the more than 400 women and men in the Syrian Democratic Forces who took my survey while they were putting their own life on the line to defeat the Islamic State. Between 2015 and 2023 I conducted over 120 interviews in Syria. I am indebted to the many people across North and East Syria who took time to meet with me: in Kobani, Derik, Qamishlo, Hasakah, Tel Tamer, Ain Issa, Manbij, Raqqa, Tabqa, Deir Ezzor, Shaddadi, Rumaylan, the Al Hol and Al Roj camps, and many small villages off the grid.

I owe thanks to many people and institutions for their support, in particular: Ambassador Mark Green at the Woodrow Wilson International Center for Scholars, Tarek Masoud at Harvard University's Middle East Initiative, Melani Cammett at Harvard University's Weatherhead Center, Steven Cook at the Council on Foreign Relations, and Charlie Glaser and Alex Downes at George Washington University's Institute for Security and Conflict Studies. I thank the many universities and institutions that invited me to present the research that went into this book, in particular: the US Commission on International Religious Freedom (USCIRF) for inviting me to provide official testimony about the situation in Northeast Syria, and the Washington Kurdish Institute, for asking me to speak at a bipartisan event on Capitol Hill alongside Senators Chris Van Hollen, Marsha Blackburn, and Mark Warner.

In the spring of 2020, I was awarded an International Affairs Fellowship from the Council on Foreign Relations (CFR), a program that allows scholars to share their expertise and serve in government. During the CFR fellowship I was seconded to two different offices at the State Department: first I worked in the Bureau of Conflict and Stabilization Operations (CSO) on the Syria/Iraq team, and then in the Office of Southern European Affairs (EUR/SE) on the Turkey Desk. Although I had already submitted the final manuscript to Oxford University Press prior to beginning to work at the State Department, I delayed publication so that the book would not be published while I was in government. The views expressed in this manuscript are solely my own, and do not necessarily represent those of the US government or any other institution.

Earlier in my life, I was an exchange student at a high school in Germany and later returned to study for my MA degree at the *Freie Universität* (FU) Berlin. During those years, I visited former concentration camps in Germany, Poland, the Czech Republic, and Belarus. One of the courses I took at the FU Berlin was about the Nazi occupation of Eastern Europe during World War II, and as part of that class we traveled to Belarus and conducted archival research in the National Archives in Minsk. As a young student in Germany studying the Holocaust, I was taught that the world had pledged *nie wieder*: to never again allow such atrocities to unfold.

By January 2015, the Islamic State had committed a genocide, set up slave markets for women and children, and seized control of territory in Iraq and Syria about the size of Great Britain. My friend Johanneke suggested we travel from Cairo to deliver aid we collected from friends to refugee and IDP camps in Turkey and the Kurdistan Region of Iraq, and I agreed. Standing on the roof of a building with a view of Kobani, I saw smoke billowing into the sky as the battle raged on the ground, and how Kurds were mobilizing on both sides of the border. It was the beginning of the US partnership with the YPG/YPJ in Syria. In the summer of 2016, I visited Sinjar, Iraq: the ancestral homeland of Yezidis and epicenter of the genocide. I wanted to understand why women and men decided to take up arms: forming the YPG/YPJ in Syria and the YBS/YJS in Sinjar, Iraq. I thought at the time that it was a small side project. I soon came to realize the global nature of problem: jihadists from more than 50 countries came to Syria to join the Islamic State. Most of them crossed into Syria via Turkey. Similarly, I came to realize that Turkey's attempts to undermine the Autonomous Administration of North and East Syria (AANES) had to be placed in a larger historical context of Turkish efforts to suppress Kurdish and Armenian demands for autonomy dating back a century. This led me to include a chapter on the Ararat Rebellion. I am grateful to Khatchig Mouradian and the Institut Kurde de Paris for helping to locate archival documents.

My heartfelt thanks are extended to many friends and colleagues: Johanneke van den Bos, Diween Hawezy, Pari Ibrahim, Lerna Ekmekcioglu, Murad Ismael, Metin Yuksel, Liesel Hintz, Khogir Wirya, Yousif Ismael, Meghan Bodette, Anne Speckhard, Dlshad and Bayan Othman, Nicholas Heras, Wladimir van Wilgenburg, Colonel Myles Caggins, and the Rojava Information Center. I am very grateful to Lukman Ahmad, a Kurdish American artist from Syria, for allowing me to use his evocative artwork on the cover. For their assistance and hospitality in Syria I would like to thank Amjad Othman and his family, Khabat Abbas, Hisham Arafat, and many others. Finally, I thank my brother Doug and his wife Kimberly, and my nieces and nephews: Rebekah, Katie, Eli, Beth, and Josiah, for always insisting I should stop working and read them stories. May the world's commitment to "never again" finally be realized in their lifetime.

1

Statelet of Survivors

Any war that is here will be the end of our people. Maybe Kurds or Arabs will survive, but not the Christians.
—Sanharib Barsoom, Head of the Syriac Union Party[1]

The Syrian army is not a national army. Its purpose is to serve the Baathist regime.
—Nisrine Abdullah, founding member of the YXG and YPJ[2]

Underground tunnels, remnants of concentration camps, and abandoned churches are all part of the geography of the Syrian-Turkish border. They are monuments to a past and present marked by escape and survival—themes that run through the history of borderland peoples. It was the survivalist instincts of fugitives seeking refuge, perhaps even more so than nationalism, that have animated attempts to carve out autonomous enclaves from those who sought to annihilate them. In a geography stained by genocide and buffeted by Turkish, Arab, and Persian nationalisms, smaller bands of minorities unable or unwilling to assimilate, have at times forged another kind of politics. Based not on a common ethnicity or language or religion—they were bound together instead by the shared desire to secure their continued existence.

These survivalist instincts are as much at the core of the Mount Ararat Republic, proclaimed in the aftermath of the Armenian genocide, as they are at the heart of the Rojava Revolution which unfolded against the backdrop of atrocities committed by the Islamic State and Assad regime. The quotes from conversations I had with YPJ commander Nisrine Abdullah and Sanharib Barsoom, Head of the Syriac Union Party, embody these instincts.

In an unexpected twist of history, those who were once considered undesirable by the Ottoman Empire and early Turkish Republic—in particular Kurds and Christians—now form the core of an alliance that governs about one-third of Syria. This book tells the story of how they created this semi-autonomous region, and the genealogy of their subterranean solidarity that dates back a century.

Statelet of Survivors. Amy Austin Holmes, Oxford University Press. © Oxford University Press 2024.
DOI: 10.1093/oso/9780197621035.003.0001

Faced with an onslaught by the Islamic State and other extremists, Kurds in the YPG/YPJ joined forces with Christians in the Syriac Military Council and Arabs in the Sanadeed Forces, even before the United States had entered the fray. Within a few years, their rag-tag militia that initially did not even have uniforms evolved into a multiethnic, multireligious force in which the diverse peoples of the region were represented: Arabs from every tribe, Assyrians, Armenians, Yezidis, Circassians, Syrian Turkmen, and Kurds joined the Syrian Democratic Forces (SDF), fighting side-by-side to defend their land and defeat the Caliphate. One grueling battle at a time, the SDF expanded far beyond the Kurdish heartland known as Rojava into Arab-majority population centers. By the time the Islamic State was vanquished in March 2019, over 11,000 young SDF fighters laid buried in cemeteries.

But their triumph over ISIS is only half the story.

In defiance of the Assad regime, the Islamic State, and Turkey, the peoples of Northeast Syria created a de facto state. While the SDF's battle against ISIS was supported by the Global Coalition against Daesh, including some 85 member countries and partners, the statelet they created is recognized by none of them.

This paradox is worth unpacking. The international community recognizes the accomplishments of the SDF on the battlefield—and by "international community" I am not merely referring to "the West," but rather those 85 countries and organizations around the world that are part of the Global Coalition. They also recognize the SDF's critical role in detaining, feeding, and housing some 50,000 people affiliated with ISIS from over 50 different countries around the world. In fact, many countries appear to prefer the SDF to bear this heavy burden indefinitely as they refuse to repatriate their own citizens who joined ISIS, or even the children whose only crime was to have been born to parents of ISIS members. The international community expects a non-state actor (the SDF) to run statelike institutions (prisons, detention facilities, and camps for displaced people) in accordance with international standards, as if it was a state. Yet they refuse to give them any political recognition whatsoever, or even to acknowledge the existence of the local governance structures they created—in part out of the necessity of housing the international community's ISIS militants. The reasons for this hypocrisy are manifold, and will be addressed in the following chapters. To justify its duplicity, the international community appears intent on either ignoring the existence of the upstart statelet, or upholding the fiction that the SDF is wholly unrelated to its civilian counterparts. In reality, the political and military institutions of the Autonomous Administration grew together organically.

In 2012, the forces of Bashar al-Assad withdrew from the north of Syria to turn their guns on rebels in the south. Into the vacuum stepped the Syrian offshoot of the PKK. As the anti-Assad protests in Damascus and elsewhere descended into a brutal civil war, which the international community dubbed the "Arab Spring," the Kurds in the north set up a rudimentary self-administration in three cantons: Afrin, Kobani, and Jazira. They were surrounded by enemies. The cantons that declared self-rule were not even connected to each other. Their chances of survival were slim. Then the Islamic State took over large chunks of Syria. While ISIS carried out beheadings on the main square of Raqqa, the Kurds audaciously promoted women into the most powerful positions of their Autonomous Administration. These women were the vanguard of a new kind of social experiment: the "Rojava Revolution." Instead of demanding the fall of Assad's regime, they wanted *autonomy* from the regime. Eight years later, they controlled one-third of Syria and two-thirds of its resources.

They then had to govern it. The state-like entity they created has changed names over the years, and is now known as the Autonomous Administration of North and East Syria (AANES). Their experiment in self-rule is more inclusive, and does more to give real power to women and minorities, than any other region of Syria.

Fractured by a decade of war, Syria is currently divided into four zones of control: the Assad regime, whose family has now ruled the country for half a century and still maintains a grip over the southern and western parts of Syria; the US-backed SDF, who holds the ground in the northern and eastern regions; Turkey and its proxies, who have carved out a swath of territory along the border; and an assortment of rebel and jihadist groups who control Idlib. Each of these four zones manifest divergent forms of governance. Bashar al-Assad, having inherited the presidential palace from his father, Hafez al-Assad, showed little interest in making even nominal concessions to the citizenry who rose up to demand democracy and human rights starting in the spring of 2011. After Russia and Iran stepped in to support him in 2015, his willingness to compromise was diminished even further. Assad now claims to have won the war, although he only controls about 60 percent of the country.

The cadres leading the Autonomous Administration claim they are not a Kurdish separatist movement. Between 2015 and 2021, I traveled to all of the regions of North and East Syria under SDF control to conduct the first ever field survey of the SDF. I wanted to understand who they really were, why they joined the SDF, what they were fighting for, and their vision for the future. My survey of over 400 rank-and-file SDF members illustrates that they, too, like their leaders, do not seek secession. Results from both 2015 and 2020 reveal that an overwhelming majority—96 percent of respondents by 2020—say they want to remain part of Syria. Even as they grew more powerful and controlled more territory, they did not fundamentally change their desire to remain part of a united Syria. Rather, they see the Autonomous Administration as a model of decentralized government that could even extend to other parts of Syria, post-Assad. It is still a work-in-progress.

Many observers have traced the origins of this movement to the founding of the Kurdistan Workers' Party (PKK) in the late 1970s that has fought an insurgency against Turkey for decades. While powerful, the PKK is only one actor to have emerged on the historical stage, and did so relatively recently. One doesn't have to adopt a longue durée perspective to recognize a simple fact: the PKK represents a contemporary iteration of a multifaceted conflict that dates back at least a century. Many of the analyses of Rojava that begin with the PKK, or describe it simply as a Kurdish movement in a Kurdish region, are ultimately ahistorical, or too narrowly focused to truly grasp both the past and present complexity of this semi-autonomous region in Northeast Syria.

To find the origins of Rojava one must begin at the time of the Armenian-Assyrian genocide and other Ottoman-era pogroms, when Kurds and Christians were faced with either annihilation or assimilation. In an attempt to secure the continued existence of their peoples, Kurds and Armenian genocide survivors forged an official alliance and created a semi-autonomous region on Mount Ararat in eastern Anatolia, on the borderlands of modern-day Turkey and Armenia.

Both the Republic of Mount Ararat and the Autonomous Administration, separated by almost a century, were based not on a common ethnicity or language or religion—but rather on the idea of equality between people of different religious and ethnic backgrounds—and on a common desire to secure their continued existence.

I contend that both Mount Ararat and the Autonomous Administration are best understood as statelets of survivors.

The ideology espoused by the Autonomous Administration is inspired by the writings of Abdullah Öcalan. Fleeing persecution in Turkey, the leader of the PKK spent some 20 years in Syria. During this time, he cultivated ties to the Syrian regime and a number of leading Arab figures, in addition to the Kurdish minority. Although often described as a separatist movement, already in 1993 Öcalan held a press conference in Bar Elias, Lebanon, where he declared a ceasefire, stating, "We are not demanding an immediate separation from Turkey. We are realistic about this subject." He went on to describe how separation could not take place because Kurds and Turks "are like flesh and bone."[3]

After being forced to leave Syria and subsequently captured and imprisoned in a maximum-security prison on the Turkish island of Imrali, he turned to writing. Inspired by an eclectic assortment of scholars, ranging from Murray Bookchin to Immanuel Wallerstein, the ideology that emerged has been referred to as "democratic confederalism." The goal of an independent Kurdish state was rejected not merely for being unrealistic, but because nation-states were seen as part of the problem that led to the subjugation of Kurds in the first place, along with women and other minorities, and therefore to be avoided. Instead of an independent Kurdistan, he urged the Kurdish movement to work toward attaining a stateless democracy. The political entity he envisioned was to be premised on secularism and full equality between all peoples, regardless of gender, religious, or ethnic identity.

However, ideology alone cannot explain the motivation of rank-and-file SDF members. I found that barely half of SDF survey respondents had ever read anything by Öcalan, as will be explained later. Instead of ideology, what drives them are the instincts of survival. Furthermore, approximately one century after the Armenian genocide and Republic of Mount Ararat, I found that Kurds and Christians in the SDF share almost identical threat perceptions. By the spring and summer of 2019, they viewed Turkey as a bigger threat to the region than ISIS. A few months later, in October of 2019, Turkey launched a cross-border operation that the highest-ranking American diplomat on the ground in Northeast Syria, Ambassador Bill Roebuck, described in an internal memo as a "catastrophe."[4]

Officials of the Autonomous Administration were guided both by the ideology of democratic confederalism, but also by the necessity of mere survival. As soon as the SDF assumed de facto control over parts of North and East Syria, officials lost no time putting these ideas into practice. A co-chair system was established where all leadership positions—from the most powerful institutions down to neighborhood communes—are held jointly by a man and a woman. The current Co-President of the Syrian Democratic Council is Ilham Ahmad, who represents the Autonomous Administration during high-level diplomatic visits outside Syria. Major battles including the liberation of Raqqa and Manbij were led by women commanders such as Nowruz Ahmed and Rojda Felat. Arab women and men have also benefited from this system and been promoted to leadership positions—although at times at considerable risk to themselves. In 2019, the year the territorial caliphate crumbled, Layla Hassan and Ghassan Al Youssef acted as Co-Chairs of the Deir Ezzor Civil Council, the largest governorate under SDF control and home to oil resources. Lelwy Abdullah, an Arab woman from Deir Ezzor, joined the SDF already in 2016, and went on to assume a leadership position. By the time I interviewed her in the fall of 2020, she had survived no less than four assassination attempts.

However, as the Autonomous Administration expanded into Arab-majority regions, they displayed flexibility in implementing their program in order to accommodate local traditions and cultural practices. Polygamy is legal in regime-held areas of Syria and was practiced also by the Islamic State, so when the Autonomous Administration abolished polygamy according to their social charter, it was seen as radical or controversial by some. Initially, however, the law was only enforced in the Kurdish regions. As a case in point, the Arab-majority city of Manbij was liberated from the Islamic State in 2016. During one of my visits to Manbij in the fall of 2021—some five years after the Autonomous

Administration assumed control of the city—I was told that the prohibition on polygamy was only being enforced for those who worked for the Administration. The law on conscription has also not been enforced or even implemented in all regions. And the new school curriculum is also still in the process of being unified across Kurdish, Arab, and ethnically mixed regions. In short, Administration officials have shown flexibility and willingness to adapt to local circumstances while implementing their governance system.

In the absence of the Assad regime, this nonstate entity has increasingly taken on state-like powers. The Autonomous Administration has established (1) military forces to defend their territory known as the Syrian Democratic Forces (SDF); (2) police forces known as Asayîş and Sutoro; (3) a new school system and curriculum that offers language instruction in Kurdish, Syriac-Aramaic and Arabic; (4) a new system of political representation based on a co-chair system where men and women share power and a quota to ensure 40 percent representation of women in all governance institutions; (5) religious freedom and recognition of the Yezidi religion for the first time in the history of modern Syria; (6) a new economic ecosystem based on their control of oil, water, and fertile farmland that offers higher salaries than those paid by the central government; and (7) a judicial system of local courts to hold terrorists and criminals accountable for the crimes they committed during the time of the Islamic State Caliphate. Finally, the Self Administration has established its own distinct diplomatic relations vis-à-vis their neighbors and the 82 countries in the Global Coalition to Defeat ISIS. And yet, although in possession of state-like powers, they are not demanding an independent state. Autonomy is their aim, not secession. The autonomous peoples of the Northeast see themselves as a model of decentralized government that could be emulated in other parts of Syria and the Middle East. My book will offer an analysis of this statelet-in-formation, and is organized as follows.

In Chapter 2, I trace the origins of Rojava to the Republic of Mount Ararat, which declared its independence from the fledgling Turkish Republic in October 1927. Ararat came about as a result of an official treaty of cooperation between the Kurdish Xoybûn League and the Armenian Revolutionary Federation (Dashnaktsutyun). I argue that the legacy of the rebellion continues to shape the present. First, many of the inhabitants of northern Syria including Kurds as well as the Syriac, Assyrian, and Armenian Christian minorities were either forcibly deported or fled across the border around the time of the Armenian genocide. They describe themselves as "descendants of survivors" of Ottoman-era pogroms. Second, the official Proclamation of the Republic of Ararat in 1927 stated "all inhabitants regardless of race or religion will be treated equally." This far-reaching commitment to equality is also ensconced in the Social Contract of the Autonomous Administration declared in 2014, and stands in contrast to the founding ideologies of Kemalism in Turkey and Baathism in Syria, that promoted Turkification and Arabization policies vis-à-vis their respective minorities.

In Chapter 3, I use my original survey data of some 400 rank-and-file SDF members collected in all regions of North and East Syria. In so doing I allow the voices of young Syrians who fought against ISIS to be heard. I also trace the history of how Kurds created the mixed-gender YXG in 2011, which then evolved into separate militias for men (YPG) and women (YPJ), which in turn evolved into the multi-ethnic Syrian Democratic Forces (SDF) announced in 2015. My survey data illustrates that Arab SDF members belonged to forty-six different tribes or sub-tribes, representing virtually all of the tribes in North and East Syria. I discuss four Christian-led units: the Syriac Military Council, Bethnahrin Women Protection Forces, the Khabur Guards, and the Martyr Nubar Ozanyan Brigade, which guard sections of the borderlands on the frontlines to Turkey and Turkish-occupied Syria, from Derik in the east to Tel Tamer in the west. I also discuss two Arab units: the Sanadid Forces based along the northeastern border to Iraq, and the Manbij Military Council in the northwest, bordering regions held by the regime and Idlib. In addition to my survey of rank-and-file members, I rely on interviews I conducted with commanders of all of these units, including but not limited to: Abu Omar al-Idliby of the Northern Democratic Brigade, Shervan Derwish of the Manbij Military Council, Ahmed Mahmoud Sultan of Jeish al-Thuwar, Bandar al-Humaydi of the Sanadid Forces, Nisrine Abdullah and Nowruz Ahmed of the YPJ, Nabil Warde of the Khabur Guards, Matay Hanna of the Syriac Military Council, Kino Gabriel, and Aram Hanna, who both served as Spokespersons of the SDF, Zenobiya and Ashurina of the Bethnahrin Women Protection Forces, and SDF Commander-in-Chief, General Mazloum Abdi.

Chapter 4 turns to an analysis of the Islamic State. Contrary to the common narrative, women were not just victims of the Islamic State. Some women participated in the enslavement of other women. I contend that ISIS governance was not just about elevating men into positions of dominance over women— but entailed using women as weapons against each other. Some women were subjugated, so they could in turn police, punish, and even enslave other women. The chapter is divided into three parts. The first part describes the "philosophy" of the Islamic State towards women, based on an analysis of documents such as "Women of the Islamic State: A Manifesto on Women by the Al-Khanssaa Brigade," which was published at the height of their power in January 2015. ISIS governed by creating a war of women against women, by attempting to destroy any bonds of solidarity between them. The second part of the chapter shows how the Islamic State strived to achieve their overall objectives in three ways: restrictions on women's freedom of movement, restrictions on women's clothing and eyesight, and restrictions on women's ability to interact with men.

The final section includes an analysis of why the Islamic State suddenly reversed course and called women to wage jihad in the fall of 2017.

The gender revolution unfurled by the Autonomous Administration is the focus of Chapter 5. The Islamic State governed by weaponizing women, thereby destroying any potential bonds of solidarity between women of different backgrounds. By contrast, the Autonomous Administration governs by giving women real power, educating them in the study of what they call *jineology*, and attempting to rebuild cooperation through the formation of economic cooperatives. With a co-chair system and 40 percent women's quota in all levels of governance, Northeast Syria has achieved a level of women's participation and leadership unparalleled elsewhere in Syria, or even the wider region. How could a small non-state actor achieve this? First, it was possible precisely because women and their male allies built a statelet where they were able to make their own laws, institutions, and promote women into positions of power. Second, the statelet was able to expand beyond the Kurdish heartland because it was supported by Arab, Christian, Yezidi, and Turkmen women. Although difficult to quantify, my observations in the field lead me to believe the project was more readily supported by women than men. Furthermore, I show how these ideas of full gender equality—not token inclusion—were developed by Kurdish women inside the movement through internecine struggles within the PKK since the 1970s. Finally, my survey data shows that the ideas of gender equality are now embraced by the rank-and-file, not just supported by the elite cadre. This chapter will explain the philosophy that guides the Kurdish movement and how it has evolved from a Kurdish separatist project to one that aims to achieve decentralization within the borders of the Syrian state. This is key to understanding how the Rojava Revolution succeeded in incorporating Arabs and expanding beyond the northern Kurdish-Christian cantons where it began.

Chapter 6 analyzes the economic underpinnings of the autonomous region, which is based on control of oil, rich agricultural lands, important waterways such as the Tabqa Dam, and local female-run communes that allow women a degree of economic independence. Despite being under embargo and under siege from all sides, the Autonomous Administration now can offer salaries to their "civil servants" that are often double what is paid by the central government in Damascus. I argue that their plan to develop North and East Syria can be divided into short-term, medium-term, and long-term strategies. In order to achieve this, officials do not appear to be following a single dogmatic theory or praxis, but are rather guided by an eclectic mix of radical feminism, a social-democratic commitment to provide a safety net for a population ravaged by war, as well as elements of capitalism in trying to promote small and medium-sized enterprises in the private sector.

Chapter 7 explains how the new education system set up by the Autonomous Administration contributed to de-radicalization after Baathist and ISIS rule, empowered ethnic and religious minorities by introducing a new Kurdish and Aramaic language curriculum, and also expanded the state-like bureaucracy. In establishing a new education system, the Administration was confronted with seven challenges, and I explain how officials have attempted to overcome each of them. One problem for which they do not yet have a solution is the refusal of the Syrian regime to recognize the degrees from their schools.

Since 2011, Syrians have lived under four regimes: the Assad regime, ISIS, the Autonomous Administration, and under Turkish occupation. Comparing how these four types of government have treated Yezidis—one of the most vulnerable minorities in the country—brings into sharp contrast the vast differences between them. That is the goal of chapter 8. Under the Baathists, Yezidis experienced systematic denial of their identity, followed by enslavement and genocide at the hands of ISIS. The AANES, however, recognized the Yezidi religion and allowed for a brief flourishing of the Yezidi religion and culture. Thanks to YPG protection, ISIS could never launch a genocidal assault on Syrian Yezidis on the scale of what happened in Sinjar, Iraq. The Autonomous Administration of North and East Syria has offered five things to the small Yezidi community: 1) recognition of their existence, 2) political representation, 3) religious freedom, 4) protection from annihilation and 5) attempts at accountability by establishing courts to try Syrian ISIS members. However, many of these gains have been rolled back in the areas now occupied by Turkey.

In the concluding chapter, I schematically compare the governance under the Autonomous Administration with the Assad regime and Turkish-occupied areas, while drawing historical parallels to the short-lived Republic of Mount Ararat. I also sketch divergent possible future scenarios. Having defeated the Caliphate, the Autonomous Administration now has authority over tens of thousands of non-Syrians, including European citizens who joined ISIS. But many countries refuse to take back their own citizens. At the time of writing, some 30,000 Iraqi citizens are detained by the AANES. If the slow pace of repatriations continues, it will take an estimated 15 years for all Iraqis to return to Iraq. Until now, the calls for an international tribunal, akin to the Nuremberg Trials after World War II, have been ignored. Officials of the Autonomous Administration have called for the creation of a hybrid tribunal. If non-Syrians are tried in courts in the autonomous region, could this result in de-facto legal recognition of their system? On the other hand, the Northeast remains excluded from the UN-led talks over the future of Syria, while the region remains surrounded by adversaries. Will the statelet persist, extend to other parts of Syria, or be erased from the map like the Republic of Mount Ararat?

A Genealogy of Rojava

Kurds and Armenians Declare the Republic of Mount Ararat, 1926–1932

"Em hene ji berê paş da qaçaxê romê ne firarê dewletê ne"

"Since the old days, we have been the fugitives of the Turk, the escapees of the state."

—From an oral poem about Ferzende Bey, military commander
of the Mt Ararat Republic[1]

O Kurds! Brethren! You are on the brink of a new massacre. Remember the hundreds of villages burnt, the thousands of Kurds killed, and the many girls and women raped. Love each other and hide your weapons and be watchful of the new cruelties which will be done to you. Forge the hostility between yourselves. The Turks want to perish our nation by using the Kurds for killing each other. We advise you again to preserve your arms, ammunition, and cohesion.

—Publication of the Armenian-Kurdish Khoyboun Society,
No. 18, circa 1930[2]

On October 8, 1927, Kurds and Armenian genocide survivors declared their independence from the fledgling Turkish Republic. Centered on the mountainous borderlands between Turkey and Armenia, they called their statelet the Republic of Mount Ararat. The rise and demise of this almost-forgotten experiment in self-rule will be the subject of this chapter. In contrast to the vast scholarship on the collapse of the Ottoman Empire, the establishment of the Republic of Turkey, and the atrocities now recognized as a genocide, the Ararat Republic itself has received less attention, although it was one of the most significant rebellions in the early twentieth century. Given the still limited scholarship on the topic, this chapter should be seen as a preliminary attempt to piece together broken fragments of the historical record, which I hope will inspire further research. My primary intention is to shed light on how Kurdish-Armenian

Statelet of Survivors. Amy Austin Holmes, Oxford University Press. © Oxford University Press 2024.
DOI: 10.1093/oso/9780197621035.003.0002

cooperation was forged in the aftermath of the genocide. I will draw from unpublished documents from the Archives of the Armenian Revolutionary Federation (ARF) in Watertown, Massachusetts, British archival documents collected in the Records of the Kurds, Turkish and American press reporting from the 1920s and early 1930s, and interviews I conducted in Syria with families of Armenian and Kurdish descent who trace their history to the Turkish side of the border.

The Republic of Mount Ararat came about as a result of an official treaty of co-operation between the Kurdish Xoybûn (Khoyboun) League and the Armenian Revolutionary Federation (Dashnaktsutyun). While Kurds in Xoybûn and Armenian Dashnaks formed the core of this alliance, it was also supported by Yezidis, Assyrians, defected Turkish army officers, deposed Ottoman monarchists, refugees, deportees, and tribal leaders. Xoybûn, or Khoyboun as it is known in French, also had international branches in France, Egypt, Syria, Iraq, Persia, Jordan, and the United States.[3]

Although the genocide is often associated with the year 1915, the decimation of Anatolian Christians and their expulsion into Syria took place over a period of some three decades, beginning with the Hamidian massacres of 1894 and then the 1909 Adana pogrom.[4] While the genocide was orchestrated by Ottoman authorities, some Kurdish tribes were also complicit. Kurds were involved in the Hamidian massacres in 1894, the genocide in 1915, and confiscation of Armenian properties.[5] In December 1900, Abdurrahman Badirkhan published an article in *Kurdistan*, the very first Kurdish journal, in which he described the deterioration in Kurdish-Armenian relations and denounced Mustafa Pasha, leader of the Miran tribe as a "traitor." It is worth quoting at length:

> Before [Abdulhamid II] ascended the throne, the Kurds were knowledgeable and civilized people, having brotherly relations with Armenians and avoiding any kind of confrontation. Then what happened? Did [Kurdish] civilization and knowledge turn into bar-barity, ignorance, and organized rebellion? Who else carries out the atrocities in Kurdistan but the members of the Hamidiye divisions, who are armed by the sultan and proud of being loyal to him? For ex-ample, there is Mustafa Pasha, the head of the Miran tribe (. . .) He used to be a shepherd ten or fifteen years ago (. . .) We do not know what he did to become a favorite of the sultan, who thought that he would assist in shedding blood and hurting people. He made him a pasha and introduced him with the title of commander of a Hamidiya division. (. . .) Would he not butcher the Armenians and pillage the Muslims?[6]

Other Kurds, however, were reportedly involved in assisting Armenians escape persecution. The two co-chairs of the Armenian mission to the 1922–23 Lausanne Conference were Gabriel Noradungian, who represented the Ottoman/Turkish Armenians and Avedis Aharonian, who represented the Russian Armenians and the former independent Republic of Armenia. Both Aharonian and Noradungian went on record at Lausanne as saying that Armenians and Kurds were generally on good terms. Noradungian reportedly made the following caveat, saying that there were "200 different Kurdish tribes" and that while the Yezidis and Kizilbashes were "friends of the Armenians" with the former reportedly sheltering some 20,000 Armenians during the deportations, the Djelalis and Hayderanlis were hostile.[7] Just a few years after the Lausanne Conference, however, the Hayderanlis were one of the main tribes that took up arms on Mount Ararat alongside Armenians.

While Christians suffered severe persecution aimed at eradicating their communities, they were not the only victims. Seda Altuğ describes how the northeastern region of Syria, known as Jazira, became the home of a checkered array of fugitives fleeing violence:

> The Syrian Jazira, with its population of displaced communities originating from across the border, is like a microcosm reflecting in reverse the dynamics of Turkey's nation-building. Its population largely consists of the last groups of the "undesirables" for whom Turkish nationalism left no space: genocide-survivor Christians belonging to different sects, among which Orthodox Armenians and Orthodox Syriacs form the majority and Syriac Protestants, Syriac Catholics and Armenian Catholics form the minority; Jews from Nisibin; nomadic and semi-nomadic Kurdish tribesmen; and some nomadic Arab tribes.[8]

It was this canton of Jazira that would later become the beating heart of the Rojava revolution. While the Kurdish-majority town of Kobani came to symbolize the armed resistance against the Islamic State, it was in the more multi-ethnic canton of Jazira where the ideas of democratic confederalism could best be put to the test.

Ras al-Ayn and the Armenian Genocide

The exact number of Anatolian Christians who were killed during this period remains a matter of dispute, and may be impossible to determine. This is in part because of the lack of agreed upon population figures prior to the eradication campaign. Estimates range from 800,000 to 1.5 million Armenians who were murdered either directly or indirectly through deportation into the Syrian desert.[9] Historical maps such as the one below (Figure 2.1) vividly demonstrate the vast geographical scope of the genocide, with deportation routes stretching from the Black Sea in Turkey in the north to the Syrian city of Deir Ezzor in the south.

The town of Ras al-Ayn (known as Serêkaniyê in Kurdish and Rish Ayno in Aramaic) should be highlighted because of its significance in 1915 and again today. Ras al-Ayn was one of twenty-five deportation or concentration camps set up by the Ottoman authorities. An estimated 65,000–70,000 Armenians were slaughtered in this city alone, making it the second-deadliest site of the genocide inside Syria. The only site in Syria where more Armenians were killed is Deir Ezzor, known as "Armenia's Auschwitz."

Although it was one of the deadliest sites of the genocide, less is known about what happened in Ras al-Ayn than other areas. It was not a significant population center like Aleppo or Van. There were no embassies or consulates based in Ras al-Ayn, and hence no foreign emissaries to report on what happened there. It was perhaps precisely for this reason that Ras al-Ayn was chosen as a

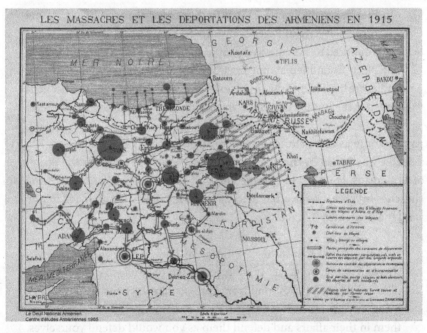

Figure 2.1 Map of the Armenian Genocide showing sites of massacres and deportation routes. Ras al- Ayn and Deir Ezzor were the two deadliest concentration camps inside Syria. *Rapport sur l'Unité Géographique de l'Arménie. Atlas Historique, Facsimilé Héliographique des 25 Cartes de l'Antiquité, du Moyen Âge, des Temps Modernes et Contemporains, Paris: s.n., 1919, carte n°24.*

site to murder Armenians en masse. The German consul Holstein was based in Mosul, more than 300 km away. The American consul, Charles P. Brissel, resided in Baghdad, some 700 km away from Ras al-Ayn. However, engineers who were working on the Baghdadbahn offered eyewitness accounts. The historian Raymond Kevorkian has relied on some of their testimonies.

The first deportees arrived in Ras al-Ayn in mid-July 1915 and were from Harput, Erzerum, and Bitlis. An engineer working on the Baghdadbahn, M. Graif, informed Dr. Niepage, a professor in Aleppo, that "along the entire trajectory of the railroad leading to Tell Abida [Tel Abyad] and Ras ul-Ayn were piles of naked corpses of raped women."[10] The German consul Holstein, who had traveled on the road between Mosul and Aleppo, said he "had seen, in several places on the way, so many severed children's hands that the road could have been paved with them."[11]

According to Kevorkian, the city of Ras al-Ayn was known as the final destination of the death marches. All of the convoys coming from the Turkish side of the border had "without exception been massacred."[12] In a report from April 27, 1916, the consul Rössler wrote:

> On the report of a perfectly trustworthy German who spent several days in Ras ul-Ayn and the vicinity . . . [e]very day, or nearly every day, three hundred to five hundred people are removed from the camp, taken to a place around ten kilometers from Ras ul-Ayn, and slaughtered. The bodies are thrown into the river known as Jirjib el Hamar . . . The Chechens settled in the Ras ul-Ayn region are playing the executioners' roles.[13]

As gruesome as these stories are, there are also stories of compassion. In 1917 a decree was issued by the Sharif of Mecca, Hussein Ibn Ali, for the protection of Armenians. His speech, inscribed on a plaque, can still be found in Armenian churches in Syria, and is often held up as an example of Arab magnanimity toward the Armenian refugees.

> We inform you that in our Gratitude to Him, we are in good health, strength and good grace. What is requested of you is to protect and to take good care of everyone from the Jacobite Armenian community living in your territories and frontiers and among your tribes; to help them in their affairs and defend them as you would defend yourselves, your properties and children.[14]

Some Arab and Kurdish families took in Armenian or Assyrian orphans and raised them as their own children. Because they were raised in Muslim families, many of these Christians came to identify as Muslims, leading to the phenomenon of "hidden Armenians" or "crypto Armenians."[15] In the fall of 2020, during one of my visits to the region of Tel Tamer, I met members of the Martyr Nubar Ozanyan Brigade. They were training in the shade by the side of a church. During the 2019 Peace Spring intervention, Turkey captured Ras al-Ayn and a long strip of Syrian territory extending to Tel Abyad. Since then, Tel Tamer has been on the frontlines of the area occupied by Turkey and its proxy forces. To my surprise, most of them identified as Muslim Armenians. Chapter 3 provides a detailed history of the Syrian Democratic Forces, including the Martyr Nubar Ozanyan Brigade.

The Seyfo Massacre of Assyrians and Syriac Christians

The Christian inhabitants of the Ottoman Empire included not only Armenians, but also another group of Christians who trace their ancestry to ancient Mesopotamia. They are known by different names: Syriacs, Assyrians, Chaldeans, Nestorians, or Aramaeans. For the sake of simplicity, I will refer to them as Assyrians or Syriacs, or at times in hyphenated form, because these are the most common terms used by the inhabitants of northern Syria today. They speak the Aramaic language, also known as Syriac.

The history of this ancient community is complex. The historian Joseph Yacoub, who was born in Al Hasakah in 1944, has written one of the most authoritative accounts of this community and the Ottoman attempts to eradicate it. In his book *Year of the Sword: The Assyrian Christian Genocide*, Yacoub explains, "Since the fall of Nineveh, Babylon and the Aramean kingdoms some 2,500 years ago, the Assyrians have been deprived of a state to protect them from age-old persecutions, which often took dramatic form from the Persian Sassanid period onwards."[16]

Similar to the Armenians, the Syriac-Assyrians constitute both an ethnic and religious minority. In contrast to the Armenians, however, who for a few years had an independent state between 1918 and 1920 before it was incorporated into the Soviet Union, the twentieth-century Assyrians were stateless, an experience they shared with their Kurdish neighbors. For the stateless Assyrians, the church became one of the key institutions they looked to for protection. The community largely belongs to either the "Jacobite" Syriac Orthodox Church of Antioch and all the East, or to the Ancient Church of the East, while those who identify more closely with the Catholic Church are known as Chaldeans. The theological and doctrinal differences between the Church of the East and the Syriac Orthodox Church date back to the time of the Council of Ephesus in 431 and the Council of Chalcedon in 451. Despite the different identities of the diverse Christian population of Anatolia, the Ottoman Turkish authorities, who had previously allowed them a certain degree of autonomy, began to view them all as unassimilable due to the simple fact that they were non-Muslims and non-Turks. One prominent member of the Assyrian community was Surma d'Bait Mar Shimun.

She was born in Hakkari in eastern Turkey in 1883 and was the sister of the patriarch Mar Benyamin Shimun. Her brother Mar Shimun was murdered in 1918 by Simko Shikak, a Kurdish agha.[17] According to her reflections on her life in Hakkari, a Turk had never set foot in Assyrian territory, which she described as "independent."[18] Surma Mar Shimun is one of the few women mentioned by name in the more than 800 pages of archival documents compiled in Volume Seven of the *Records of the Kurds*.[19] The lack of archival documents, and the absence of women in those documents that do exist, is one of the many reasons why our understanding of the Ararat Republic remains fragmentary. Similarly, Kurds under the Ottoman Empire also enjoyed a degree of autonomy from Constantinople and practiced a certain degree of self-rule. This is one of the reasons why some of the insurgents on Mount Ararat supported the deposed Sultan, because he had granted them self-rule, while Mustafa Kemal Atatürk, the new leader of the Republic Turkey, had taken it away. Although their demand for an "Armenian National Home" had been rejected at the Lausanne Conference, through the creation of the Ararat Republic, Kurds and Christians were attempting to establish facts on the ground that would entail a continuation of their autonomous status, and to maintain political and cultural rights which they previously enjoyed, but had lost.

The persecution of the Armenians has now been widely recognized as a genocide, although it took 106 years for an American President to officially recognize it as such.[20] By contrast, the persecution of Syriacs and Assyrians has received far less attention, leading Joseph Yacoub to refer to it as a "hidden genocide." It was a time when "the Ottomans sought to extirpate the Aramaic-speaking Assyrian, Syriac and Chaldean Christians of the Middle East."[21] Syriacs and Assyrians often refer to these events as "Seyfo," which is the Aramaic term for sword, as it was the weapon used for slaughter.

The Breakup of the Ottoman Empire

The Treaties of Sykes-Picot, Sèvres, and Lausanne

The demise of the Ottoman Empire had been a slow process set in motion already in the nineteenth century. The final collapse after some 600 years came about rather abruptly in the aftermath of World War I. In November 1922 the Ottoman Sultanate was abolished; in October 1923 Turkey was declared to be a Republic; and in March 1924 the Ottoman Caliphate was also finally abolished by decree of the Turkish Grand National Assembly. After more than six centuries, the Ottoman Empire had become a relic of the past.

Even before World War I was over, European colonial powers were making plans for how to divide up the Middle East. In May 1916 the secret Sykes-Picot Agreement was signed between Sir Mark Sykes of Great Britain and Georges Picot of France. The Agreement effectively handed control of Syria, Lebanon, "Turkish Cilicia," "Turkish Armenia," and "northern Kurdistan" to France, while Russian influence was also acknowledged in the latter two regions.[22] Palestine, Jordan, Baghdad, and the Persian Gulf areas were effectively given to the British. While neither France nor Britain owned these territories, as mandate powers, they were endowed with wide-ranging administrative control. Archival documents reveal that British officials in Iraq used their powers to disrupt the activities of Khoyboun, the Kurdish organization that formed an official alliance with Dashnaksutyan, as described later in the chapter. British officials in Iraq denied visas to Kurds and Armenians, confiscated their newsletters, and threatened financial sanctions against Kurdish leaders unless they ceased their activities, thus contributing to the failure of the movement even before the insurgents were crushed by the Turkish military.[23]

At the Paris Peace Conference in 1919, in addition to the "Big Four"—Lloyd George of Britain, Vittorio Emanuele Orlando of Italy, Georges Clemenceau of France, and Woodrow Wilson of the United States—Kurdish and Armenian delegates were also in attendance. The Kurds were represented by Sharif Pasha while Armenians were represented by Boghos Nubar Pasha. Arshak Safrastian, an Armenian from Van, was nominated to be part of Nubar Pasha's delegation. He describes the surprise of observers that Kurds and Armenians were able to compromise despite competing territorial claims:

> As some of the Kurdish territorial claims clashed with those of Armenia, the principal representatives of the two nations, Boghos Nubar Pasha (Armenia) and Sharif Pasha, signed an agreement as to the common pursuit of the interests of these two countries. European diplomats, experts, third-rate journalists in every camp were dumbfounded at this Armenian-Kurdish understanding, because for nearly half a century they had recorded and proclaimed that the two neighbouring races were "deadly enemies" and could never work together.[24]

The 1920 Sèvres Treaty provided for the allotment of certain lands in Turkey to Armenia, the exact boundaries of which were to be defined by the President of the United States, see Box 2.1. At the time the Sèvres Treaty was signed in August 1920, an independent Armenia already existed, which had been established May 1918. But by December 1920, it had become incorporated into the Soviet Union.

Box 2.1 The Treaty of Sèvres: August 10, 1920

The Treaty of Sèvres also provided for the creation of an autonomous Kurdish region that should include "full safeguards for the protection of the Assyro-Chaldeans." The three Articles concerning Kurdistan and the Assyrians were as follows:

Article 62

A Commission sitting at Constantinople and composed of three members appointed by the British, French and Italian Governments respectively shall draft within six months from the coming into force of the present Treaty *a scheme of local autonomy for the predominantly Kurdish areas lying east of the Euphrates,* south of the Southern Boundary of Armenia, as it may be here-after determined, and north of the frontiers of Turkey with Syria and Mesopotamia, as defined in article 27, II, (2) and (3). If unanimity cannot be secured on any question it will be referred by the members of the Commission to their respective Governments. *The scheme shall contain full safeguards for the protection of the Assyro-Chaldeans and other racial or religious minorities within these areas,* and with this object, a Commission composed of British, French, Italian, Persian and Kurdish representatives shall visit the spot to examine and decide what ratifications, if any, should be made in the Turkish frontier where under the provisions of the present Treaty, that frontier coincides with that of Persia.

Article 63

The Turkish Government hereby agrees to accept and execute the decisions of both the Commissions mentioned in Article 62 within three months from their communication to the said Government.

Article 64

If within one year from the coming into force of the present Treaty the Kurdish peoples within the areas defined in Article 62 shall ad-dress themselves to the Council of the League of Nations in such a manner as to show that a majority of the population of these areas desires independence from Turkey, and *if the council then considers that these peoples are capable of such independence and recommends that it should be granted to them, Turkey hereby agrees to execute such a recommendation, and to renounce all rights and title over these areas.* [Emphasis added.]

Importantly, the Treaty of Sèvres also imposed limitations on the Ottoman military: it was not allowed to have an air force, the army was limited to 50,000 men, and the navy was limited to 13 boats. The 1923 Treaty of Lausanne, which later annulled the Treaty of Sèvres, did not stipulate such limitations. The fledgling Turkish Republic went on to develop an air force, which for the first few decades of its existence was used for the sole purpose of crushing Kurdish-led rebellions.[25]

Wilsonian Armenia

In November 1920 the Arbitral Award on the Turkish-Armenian boundary was published by President Woodrow Wilson (Figure 2.2). The book-length document had a long title: "Decision of the President of the United States of America respecting the Frontier between Turkey and Armenia, Access for Armenia to the Sea, and the Demilitarization of Turkish Territory adjacent to the Armenian Frontier."[26]

Figure 2.2 Map of Wilsonian Armenia

However, the 1923 Treaty of Lausanne replaced the Treaty of Sèvres. In the words of Arshak Safrastian: "in spite of all their promises and the signing of the Treaty of Sèvres, the Allied powers betrayed both Kurdistan and Armenia."[27] The collapse of the First Armenian Republic and its absorption into the Soviet Union also prompted the Armenian Revolutionary Federation (ARF) to rethink their strategies. The First Republic had been governed by the ARF, and after Sovietization they were exiled in toto. It was against this backdrop that a provisional agreement was reached between Kurdish notables and Dashnak. According to Garo Sasuni, head of the Dashnak branch in Beirut, this agreement was reached already in 1924, even before the Sheikh Said rebellion in 1925.[28]

The early Turkish Republic was characterized by numerous uprisings against the new government in Ankara led by Mustafa Kemal Atatürk. In the fifteen years from 1924 to 1938, the encyclopedia of the official Ataturk Research Center lists no less than twenty mass uprisings, beginning with the Nestorian revolt in 1924. All of them were concentrated in the eastern provinces. Of these 20 officially recognized rebellions, three of the most significant were arguably the Sheikh Said Rebellion, the Ararat Rebellion, and the Dersim revolt (Figure 2.3). Armenians were involved in all three. According to Garabet K. Moumdjian, Turkish authorities "spearheaded a media campaign where they underlined the participation of Armenian and Assyrian militants in the Sheikh Sa'id Rebellion."[29] The participation of Armenians in the Mount Ararat Republic was based on an official treaty of cooperation between Dashnak and Xoybûn, as described in more detail in the next section.

The 1923 Treaty of Lausanne shattered all dreams of autonomy, shared by both Armenians and Kurds. Armenians remained divided between what they refer to as Western and Eastern Armenia. Kurds were divided between four countries, or what they refer to as four parts of Kurdistan: Bakur (northern Kurdistan in Turkey), Başûr (southern Kurdistan in Iraq), Rojhelat (eastern Kurdistan in Iran), and Rojava (western Kurdistan in Syria).

In the new Turkish Republic, non-Muslims including Armenians, Assyrians, Greeks, and Jews were recognized as official minorities. By contrast, the new Turkish leadership believed that Kurds, despite speaking a different language, could be assimilated or Turkified. Deprived of the meager recognition that other minorities enjoyed, Kurds were deemed "Mountain Turks." After 1923, state-sponsored attempts to (forcibly) Turkify the Kurds accelerated.[30]

While some Kurdish intellectuals may have supported Atatürk's reforms, the vast majority of Kurds took a dim view of these decisions, which were tantamount to asking Kurds to renounce both their religion and their national

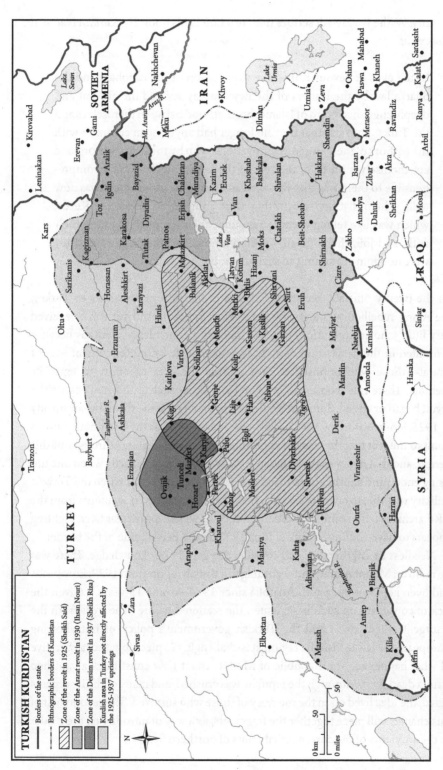

Figure 2.3 Map of the Sheikh Said, Ararat, and Dersim Rebellions

Source: From the memoirs of Ihsan Nouri Pasha, "La Revolte De L'Agri Dagh." Ihsan Nouri Pasha, *La Révolte de l'Agri Dagh: "Ararat" (1927–1930)*, (Genève: Editions Kurdes, 1986).

identity. Wadie Jwaideh describes their reaction in his book *The Kurdish National Movement*:

> In the eyes of devout Kurds, the suppression of the caliphate and the Shari'a law by the leaders of the new Turkey severed the ancient and deeply cherished bond of Islamic brotherhood between themselves and the Turks. They felt that they no longer had anything in common with the authors of these impious innovations, who by their own actions had cut themselves off from the rest of the faithful. What was incomprehensible to them was that this alien and renegade government was now telling them that henceforth they were going to be Turks, not Kurds, which was like telling them to renounce their nationality, adjure their faith, and join the company of the impious and the iniquitous. They were not going to submit to such dictation.[31]

Of the twenty officially recognized risings in the eastern provinces of Turkey, the Ararat rebellion was arguably the most significant. And yet it has received very little scholarly attention, which is unlikely a coincidence. Perhaps because it resulted in the declaration of an independent state—the Republic of Mount Ararat—those who opposed it have exerted the greatest effort to erase its memory. There is no consensus even on basic issues such as to when exactly the revolt began or ended. Some archival documents suggest the revolt began already in 1925, while historians have usually considered 1927 as the beginning. Others point to the fact that there was a continuum of armed rebellions throughout this period, and that it may make little sense to try and decipher exactly when one uprising ended and another began. The year 1930 is often cited as when the Turkish military was able to crush the revolt. However, unpublished documents from the ARF archives tell a somewhat different story, as will become clear later. Fighting appears to have continued until at least 1932 on the Persian side of the border.

Needless to say, there are still considerable gaps in our knowledge. There was no radio on Mount Ararat, and according to a British report from 1929, Europeans had been kept out of eastern Anatolia since 1914—some 15 years.[32] Given the lack of consensus on such basic issues, the scattered nature of sources from the insurgents themselves, and the Turkish government's policy of not allowing European officials to visit the region, it is challenging to piece together a narrative of what happened. The Republic of Mount Ararat now constitutes a vanished state, a dead state. Although the republic was crushed, and many of the insurgents killed, the idea lived on in the memory of those who survived. The second half of this chapter will piece together the fragments, as a way of introducing the reader to the ancestors of the current inhabitants of northern Syria.

The Republic of Mount Ararat

Avec l'aide et la grâce de Dieu, il a été mis fin aujourd'hui, à l'occupation turque dans la patrie kurde, et un gouvernement national kurde y a été institué.

With the help and the grace of God, the Turkish occupation of the Kurdish homeland has ended today, and a Kurdish national government has been established.[33]

With this statement, the Republic of Mount Ararat was declared. Centered on the Ağrı (Ararat) Province of eastern Turkey, it represents one of the most important early attempts to establish an independent Kurdish state—and was supported by Armenians. Atop the craggy slopes of Ararat, the insurgents hoisted a flag, wrote a national anthem, and pledged to expel all Turkish soldiers. But more significant than these proclamations and symbolic trappings of statehood, is the sheer size of territory that declared independence, its duration, and that it was supported by Kurds from all four regions of Kurdistan, an area that encompasses parts of what is now modern-day Turkey, Iran, Iraq, and Syria. It was also supported by defected officers of the Turkish army, and deposed royalists including Prince Selim, the son of the former Sultan Abdul Hamid II, Yezidis, and Assyrians.

Perhaps most significantly, the Ararat Republic came about due to an official treaty of cooperation between Kurds and Armenians—just ten years after the Armenian genocide, when some Kurdish tribes assisted the Ottoman army in the massacre and deportation of Armenians from Anatolia.[34] Finally, in contrast to other Kurdish-led rebellions in the early years of the Turkish Republic, such as the Sheikh Said Rebellion and the Dersim Revolt, the insurgents on Mount Ararat were not only able to control territory, but attempted to form the rudimentary building blocks of a state and abolish, albeit temporarily, Turkish sovereign control over the area. It was a statelet of survivors.

According to news reports at the time, Turkish officials admitted that the Ararat rebellion represented a much more "serious" challenge than the Sheikh Said Rebellion in 1925,[35] which had been defeated after just a few months, and had been limited primarily to Zaza-speaking Kurds in areas surrounding Diyarbakir and Mardin. By contrast, the insurgency on Mount Ararat lasted for seven or eight years. By some accounts, the uprising began in the immediate aftermath of the defeat of Shaikh Said in 1925, or by May or June of 1926 at the latest, and continued even after Turkish officials proclaimed victory in 1930. Fighting on the Persian side of the border continued until 1932 and was not resolved until Persia and Turkey agreed to cooperate in the suppression of the rebels, officially swap territory, and readjudicate the national borders between the two states.[36]

The question of how this statelet came about is, at least to my mind, more intriguing and in need of explanation than the issue of how it was crushed. The Turkish Republic was in command of a much larger army and communications network than the insurgents, and had airplanes and political recognition while the rebels had neither.[37] The creation of this Kurdish-led statelet was inextricably linked to the dissolution of another state, the Republic of Armenia, which had gained independence in 1918 but was subsumed into the Soviet Union in late 1920.

When the fledgling Republic of Armenia was taken over by the Soviet Union, the leadership of the ARF was expelled. A few years later, the ARF held its Tenth World Congress in Paris in 1925—the same year as the Sheikh Said uprising in Turkey. During this congress the ARF reconfirmed their decision to support and participate in the Kurdish rebellions that were already underway. Moumdjian describes this as a "core strategic decision" of the Tenth World Congress. If the Kurdish rebellions were successful, they would have potentially allowed Dashnak to achieve its own goals: in particular the repatriation of the Armenian diaspora and deportees back to their ancestral homeland.[38] The Turkish Republic had notably refused to allow the Armenians who had survived the deportations to return to their homes in Turkey, even though they had Turkish citizenship.[39]

In the spring of 1927 a Kurdish National Congress was held in a location described as "one of the mountains of Kurdistan."[40] The meeting was initiated by Kurds from Syria and attended by delegates from various tribal and urban organizations as well as delegates representing the insurgents who were already fighting on Mount Ararat. In May–June of 1926 the Jalali and Haydaranli tribes had risen up to protest the fact that they were being subjected to deportations, which Ankara had ordered as punishment for the Sheikh Said rebellion, although they themselves had not participated in that rebellion. As previously noted, the Sheikh Said rebels had been primarily Zaza-speaking Kurds while the Jalali and Haydaranli tribes, and many of the other Mount Ararat insurgents, were Kurmanci-speaking. This was neither the first nor the last time that the collective punishment of the Kurds would result, not in quashing the rebellion, but in ensuring that it continued. In a confidential dispatch from August 1927, Sir George Clerk wrote to Foreign Secretary Sir Austen Chamberlain that the transfers of Kurds from eastern to western Turkey were increasing, highlighting ominously that "they are now taking place on a scale which to some extent recalls the mass deportations of Armenians in 1915."[41]

At this meeting in the spring of 1927, the Kurdish leaders decided to: dissolve all existing Kurdish nationalist organizations and to amalgamate them into a single organization which they named Xoybûn, meaning "Independence" or to "be oneself." They also vowed to create an army by unifying the various tribes into a single command structure, to establish supply and munitions depots, to overcome Kurdish-Armenian differences and actively collaborate for the liberation of both Kurds and Armenians, to designate Kurdava as the provisional capital until Diyarbakir could be made the permanent capital, and to continue their struggle "until the last Turkish soldier had left Kurdish soil."[42]

In October 1927 another meeting was held, this time at the summer residence of ARF leader Vahan Papazian in Bhamdoun Lebanon. It was here where the Xoybûn organization was formally announced. The Executive Committee consisted of Sureyya, Jeladet, and Kamuran Bedirkhan, all brothers belonging to a princely family, in addition to Memduh Selim Bey and Shahin Bey. At this meeting, Ihsan Nouri was appointed "General Commander of the Kurdish Forces." He was given the task of unifying the Kurdish tribes and "survivors of the deportations" into a single force structure.[43] Ibrahim Heski Tello was appointed Head of the Civilian Administration. Jeladat Bedirkhan remained President of the Executive Committee of Xoybûn from 1927 to 1932.

While the leadership of Xoybûn were primarily Kurds from Turkey, efforts were made to organize Kurds from Iraq as well. During the same month of October 1927, a Kurdish delegate by the name of Ali Ilmi who resided in Beirut, was authorized by the Kurdish Revolutionary Committee in Iraq to continue negotiations with Papazian, the Dashnak emissary. The Kurdish Revolutionary Committee in Iraq instructed Ali Ilmi to put the following questions to Papazian:

(a) What financial and other material support would the Greeks and Italians be willing to furnish?

(b) What form of insurrection would be proposed and in what area would it be required to take place?

(c) How would the Greeks and Italians cooperate with an actual insurrection?

(d) What are the plans of the Dashnak Committee and what do they expect from the Kurds?

On October 25, Papazian replied as follows:

We are prepared to come to an understanding with the Kurds and we can secure all necessary assistance from the Italians and the Greeks on condition that:

(a) The Kurds come to an understanding amongst themselves and form a central organization invested with the sole authority to represent the majority of the important tribes.

(b) Sayed Taha's written authority to be added to that of the Kurdish Committee for any further negotiations.

(c) Further negotiations be undertaken with a duly authorized representative of Sayed Taha as well as with the Kurdish Committee."[44]

The question of how many Armenians fought alongside their Kurdish comrades remains unclear, in part due to the lack of archival sources, but also because some Armenians concealed their identities. For example, one of the most famous rebel leaders on the mountain was known as Ziylan Bey. It was only revealed later that his real name was Ardashes Mouradian, and that he was Armenian. Born in 1894, Mouradian spoke both Armenian and Kurdish. His father Hagop had been a close associate of Sheikh Said, who led the revolt in 1925, and Mouradian himself was also reportedly close to the son of Sheikh Said, Ali Riza.[45]

Ardashes Mouradian had been sent to Ararat secretly by the ARF with the purpose of "strengthening Armenian-Kurdish relations and helping the Kurds in their utmost struggle."[46] This required, among other tasks, maintaining open channels of communication between the insurgents fighting on a mountain in a remote region of Turkey and the ARF Central Committee in Paris, as well as their numerous regional offices. According to recently discovered documents, Mouradian wrote some of his letters in code and with invisible ink. His letters were intercepted, decoded, and then provided to Turkish and Soviet officials as evidence that the Persian authorities were turning a blind eye to the activities of Kurdish and Armenian revolutionaries.

The exact circumstances of Mouradian's murder remain unclear. Based on newfound documents uncovered by Aram S. Sayiyan, it appears Mouradian was arrested by Armenian Bolsheviks who summoned him to a meeting in the border area near the river Araxes, where he was ambushed and smuggled to Soviet Armenia. Ihsan Nouri learned only some time later that his co-conspirator had been exiled to Siberia.[47] According to Sayiyan, it was only after the collapse of the Soviet Union that declassified documents revealed that this leader of the revolt had been shot in a Soviet gulag in 1938 in the Arkhangelsk region, more than 3,600 km to the north of Mount Ararat.

According to Garo Sassouni, Ziylan Bey/Ardashes Mouradian was only one of many Armenians who fought on Mount Ararat. The fact that he was an important leader of the rebellion is clear, however, due to the simple fact that he was photographed next to Ihsan Nouri, the Kurdish commander-in-chief of all the forces fighting on Ararat (Figure 2.4). After Mouradian was captured, the ARF sent another Armenian to act as the new liaison with the Kurdish forces. He was known by the nomme de guerre Vali Bey, or Sev Vahan. His real name was Vahan Kalusdian, and he was none other than a captain in the army of the (formerly) independent Republic of Armenia.

The ARF and the Kurdish Nationalist League Xoybûn signed a Treaty of Collaboration in which they agreed to cooperate for the liberation of Armenians and Kurds. The five-page treaty was written in French and signed by eight members of Xoybûn as well as Vahan Papazian, representing the Dashnaksutyun.

Figure 2.4 Photo of Ardashes Mouradian (Zilan Bey) and Ihsan Nouri, Armenian and Kurdish commanders on Mt Ararat. Credit: ARF Archives in Watertown, Massachusetts.

The ARF agreed to carry out public relations efforts among Western powers, provide temporary economic and material aid, establish diplomatic relations, and train Kurdish organizers, technicians and propagandists.[48] The prerequisite for this support was that the Kurds should overhaul their organization. The Xoybûn Oath stated:

> I do hereby swear on my honor and religion that from the date of my signing of this undertaking to a period of two years I do not use arms against any Kurd unless an attack is made by him on my life and honour [. . .] I do postpone to the expiry of these two years all blood feuds and other disputes, and do my utmost to prevent bloodshed among two Kurds on private matters. Any Kurd who acts in contravention of this

undertaking is regarded a traitor of his Nation, and the murder of every
traitor is a duty.[49]

As the oath makes clear, the ARF's support for Xoybûn was contingent on Kurds
overcoming their political and tribal divisions. However, Armenians themselves
remained politically divided, most significantly between those who supported
the Sovietization of the First Armenian Republic, and those who did not. While
disagreements did emerge within the ARF-Xoybûn alliance, it was arguably
divisions *within* the Armenian and Kurdish communities themselves that would
prove most fatal.

The Ideology of the Ararat Insurgents

As the twelve-point proclamation in Box 2.2 makes clear, Xoybûn was to make
all decisions regarding the military and civilian administration including personnel decisions. Everyone living in the areas under control of the insurgents
was called upon to support the army including by preparing food and providing transport. Anyone who refused to fulfill these duties was considered
a traitor. Furthermore, the inhabitants of the area were "invited" to deliver,
within a 24-hour period, all "objects, currency, or weaponry belonging to the
state."

Point number seven proclaimed that "all inhabitants regardless of race or religion will be treated equally, provided that they obey all the regulations and laws
of the Kurdish government." This emphasis on equality between peoples of different religious and ethnic backgrounds deserves to be highlighted as it stands
in sharp contrast to the policies of the central government that was attempting
to create a homogeneous nation-state through genocide against Anatolian
Christians, and forced assimilation or Turkification of Kurds. Just a few years
earlier, Sheikh Said had nominated a caliphal not a Kurdish candidate to his
proposed throne of Kurdistan. As David McDowall points out, this suggests that
"his idea of 'Kurdishness' was based less on ethnicity per se than on Kurdish religious particularism."[50]

Presumably, in order to avoid a situation of anarchy, point eight decreed
that Turkish law would continue to be enforced until the promulgation of
Kurdish law. Point nine repealed the obligation for wearing a hat and using Latin
characters. Everyone was free to dress according to his or her will. The declaration illustrates the far-reaching intentions of the insurgents, with new laws which
were to regulate everything from taxation to conscription to how women and
men were allowed to dress. In the assessment of Wadie Jwaideh, "By 1928, a
miniature Kurdish state had been created at Agri Dagh."[51]

Box 2.2 **Proclamation of Ararat Republic**

CADN, Fonds Beyrouth, Cabinet Politique 1055. « Proclamation de l'occupation effective et de l'institution du gouvernement ». Services civils du Délégué n° 1982. Alep, le 23 mai 1933.[a]

TRANSLATION FROM FRENCH

Proclamation of Effective Occupation and Institution of Government

1. With the help and grace of God, today the Turkish occupation in the Kurdish homeland has been ended, and a Kurdish national government has been established there.

2. Government affairs will be regulated and directed by the military command of "Khoyboun." The organization of administrative and military services, the appointment or dismissal of civil and military officials, the making or annulment of all decisions relating to the various branches of government, will be the competence of the said commanders.

3. Anyone from the territories gradually occupied by the Kurdish armies is called upon to assist this army and to discharge all the duties incumbent upon him to ensure its salvation. The preparation of means of transport and food is part of these duties. Any deviation from this will be considered a betrayal of the Fatherland.

4. Officials and residents are invited to deliver, within 24 hours, to the command or the authority designated by it, all objects, currency or weaponry belonging to the State.

5. Those who know the places where the objects mentioned in article 4 are hidden, are invited to notify the same authorities within the same period.

6. The security of foreign consular establishments is guaranteed, under the guarantee of the Kurdish government.

7. All residents, regardless of race and religion, will be treated equally provided they obey all the regulations and laws of the Kurdish government. It is absolutely forbidden to pillage private or state property. The freedom of relations is safeguarded.

8. Turkish law will be in force in the country until the promulgation of Kurdish law.

9. The obligation to wear a hat and use Latin characters is abrogated. Everyone is free to dress as they wish. Taxes and fees imposed arbitrarily will be reviewed and amended at the earliest opportunity.

10. No account will be taken of the sentences handed down by the Turkish courts on the Kurdish question. On the other hand, people who have been convicted of common law crimes are granted amnesty.

11. From the moment of the distribution of this proclamation, martial law will be in force in the country. It is forbidden to walk in the street from sunset until dawn. It is also prohibited to hold meetings during the day or at night, either indoors or outdoors. Bars and cabarets are permanently closed and cafes can only be opened until sunset.

12. The slightest deviation from the prescriptions of this proclamation, which has the force of law, will be considered as a disobedience to the Kurdish government and a betrayal of the Fatherland. Offenders will be sentenced to death.

---

[a] Tejel, *La Ligue Nationale Kurde Khoyboun*, 56–57

As some of the points in this declaration make clear, the Ararat Rebellion was in some ways in reaction to the secularist and modernizing reforms initiated by Ankara. These included closing down the religious madrasas, dissolving the Caliphate in 1924, and the reform of the alphabet in 1928.[52] According to a news report at the time, one of the insurgents reportedly killed a teacher for holding classes in a school instead of a mosque.[53]

However, other elements were more forward-looking, such as the proclamation of ethnic and religious equality, and the decision to cooperate between Kurds and Armenians. The signing of a Treaty of Collaboration is significant, especially because some of the Kurdish population were complicit in assisting in the genocide of Armenians just a few years earlier. This tragic irony was not lost on the British Ambassador Sir George Clerk, who reported about a new law in June 1927 which empowered the government to

> transport from the Eastern Vilayets an indefinite number of Kurds or other elements . . . the Government has already begun to apply to the Kurdish elements . . . the policy which so successfully disposed of the Armenian Minority in 1915. It is a curious trick of fate that the Kurds, who were the principal agent employed for the deportation of Armenians, should be in danger of suffering the same fate as the Armenians only twelve years later.[54]

The question of Kurdish complicity in the persecution of the Christian population of Anatolia has led to major divisions within subsequent Armenian and Assyrian political parties that continue until today. While some organizations remain skeptical of any engagement with the Kurds, others have actively tried to overcome these past grievances and work together as allies. How one interprets the Armenian genocide, Seyfo massacre, the persecution of the Kurds, and other tragedies that occurred during this time, has been key in shaping the

consciousness of the inhabitants of northern Syria, and hence their current political projects. This leads us to the question of ideology.

The scholarly debate on whether the Ararat Republic was motivated more
by nationalistic sentiment or religious fervor is somewhat curious. If one pays
attention to what the rebels actually did (as opposed to the propaganda used
against them) their aspirations for autonomy become clear: they declared a republic, hoisted a flag, wrote a national anthem, and demanded that all Turkish
soldiers leave. They appeared to have created a court-martial to try Turkish
officers they captured.[55] Ibrahim Pasha Heski Tello was made head of the civilian administration. While the extent of any state-like administration remains unclear, the insurgents proclaimed that Turkish laws and decrees were
abolished, created their own laws, controlled a large swath of territory, and had
an impressive array of external relations with Persia, the mandatory powers in
Syria and Iraq, the League of Nations, and the Second International. In Syria
alone, the Xoybûn League had branches in Aleppo, Damascus, Antioch, Hama,
Jarablus, and Al Hasakah. In Iraq, there were branches in Baghdad, Mosul, and
Zakho. Further afield, Xoybûn had branches in Beirut, Cairo, Amman, Paris,
and Detroit.[56]

Given how obvious their aspirations for autonomy were, one has to wonder
why Turkish officials and Kemalist-inclined historians tried so hard to claim otherwise? Jwaideh argues that it had to do with Turkish demands to control the oil
around Mosul. Extending Turkish sovereignty to that region required claiming
that the people of that area actually wanted to be part of the Turkish Republic.

> The Turkish government's official acknowledgement of the nationalistic
> character of the Kurdish rebellion would have completely undermined
> Turkey's case. The Turks could not very well admit that Kurds north of
> the Brussels Line were engaged in a bloody struggle for their indepen-
> dence against the Turkish army, while contending that Kurds south of
> that line were eager to rejoin the Turkish state.[57]

By contrast, I suggest that what the Kurds and Armenians were doing on Mount
Ararat was in many ways ahead of their time, and cannot be grasped within the
scope of a debate limited to nationalism or religious fervor as the two frames of
reference.

Women of Ararat

Of all the many gaps in our knowledge about the Mount Ararat revolt, the question of women's participation in these events is perhaps the biggest lacuna.
British colonial officers recorded reams of pages and were in some cases quite
perceptive. Yet they were seemingly unable to overcome their gender biases. Very

few women are mentioned in the 805 pages of archival documents collected in
Volume Seven of the *Records of the Kurds* which covers most of the period of the
Ararat revolt. We do know that already during the 1914 Bitlis revolt, women not
only provided food but fought as insurgents alongside the men, as documented
by Celîlê Celil based on an analysis of Armenian newspapers from the time.[58]
Women also appear to have fought as insurgents during the Mount Ararat revolt.
We know this because it was documented by another woman: Rosita Forbes, a
British journalist and traveler. Although Forbes was an outside observer and her
account may reflect the attendant biases and a somewhat romanticized notion
of the events, she deserves credit for chronicling the participation of women at
all. Furthermore, she had actually visited the region of eastern Anatolia whereas
many of the (male) British colonial officials had not. She wrote,

> As Sultan el Atrash was to the Druses, so was Tello to the frontier Kurds.
> His fame had already passed into song, and encouraged by his shouted
> name, women would take up the rifles dropped by the wounded.
> Fighting side by side with their men, they seemed to enjoy the sport,
> for they returned to their villages, blood-stained and smiling with the
> boast, "We are not afraid of our enemies. When we see them coming,
> we laugh, for how can an army reach us here?"[59]

Persian documents also attest to the presence of women, and how they were executed for their role in the rebellion, just as men were. On December 20, 1930—
after the Turkish government officially declared that the rebellion had been
crushed—some thirty Kurdish women were reportedly executed by a firing squad
in Bayazit by Turkish forces. A Persian document notes that the Turks shoot all
men, women and children who they take as prisoners from the Kurds. The same
document notes the following: "the decision has been taken to annihilate the
Kurdish element (*mahve onsore Kord*) like the Armenians (*mesle Araminah*)."[60]

Repression, Deportation, and Turkification

Although British officials were seemingly blind to the role of women in these
tumultuous events, they did see very clearly, and report about, the level of repression. They also recognized that state violence was not only sanitized by
the official media, but presented as the very opposite. Sir George Clerk, British
Ambassador to Turkey, wrote in a memo already on October 4, 1927:

> in every press article, the policy of stern repression, if not of exter-
> mination which the Turkish Government is relentlessly pursuing
> towards its Kurdish minority, is solemnly presented as civilization and
> enlightenment.[61]

The repression of the Ararat Republic was severe, and widely reported about in American newspapers including the *New York Times, Washington Post, Los Angeles Times,* and even smaller regional media outlets such as the *Hartford Courant* (see Box 2.3). The American media was also quite explicit about the level of violence, even warning of "extermination" of the Kurds, as this excerpt from the *New York Times* makes clear:

> it was regarded as apparent by many that Turkey would desire to pursue the Kurds across the Persian frontier if Persia did not cooperate in their extermination.[62]

Multiple military offenses resulted in the Zilan massacre in July 1930. Estimates are that somewhere between 15,000 and 47,000 insurgents were killed. Despite the brutal level of repression, archival documents illustrate that even a year after the Zilan massacre, insurgents continued to fight, and the Kurdish-Armenian alliance continued to send funds to support the rebels on Ararat and expand the geographical scope of their operations.

Yet rifts were emerging. At a joint meeting on May 28, 1931, both Dashnak and Xoybûn agreed to "organize the bases of insurrection" in a vast region from Mount Ararat to Erzerum, Muş, and stretching south to the Syrian border.

They unanimously agreed to not only continue the insurrection, but to expand it. The minutes from the meeting, taken in French, are ten pages long and state their intentions quite clearly:

> The common task of Hoyboun and Dashnak must be above all to organize the bases of insurrection and resistance in the following districts:
> 1. Ararat, including all areas north of Alashkert Erzerum and the Soviet border
> 2. Zilan extending south to Van and Muş
> 3. Hakkâri i.e., the region between Iraq and Persia up to Van and Bitlis
> 4. Botan encompassing Jazira, Siirt, Midyat up to Hakkâri
> 5. Sassoun encompassing the region from the Syrian border to Muş
> 6. South of Dersim to Mazıdağı and Divrek
>
> As their financial resources increase, the two parties, by mutual agreement, will introduce revolutionary agents into the regions, either to strengthen the organizations already existing in some places, or to set up these new organizations.[63]

However, the ARF and Xoybûn disagreed over the course of action in Iraq. The ten-page-long minutes of the meeting include separate sections where Xoybûn and Dashnak explain their positions. Xoybûn declared they would "grant the Kurds of the South their political and moral assistance" while Dashnak voiced "great concerns" about their support for the Kurdish national movement of Iraq, wanting instead to remain focused on their common struggle on Mount Ararat.[64]

The following month, on June 18, 1931, Sureya Bedirkhan wrote a letter to the ARF Central Committee in Paris. He complained that the ARF regional offices in Persia and Iraq exhibited "great nonchalance" in acting as liaison with the Kurds. In a response dated July 20, 1931, the ARF Central Committee requested further information as to who had allegedly failed in their duties, and that their own information contradicted his: "Our comrades are in communication with Ihsan Nouri Pasha at the risk of their lives and they have given him their moral and material assistance."[65]

Eventually, the Ararat revolt was crushed. Some Turkish officials saw this as not merely a military defeat, but as having entirely resolved the Kurdish issue, or rather buried it. Tevfik Rustu Bey, the Turkish Minister of Foreign Affairs and a known perpetrator during the Armenian genocide, is reported to have said at a meeting with journalists in Tehran, "There is no longer a problem by the name of Kurdish and this question has become a part of history."[66] On September 19, 1930 the nationalist *Milliyet* reportedly published a cartoon (Figure 2.5) showing Mt Ararat with a grave bearing the inscription "Imagined Kurdistan is buried here."[67]

dessin paru dans le journal turc "Milliyet"
après la fin de la révolte de l'Agri-Dagh,
avec l'inscription sur la pierre tombale :
Le rêve d'un Kurdistan libre est enterré ici.

Figure 2.5 Historical cartoon showing Mt Ararat with a grave bearing the inscription "Imagined Kurdistan is buried here." Reportedly published in Milliyet after the Mt Ararat Republic was crushed.

Box 2.3 **American Newspapers**

EXCERPTS FROM AMERICAN NEWSPAPERS ABOUT THE
REPRESSION OF THE MOUNT ARARAT REVOLT AND FORCED
RESETTLEMENT OF KURDS 1930–1931

**"Kurdish Rebels Use New Machine Guns: Turkish Exiles Believed
to Be in Command of Tribesmen Around Mount Ararat.** FIGHT
AGAINST MODERNISM Spokesmen Say Allah Sent Them to Wreak
Vengeance on Turks for Quitting Old Customs. Revolt Aimed Against
Modernism." *New York Times* July 13, 1930.

Although dressed like savages in white trousers and sheepskins, the
Kurdish rebels are armed with the latest model machine guns and
are believed to have some Turkish exiles in command. Witnesses of
the trouble at Erzinjan say the Kurds are cutting the rims from their
captives' hats to make them resemble fezes. The rebels killed a teacher
because he held classes in a school instead of a mosque. Attempts to
break the Turkish blockade around Mount Ararat have failed and the
rebels, running short of food, are threatened with starvation. Much
propaganda material was found on prisoners taken by the Turks.

"Turkey Herds Kurds from Noah's Refuge." *Washington Post,* **December
27, 1931.**

Turbulent Kurds who launched revolt against the Turkish Republic
from the crag where the Ark grounded, are being shipped to Turkey's
peaceful western provinces. To avert further rebellions, the Turkish
government is moving thousands of the Halikanli tribe to the shores
of the Marmora. With tents, cattle and swarms of women and children, these Kurds are trekking to lands which the government has
allotted them in the hope that they will become peaceful farmers.

Turkish government officials made little effort to hide their contempt for
non-Turks. Judging by their public statements, it would appear that the more explicit they were in expressing their belief in the ethnic superiority of Turks, the
easier it was to justify assimilation or Turkification. Mahmud Esad Bozkurt, the
Interior Minister of Turkey at the time and also a perpetrator of the Armenian
genocide, exemplified this in the following statement in 1930:

Only the Turkish nation has the privilege of demanding national
rights in this country. There is no possibility that other ethnic groups'

demands for such a right will be recognized. There is no need to hide the truth. The Turks are the sole owners and the sole nobles of this country. Those who are not of Turkish origin have only one right: to serve and be the slaves, without question, of the noble Turkish nation.[68]

The severe repression of the insurgents on Mount Ararat was just the beginning of numerous military operations to put down Kurdish rebellions. Between 1924 and 1938, only 1 out of 18 Turkish military engagements occurred outside Kurdistan. After 1945 until the end of the Cold War, apart from the Korean War (1949–1952) and the invasion of Cyprus (1974), Turkish army operations continued to be directed against the Kurds.[69]

Until today, the region of Ararat continues to be the poorest province within Turkey in terms of GDP per capita. According to data from the OECD and the Turkish Statistical Institute, the GDP per capita of Ararat in 2018 was $8,958, or less than one-fifth that of Istanbul, the wealthiest region, with a GDP per capita of $45,771.[70]

Regional Impact of the Ararat Republic in Turkey, Syria, and Persia

The crushing of the Ararat Republic had reverberations across the region. In Turkey, there was a turn to severe Turkification. In Persia, authorities feared another revolt was in the offing, which then happened in 1946 with the declaration of the Mahabad Republic, and in Syria, the exiled leadership of Khoybun continued their activities. Kurds and Armenians who had escaped from Turkey formed a movement demanding political autonomy between 1936 and 1939 in the Jazira region of northeastern Syria. As Jordi Tejel Gorgas explains, the origins of the autonomist movement can be found in the *"bloc kurdo-chrétien"* or Kurdish-Christian alliance.[71] However, although most of their demands were rejected by the French mandatory authorities—including the establishment of Kurdish language schools, recognition of Kurdish as an official language, and the appointment of Kurdish administrators in Kurdish areas, and one of their leaders, Osman Sebrî, was even exiled to Madagascar—their activities were still "tolerated" by the French.

This Kurdish-Christian alliance that blossomed on the slopes of Mount Ararat has been rekindled in northeastern Syria. As explained in the following chapter, Christians in the Kurdish-led Syrian Democratic Forces (SDF) are organized in four units. Those who identify as Syriac Christians are mainly organized in the Syriac Military Council and the Bethnahrin Women Protection Forces, while Assyrians in the region around Tel Tamer are organized in the Khabur Guards. Finally, those who identify as Armenians—including those who are still Christian today and those whose ancestors converted to Islam to escape persecution—are organized in the Martyr Nubar Ozanyan Brigade. It is to them we turn next.

3

The SDF

The Evolution of the YPG into Syria's Second-Largest Armed Force

[After the uprising started in 2011] . . . *"We talked to politicians in Aleppo, Afrin, and Kobani about creating a military unit—and people would laugh at us. They told us: 'We don't have weapons and we don't have a mountain. We don't need a military, after a few weeks Bashar al-Assad will be gone.' Then in February 2012, because of the civil war in Deraa and other places, people started to give us weapons."*
—Polat Can, founding member of the YPG[1]

Syrian Kurds had been persecuted for decades under the rule of the Baath Party, but the 2004 uprising that started in Qamishli marked a turning point. Some began advocating for Kurdish administration of Kurdish areas, while others became convinced of the necessity of creating an armed group to defend themselves from Assad's brutal security apparatus.[2] The clashes began after a football match when supporters of the team from Deir Ezzor began chanting loudly in support of Saddam Hussein, and insulting Iraqi Kurdish leaders Barzani and Talabani as traitors. Brandishing posters of Saddam, whose Anfal campaign had killed hundreds of thousands of Kurds in Iraq, quickly transformed the football match from a sporting event to a political battle between those who supported and opposed the Baathist regimes on both sides of the border.[3] The skirmishes escalated into larger antigovernment protests and spread to other Kurdish areas of Jazira, Afrin, as well as Aleppo and Damascus.[4] Rioters toppled a prominent statue of former President Hafez Al-Assad in Qamishli, reminiscent of the much more publicized events in Baghdad in April 2003 when a protester took a sledgehammer to the statue of Saddam Hussein. Security forces cracked down hard across northern Syria, killing 36 people and arresting more than 2,000 Kurds.[5] The Kurdistan Workers' Party (PKK), having been expelled from Syria five years earlier, watched the events from their perch in the Qandil mountains of Iraq.

Statelet of Survivors. Amy Austin Holmes, Oxford University Press. © Oxford University Press 2024.
DOI: 10.1093/oso/9780197621035.003.0003

In March 2005, on the anniversary of what Joseph Daher referred to as the "Kurdish *Intifada*," the Kurdish Youth Movement in Syria (*Tevgere Ciwanên Kurd*) was established. Known by the acronym TCK, the youth organization had to operate underground.[6] The Assad regime was able to maintain its iron grip on the north, making it virtually impossible to engage in peaceful opposition activities, not to mention organizing a militia or procuring weapons.[7] The TCK went on to become one of the largest political youth groups and played a key role in the protests in 2011.

The 2004 uprising also happened around the same time the PKK was undergoing a paradigm shift and its most severe internal crisis since it was founded in the late 1970s. As discussed in Chapter 5, the capture of Abdullah Öcalan in 1999 had a profound impact on the PKK's ideology and strategy, as did the US invasion of Iraq in 2003. Perhaps influenced by the rise of the semi-autonomous Kurdistan Region of Iraq in the wake of the US invasion, the PKK shifted to a regional strategy in each of the four countries with large Kurdish minorities. This culminated in the creation of the Kurdish Free Life Party (PJAK) in Iran, the Kurdistan Democratic Solution Party (KDSP) in Iraq, and the Democratic Union Party (PYD) in Syria.[8]

The power struggles within the PKK at the time were complex. There were differing assessments of the changing geopolitical landscape, but also disagreements over the rigid behavioral guidelines for cadres that prohibited marriage and sexual relations, as discussed in Chapter 5. As a result of the PKK's inability to resolve these differences, two separate factions defected from the organization—together totaling several thousand people. It was a decision that could have cost them their lives. One faction centered around Osman Öcalan, a Kurd from Turkey who had been one of the cofounders of the PKK, but perhaps best known as the brother of Abdullah Öcalan. The second faction included many Syrian Kurds, such as Hozan Afrini. Members of his group moved to the region around Suleimani, and although they lived in military camps, in the assessment of one senior cadre, other than training, "they didn't do anything."[9]

Whether one looks at the power struggles within the PKK, or the football match in Qamishli in 2004, which escalated into deadly clashes because of references to events in Iraq, it is clear that any attempt to analyze Kurdish history must take into consideration their transnational connections.

Nisrine Abdullah's family exemplifies these interconnections. She was born in Derik in 1979, and later went on to serve as spokesperson of the YPJ. I had the opportunity to interview her twice during my field work in Syria. During the first interview in March 2018, she related to me how she came from a family with a long history of participation in Kurdish rebellions, dating back to the Sheikh Said uprising in Turkey in the early twentieth century. She explained how members of her extended family had fought in three of the four countries that contain Kurdish minorities:

> My great grandfather and his brother took part in the Sheikh Said uprising. They were both sentenced to death by the Ottomans. They were later given amnesty on the condition that they leave the country. That's why they came to Derik [...] Two of my cousins fell fighting in the PKK; that was fifteen years ago. Some of my other relatives are now among the Peshmerga in Iraqi Kurdistan. My brother and I are fighting here in Rojava.

Almost as an afterthought, she laughed, and said, "Only *Rojhelat* is missing."[10]

The Mixed-Gender Yekîneyên Xweparastina Gel (YXG): The First Syrian Kurdish Militia

It was not until early 2011, when the so-called Arab Spring protests were sweeping the country, that the opportunity arose for the Syrian Kurdish militias to begin to operate in the open. The withdrawal of regime forces created a vacuum, allowing the militias to emerge from the underground. But many of the same hurdles they faced in 2004 remained.

In the summer of 2011 a small force called Yekîneyên Xweparastina Gel (YXG) or People's Self-Defense Units was created, which can be considered the predecessor of what is now known as the People's Protection Units (YPG) and Women's Protection Units (YPJ). Born into a family with a long history of involvement in the Kurdish struggle, Nisrine Abdullah was politicized at an early age. When she was 16 years old she was arrested for participating in Kurdish politics, and spent three months in prison in Damascus. She went on to become one of the cofounders of the YXG. When I interviewed her a second time, in September 2020, I asked her about the YXG and how they decided to create it. Although important as a precursor to the YPG and YPJ, outside of local Kurdish news media, not been much had been written about the YXG.

> So the Kurds of Rojava were always linked to others . . . But, in contrast to the other three parts of Kurdistan, which all had military units or political parties with military wings, in Rojava we had none . . . This is why it was a challenge not just to create the YXG, but also how to announce it. So, the YXG was never formally announced. But the people knew.[11]

There were small units all over northern Syria, including in the Kurdish neighborhoods of Aleppo and Damascus. At the time, their numbers were small: some 2,000 to 3,000 people in total. Women were already part of these groups, although not yet as an independent women's militia, which the YPJ later became. Polat Can described to me how they were not only small in number, but utterly underequipped: "We didn't have real weapons, we only had knives and pistols. I was living in Aleppo, but my pistol was in Derik."[12] The distance between these two cities exceeds 500 km. Presumably because of the checkpoints along the road between the two cities, he had to take precautions. He continued, "I asked my sister to get my pistol, but it took her three visits. First she brought the bullets, then the piston, then the pistol. We didn't have Kalashnikovs, only some had a pump gun for hunting." Some of the very few published interviews with other members of the YXG confirmed the lack of equipment. Lorin Efrin, a female combatant who was part of the armed mobilization since 2011, said the YXG was "semi-professional and lacked armaments. But it had a lot of faith and determination."[13]

On March 11, 2012 the YXG fought in Aleppo against pro-regime forces known as "Shabiha."[14] The fighting ensued after the pro-regime forces attacked the Kurdish neighborhood of Sheikh Maqsood, killing a Kurdish woman by the name of Gulay.[15] The group didn't have an official name, or a flag, or a commander. Unofficially, Polat Can, a Kurd born in Kobani in 1980, acted as their de facto commander. After a battle lasting some four to five hours, they managed to force the regime to retreat. They were only 15 people, fighting with pump guns, and without much training. Of the 15, 11 or 12 were injured, and three were killed. Sheikh Maqsood was the first battle the Kurds fought against the Syrian regime.

By the summer of 2012, the ranks of the YXG had swelled, and it became necessary to formalize the informal units into a new structure. It was during the summer of 2012 that the YXG was restructured into the YPG. Xebat Dêrîk, a former PKK commander, was one of the cadres involved in setting up the YPG.[16]

The Assad Regime Withdraws from Northern Syria and Kurds Declare Formation of YPG

The withdrawal of regime forces from northern Syria in the summer of 2012 has been interpreted as both a sign of Syrian Kurds' collusion with the Assad regime, and as a form of rebellion against it. There are elements of truth to both interpretations.[17] What is not in question, however, is that the regime was confronted with an armed uprising and unable to fight on multiple fronts at the same time. Assad's decision to withdraw from the north allowed his military and security forces to turn their guns on rebels in the south.

On July 19, 2012, the Mukhabarat and internal security forces withdrew from Kobani. Large anti-government demonstrations had been taking place, with protests in front of the police department and various security offices, demanding that they drop their weapons and leave the city. At the time, Idris Nassan was working as a teacher. He was a member of the Democratic Party of Kurds in Syria (PDKS), known in Kurdish as *Partiya Demoqrat a Kurdî a Sûrî*.[18] The PDKS had split off from another party in 1970. Without going into the details of the many Kurdish political parties and their various splinter groups, suffice it to say that in early 2011, the PDKS (without a hyphen) was more closely aligned to PDK-S (with a hyphen) and was part of the Kurdish National Council, in opposition to the PYD. Mr. Nassan received a phone call from one of his fellow party members, who told him to stop whatever he was doing, and take part in the demonstrations so they could occupy a building. The plan was to seize an abandoned government building and turn it into the headquarters of their political party. According to Mr. Nassan, the regime employees in the Kurdish-majority city of Kobani were mainly Arabs who were from other regions in the south of Syria. He recalled: "Even their cars we took from them—they are after all public cars. The regime got in minibuses or other types of public transport, and left."[19] While the PYD and YXG may have been the driving force, there were other political actors who were involved in—and had an interest in—the withdrawal of the Baathist security apparatus.

Soon thereafter the security forces were also expelled from Afrin and Derik. After another month or two, they retreated from Amude, Derbesiye, then later they were kicked out of Rumeilan and Girkê Legê (Al-Muabbada). According to Polat Can, "we were working for four to five months for all regime guys to leave."[20]

Local people created popular committees, known in Arabic as *legaan shaabeya* to fill in the security vacuum—similar to the neighborhood committees created in Egypt and Tunisia when the police withdrew and were absent from the streets for six months or more during the revolution in 2011. But unlike Egypt and Tunisia, where the police later returned to their police stations and the *legaan shaabeya* faded away, in the Kurdish region of Syria, the newly created security forces retain control. The Kurdish-led *legaan shaabeya* became institutionalized as a local police force and known as the *Asayîs*, eventually engaging in arrests just as regular police forces do. Members of the Syriac-Assyrian Christian minority affiliated with the Syriac Union Party (SUP) also organized police forces to protect their areas, which they referred to as *Sutoro*.

The YPG was officially announced at a three-day conference that began on July 19, 2012 the same day the regime withdrew from Kobani.[21] The Kurds didn't want to take any chances that another armed actor may step in to fill the vacuum. Both the timing and location of the conference, held at a base that formally belonged to the Special Forces of the Syrian Army (*Quwat al Hassa Geish al Suriye*), suggest there was prior knowledge and coordination between the regime and the PYD. The formal announcement took place on the last day of the conference, which was attended by other Kurdish political parties as well, including the Hizb al Takadum al Dimokraty, which did not have a military wing. Nisrine Abdullah described the fact that other non-PYD political parties attended the conference and sent their youth to join the YPG, as a sign that the newly formed YPG represented Kurds of various political affiliations, although the dominance of the PYD clearly continued. At least two other factors also contributed to the growing strength of the YPG, even prior to the beginning of US support. First, with the militarization of the conflict, Islamist forces began to gain ground and encroach on Kurdish and Christian-inhabited regions of northern Syria. As a result, even those who had previously been outspoken critics of the PYD began to voluntarily join the ranks of the YPG, seeing it as the lesser of two evils and necessary for the sake of survival.[22] Second, the inability of the KNC to exert real influence on the ground, and the PYD's unwillingness to allow KNC-linked fighters to form a separate unit outside the command structure of the YPG, also contributed to ensuring that the YPG began to assume a de facto monopoly on the use of force in areas under its control. Syrian Kurds organized in the Rojava Peshmerga, or Roj Pesh, had withdrawn to Iraqi Kurdistan and were supported by the KDP. In order to maintain a unified command structure, the PYD had offered to allow the Roj Pesh to return to Syria as individuals, but not as a separate brigade under a different command structure. While the KNC sees the decision as an example of the PYD's unwillingness to share power, it has also until now prevented the creation of competing militias which could potentially lead to an intra-Kurdish civil war, as happened between PUK and KDP Peshmerga in Iraqi Kurdistan in the 1990s.

Perwerde: Ideological Training

Unconsciously, every Kurd wants a Kurdish state. So we actively try to change that thought.

—Nisrine Abdullah, cofounder of the YPJ

The first ideological training academies were established in mid-2012, around the same time as the YPG was formally announced. The first academy was created in a village in the countryside of Derik. Ms. Abdullah explained that it was General Mazloum Abdi who asked her to create the academy. Back then, one training cycle lasted just ten days. In later years, the training cycles reportedly lasted six months or more. During the first three cycles, there were no women. But that changed during the fourth cycle. The amount of time dedicated to ideological training likely varied depending on the conflict, but it appears that the bulk of their training has always been dedicated to ideology. In their 2015 book,

Figure 3.1 YPJ Women wearing vests before they had uniforms

Anja Flach, Ercan Ayboğa, and Michael Knapp claim that most of the YPG's education is political in nature.[23] When I spoke to Ms Abdullah in the fall of 2020, she claimed that about three-fourths of their training is ideological, while only one-fourth is military training.

Ms. Abdullah explained that back in 2012, they still did not have uniforms, and no money to make uniforms. So the YXG were initially wearing civilian clothes. Her brother, however, was a tailor and offered to make vests for them. Vests were cheaper to make than entire uniforms, and were worn on top of civilian clothes (Figure 3.1). He reportedly made ten vests because there were just ten participants. But then in the next cycle, there were thirteen participants, so three did not have any vests. The ideology of democratic confederalism is described in more detail in Chapter 5.

Yekîneyên Parastina Jin (YPJ): Kurdish Women Form Their Own Militia

On April 4, 2013 the *Yekîneyên Parastina Jin* (YPJ) was formally announced. Based on the PKK's model that Kurdish women had fought for years to achieve, the YPJ was to be a women's army, separate and distinct from the men. The conference was held in Derik in the same base that used to belong to the Special Forces of the Syrian Army. According to Ms. Abdullah, at that time there were less than one thousand women in total who belonged to the YPJ, and all of them were Kurds. Even prior to the official creation of the YPJ, individual all-women's units existed in the YPG. The first one was the Martyr Ruken Battalion in Jinderes, Afrin in February 2013.[24]

Years prior to this, women in the PKK were already organized in separate all-female units. In the 1990s, the PKK underwent a sea change in which gender inequality shifted from being a secondary to one of the primary goals of their struggle. As explained more in Chapter 5, after being imprisoned Abdullah Öcalan began to write extensively about the creation of patriarchy and the growth of the state as leading to the enslavement of women. This new paradigm resulted in the PKK renouncing its goal of wanting to achieve an independent Kurdistan and instead fought for decentralization and gender equality in what it calls "democratic confederalism."[25] While some of the other male leaders in the PKK opposed the autonomous units of female warriors, women fought to keep them.

The creation of the YPJ in Syria was an outcome of this internal conflict within the movement, one that women had won. Already during the early days of the YPJ, Yezidi women had also joined the ranks. In May 2013, the first YPJ woman fell as a martyr in Afrin, Meryem Mihemed.[26] Later in the year, a Yezidi woman by the name of Berivan Fazil, was killed while fighting against Jebhat al Nusra in the region around Serêkaniyê.[27] While exact numbers are impossible to verify, (Table 3.1) provides a rough estimate of the rapid expansion of YPJ forces since 2013.

The spectacle of armed Kurdish women defeating ISIS captured the imagination of people around the world. The Western media in particular produced salacious images of Kalashnikov-toting young women, and yet a lot of the coverage remained relatively superficial.

My own involvement began in January 2015, when I traveled by car along the Turkish-Syrian border, and then by bus at night across the border, via

Table 3.1 **YPJ Forces**

Year	Estimated YPJ Forces
2013	1,000
2014	7,500
2016	7,500–10,000
2017	24,000

the outskirts of Mosul, eventually arriving in Erbil, the de facto capital of the Kurdistan Region of Iraq. A friend in Cairo who had organized aid to deliver to Syrian refugees in Turkey and the Kurdistan Region of Iraq asked if I wanted to join her. It seemed like a good way to spend the winter break. In Turkey, we visited numerous refugee camps, including one run by the Turkish government, and several others run by the Kurdish-led HDP party. In the government-run camp in Islahiye, I asked the man who worked there how many of the Syrian refugees were Kurds, as opposed to Arabs or other ethnic groups. His response was simple but startling: "We don't count Kurds."

Maybe for this reason, most Syrian Kurds who fled to Turkey as refugees seemed to prefer to live in the camps run by the HDP. I was told that the HDP was paying for the camps on their own, with no support from the government.

On a cold day in January, I remember standing on top of a building on the outskirts of Suruç, watching the liberation of Kobani just across the border. Then in June 2015 I made my first trip to Rojava, where I witnessed the liberation of Tel Abyad and also conducted a survey of the YPJ with a women's unit stationed in Kobani. During this very first trip in June 2015, I was able to conduct the survey with 46 people—all unmarried Kurdish women between the ages of 18 and 34, many of whom fought in the battles in Kobani, Tel Abyad, and elsewhere (Table 3.3). For now I will just highlight four of my findings from this initial round of the survey in 2015.

First, I found that 44 out of 46 respondents did *not* want to establish an independent Kurdish state, but wanted to remain part of Syria.[28] Although the sample size was still small, my early findings highlighted several issues of larger significance. First, I conducted this initial round of the survey in the summer of 2015, at a time when Kurdish leaders in Iraq had declared their intention to move forward with an independence referendum. My findings complicated the assumption held by many Western observers that all Kurds inherently want a state. Second, while several scholars have highlighted the ideological transformation that Öcalan had undergone, in which statehood was rejected as inherently repressive, and the rise of the notion of a "stateless society," my survey indicated that these ideas were not only embraced by cadres, but also by the rank-and-file.[29] Third, the views of the women in the survey also corroborated Article 12 of the Rojava Social Charter, which reads: "The Autonomous Regions form an integral part of Syria. It is a model for a future decentralized system of federal governance in Syria."[30]

Fourth, I found that many of the Kurdish women said that they were fighting not only against the Islamic State but also against the patriarchal norms of their own culture. A 24-year-old from Afrin said she joined the YPJ because there was "no equality between men and women in the society." A 22-year-old from Cizire said she joined because "of the suffering of women, and the YPJ was solving problems of women." A 21-year-old from Kobani said she joined simply because she "saw freedom in the YPJ."

The reasons for deciding to abandon the goal of establishing an independent Kurdistan were complex, but happened in part because Öcalan was "following the lead of the PKK women."[31] For years, women had fought alongside men in the PKK and other national liberation struggles. Despite making huge sacrifices, women often found themselves marginalized either within their own movement—as in the PKK—or after achieving independent statehood—as in the Algerian FLN—or both. In order to prevent the kind of marginalization that has occurred in the past, the YPJ was established as an independent women's unit, rather than being subsumed under the men's YPG (People's Protection Units).

Kurdish women's units also emerged in the Sinjar Mountain region of Iraq, a disputed territory claimed by both the Kurdistan Regional Government in Erbil and the central government in Baghdad. In August of 2014, it was about a dozen PKK veterans and YPG fighters who showed up to protect thousands of Yezidis after other security forces had withdrawn. Stranded on a mountaintop, the Yezidis were left defenseless just as ISIS militants had encircled them. By opening up a corridor, the Yezidis who had been entrapped on the Sinjar Mountain were able to escape to safety. It was this operation that impressed American officials about the YPG's "ability to quickly get things done."[32]

In the aftermath of the genocidal assault in Sinjar in August, young Yezidi women and men have also joined the self-defense forces. By the end of August 2014, or within a few weeks of the assault against the Yezidis in Sinjar, the YPG created local Sinjar defense forces, known as the Sinjar Resistance Units (YBS) and Women's Protection Units-Sinjar (YJS). In Rojhelat or Western Iran the women's militia is known as HPJ, while the YRK is the men's militia. All of these are considered local defense forces which operate in their respective corner of Kurdistan. Their purported goal is to act as a self-defense force for the local people, whether they are Kurds, Yezidis, Assyrians, Arabs or any other ethnic or religious group. By contrast, the militias directly under the command of the PKK are the Free Women's Units (YJASTAR) and People's Defense Forces (HPG), which may be deployed to any of the four regions of Kurdistan (Table 3.2).

July 19, 2012—the day the Assad regime withdrew from Kobani—came to symbolize the beginning of the Rojava Revolution. The day henceforth became a holiday, celebrated annually. Seven years later, I attended one of those celebrations in Qamishli on July 19, 2019. Walking from the hotel where I was staying, I found my way to the large stadium where the festivities were held. With both solemn speeches to commemorate the thousands of martyrs, and spirited dancing, people celebrated seven years of autonomy from the Assad

Table 3.2 **Kurdish Forces**

Kurdish Forces in Syria, Iraq, Iran, and Turkey			
Acronym	English Translation	Gender	Area of Operation
YPJ: Yekîneyên Parastina Jin	Women's Protection Units	Women	Northern Syria/ Rojava
YPG: Yekîneyên Parastina Gel	People's Protection Units	Men	Northern Syria/ Rojava
YJS: Yekîneyên Jinên Şengalê	Women's Protection Units Sinjar	Women	Sinjar Mountains/ Iraq
YBS: Yekîneyên Berxwedana Şengalê	Sinjar Resistance Units	Men	Sinjar Mountains/ Iraq
HPJ: Hêzên Parastina Jinê (HPJ)	Women's Defense Forces	Women	Western Iran/ Rojhelat
YRK: Yekîneyên Parastina Rojhilatê Kurdistan	Eastern Kurdistan Defense Units	Men	Western Iran/ Rojhelat
YJASTAR: Yekîneyên Jinên Azad ên Star	Free Women's Units	Women	All regions of Kurdistan
HPG: Hêzên Parastina Gel	People's Defence Forces	Men	All regions of Kurdistan

regime. Images of the President of Syria were nowhere to be seen, but there was a large banner with Öcalan's visage. Until now, the significance of the holiday is not fully appreciated.

Other anniversaries of the Syrian conflict were often used by analysts and activists to remind anyone who needed reminding that the Assad regime was vicious, corrupt, utterly undemocratic, and so forth. But the fact that one-third of the country had achieved a considerable degree of autonomy from Assad—and the holiday that symbolized and celebrated that remarkable achievement—is still often ignored. Even by people who openly advocated for the fall of the Assad regime.[33]

Be that as it may, by that point it had become more common to call it the "July 19 Revolution" rather than the Rojava Revolution. Perhaps because by then part of Rojava had been lost, as Afrin was under Turkish occupation, but the Autonomous Administration was in control of Raqqa, Deir Ezzor, and many other Arab regions far beyond the Kurdish heartland. The story of how that happened requires an understanding of how the Syrian Democratic Forces (SDF) evolved out of the YPG/YPJ into a multiethnic, multireligious force.

The YPG Evolves into the SDF

Of all the actors in the Syrian conflict, the SDF is perhaps the most misunderstood. This is in part due to the complexity and opaque connections between the various Kurdish armed groups operating in Syria, Turkey, Iraq, and Iran. In order to obtain continued American support, the YPG and YPJ were obliged to rebrand themselves as the SDF, emphasize their Syrian identity over their Kurdish identity, launch operations against ISIS in non-Kurdish areas of Syria, and drop their connections to Kurdish forces operating outside of Syria. The extent to which the latter has happened remains a matter of some dispute.

Between 2015 and 2020 I conducted the first field survey of the SDF through multiple visits to all of the governorates of North and East Syria under SDF control. This chapter is based on both my field survey of the rank-and-file and interviews with SDF commanders (Table 3.3 and 3.4).

Table 3.3 **Main Battles Fought by the YPG and Allies before the Creation of the SDF**

Battle	Date	Notes
Ras al-Ayn/Serekaniye	November 2012–September 23, 2013	Against the Al-Qaida affiliated Al Nusra Front and their allies.
Tel Kocer (Yarubiya)	October 2013	Against Al Nusra Front, who wanted to control Yarubiya/Tel Kocer border gate.
Sinjar	August 2014	First indirect contact between YPG and the United States. UN Commission Report "They came to destroy" credits YPG with saving thousands of people's lives.
Kobani	September 2014–January 26, 2015	According to YPG fighters ISIS allegedly attacked with support of Turkey (Turkey also allowed Pesh/FSA in at later stage). Global Coalition to defeat ISIS gave direct support to YPG after October 1, 2014.
Qamishlo southern countryside/Tel Hamis/Tel Brak	Liberated February 27, 2015	Coordination between YPG and Al-Sanadid Forces.
Kobani southern countryside/Sheikh Tahtany	Liberated March 5, 2015	

Table 3.3 **Continued**

Battle	Date	Notes
Abdulaziz Mountains/ Mount Kizwan	Liberated May 21, 2015	
Tel Tamer countryside and Serekaniye countryside	Operation began June 6, 2015. The Tel Tamer countryside had been attacked by ISIS on February 23, 2015.	
Operation Euphrates Volcano	Suluk liberated on June 14, 2015 and Tel Abyad/Gire Spi on June 15, 2015.	Cut off main supply route used to transfer wounded ISIS members to hospitals in Turkey.
Ain Issa	Liberated June 7, 2015	
Sarrin (south of Kobani)	Liberated September 27, 2015	

Table 3.4 **Battles Fought after Creation of the Syrian Democratic Forces**

Battle	Dates	Notes
Al-Hol offensive (southern Hasakeh countryside)	October 2015–November 2015	First offensive declared by the Syrian Democratic Forces after their official founding.
Tishrin Dam offensive	December 2015	Strategic dam captured north of Raqqa, cutting ISIS supply lines.
Manbij	May 31, 2016–August 27, 2016	
Tabqa	March–May 10, 2017	SDF capture Tabqa dam and first land south of the Euphrates.
Operation Wrath of Euphrates (Raqqa and surrounding countryside)	Campaign announced November 6, 2016. Raqqa city fully liberated October 20, 2017.	Raqqa was considered the de facto capital of ISIS prior to its liberation.
Operation Jazira Storm (Deir Ezzor countryside)	Campaign announced September 9, 2017. Final ISIS pocket in Baghouz liberated on March 23, 2019.	The end of this battle marked the territorial defeat of ISIS.

The SDF was founded in October 2015 as an alliance of the YPG/YPJ and various FSA groups that had previously formed the Euphrates Volcano in Hasakah province of northeast Syria. Because the SDF grew out of predominantly Kurdish forces in the YPG/YPJ, some observers continue to refer to the SDF as "Kurdish forces." But this characterization is inaccurate. By 2019, and possibly even earlier, Arabs constituted more than half of all SDF fighters. This is because as the fight against the Islamic State continued and major Arab population centers were liberated such as Manbij, Raqqa, and Deir Ezzor, more and more Arabs from those regions were incorporated. My survey respondents belonged to forty-six different Arab tribes or sub-tribes, representing the tribal diversity of the region. Fighters from all of the seven governorates of northern and eastern Syria now belong to the SDF, as well as some who joined from territories controlled by the regime of Bashar al-Assad. More than 20,000 square miles of land—about one-third of Syria—is now under the control of the SDF. This territory is about the same size as Croatia or Costa Rica.

Led by Kurds, the YPG evolved over time into the SDF: a multiethnic, multireligious force in which all the indigenous peoples of the region are represented. Arabs, Assyrians, Armenians, Yezidis, Circassians, and Turkmen fought alongside Kurds to defend their homeland. By 2019, when the SDF had liberated all of Syrian territory from the ISIS Caliphate, there were some 100,000 fighters (including SDF and Internal Security Forces) under the leadership of SDF commander-in-chief Mazlum Abdi, a Syrian Kurd and former PKK cadre.[34] The majority of his rank-and-file fighters, however, were Arabs. While conscription can account for some of this growth, it does not tell the whole story. Until today, the rules on mandatory conscription have never been implemented in several Arab-majority regions; in previous years there was even less enforcement. Furthermore, conscription only applies to men and is currently limited to one year, although the length of conscription has varied over the course of the conflict. How was the PKK's sister militia in Syria, an organization that historically fought for an independent Kurdistan, able to successfully recruit and retain tens of thousands of Arabs—as well as Christians, Yezidis, and Turkmen, for multiple years? What sort of a political project did they create and promise, which retained the loyalty of an ethnically diverse coalition?

In a previous era, Kurdish and Palestinian guerrilla fighters had rubbed shoulders and at times trained together in the Bekaa Valley of Lebanon. But the PKK, being a Kurdish movement that waged a war of national liberation in Turkey in pursuit of an independent Kurdistan, had always been dominated by Kurds. While there were some Arabs who joined the PKK, Aziz Arab being known as the PKK's first Arab martyr in 1986, he was an exception. For most of its history, the PKK had never incorporated Arabs in any significant numbers into its ranks.[35]

My field survey of over 400 SDF members reveals that there are three main reasons for the SDF's success in recruiting and retaining non-Kurds: First, the SDF offered material incentives such as salaries and training opportunities.[36] Second, the existence of a common threat—first ISIS and now Turkey—solidified bonds between Kurds and Arabs and also prompted many to enlist. Third, the survey shows that many Arab members of the SDF support at least some, if not all, of the basic political principles upon which the SDF and the Autonomous Administration of North and East Syria (AANES) are based. While the SDF is often portrayed as the Syrian offshoot of the PKK, I found that out of 386 respondents only 202 (52.3%) reported that they had ever read anything by Abdullah Öcalan, while 184 respondents (47.7%) said they had not. For more on the evolution of the ideology known as "Democratic Confederalism," see Chapter 5.

To highlight the religious and ethnic diversity of the SDF, in what follows I will describe the Syriac-Assyrian Military Council (MFS), the Bethnahrain Women's Protection Forces (HSNB), the Al Sanadid Forces of the Shammar Tribe, the Manbij Military Council (MMC), and the Martyr Nubar Ozanyan Brigade (Figure 3.2). The Yezidi minority joined the SDF as individuals, but did not form a separate Yezidi unit, as happened in the Sinjar region of Iraq in the aftermath of the genocide in 2014. In Sinjar, a disputed territory, the PYD-aligned militias were known as Yekîneyên Berxwedana Şengalê (YBS) or Sinjar Resistance Units and Yekîneyên Jinên Şengalê (YJS) or Women's Protection Units/Sinjar. In the summer of 2016 I spent three weeks conducting fieldwork in Sinjar where I was able to carry out the survey with members of the YBS and YJS. However, as the YBS/YJS are located on the Iraqi side of the border and not part of the SDF; they are not included in the current chapter. During the course of my survey research in Syria, purely by coincidence, I met several Yezidi men who were rank-and-file members of the SDF. According to General Mazloum, there were two Yezidis also serving as military commanders. However, they were based in Shahba, the region where many people from Afrin fled to after the Turkish occupation.[37]

The Dawronoyo and the Syriac-Assyrian Military Council (MFS)

Of all the diverse components of Syrian society, the Christian minority was one of the first to strike a deal with the Kurds as brothers-and-sisters-in-arms. There was a history to it.

The Christian minority in the Northeast identify variously as Syriacs, Assyrians, Armenians, Chaldeans, and Aramaeans. As explained in Chapter 2, many of them settled in the region after fleeing persecution during the time of the Ottoman Empire. While the atrocities visited upon the Armenians

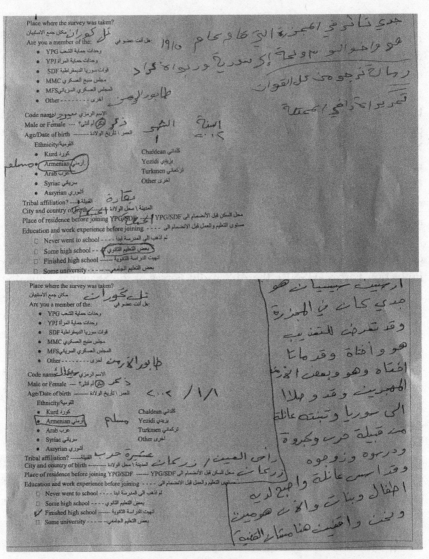

Figure 3.2 Armenian Muslims in the Martyr Nubar Ozanyan Brigade – Hand-written survey answers Source: **Sirob**: Armenian Muslim, age 22, born in Al Hasakah, belongs to Baggara tribe. Some high school. Joined September 2019. Fought in Ras al-Ayn (Hand-written in Arabic) "My grandfather was in the massacre of 1915. He and his 3 brothers they went to Syria, the Kurds adopted them. My message to the Global Coalition: liberate the occupied areas."

Source: **Sivak**, age 22, born in Ras al-Ayn, belongs to Harb tribe. Finished high school. Joined March 2019; fought in Ras al-Ayn against the FSA. (Hand-written in Arabic) "Arsin Sissisyan was in the Armenian massacre, he was tortured, and his two sisters. They came to Syria with other Armenian IDPs. The Harb tribe adopted them, they got an education, had a family. We are here now for the Armenian cause."

have slowly gained recognition as a genocide, the persecution of Syriacs and Assyrians that culminated in the Seyfo Massacre in 1915, has not. Although often portrayed as a religious minority, the Christian communities in fact constitute both an ethnic and a religious minority. They call their people Suryoye (Syriacs) and their homeland Bethnahrain (Mesopotamia). Their language, referred to as Aramaic or Syriac, is the language historians believe was spoken by Jesus.

Ravaged by waves of violence, a small community of Syriacs persisted in the Syrian-Turkish borderlands, concentrated mainly in the Tur Abdin region of southeastern Turkey and the Jazira region of northeastern Syria. In the 1980s, there was an increase in attacks against Syriacs in Turabdin by unknown perpetrators. Whether the killers were religious extremists, or ultranationalists, or someone else, was never uncovered. The effect was to further decimate the tiny Christian population of Turkey. Over the course of the 1980s and 1990s, almost the entire Syriac community left Tur Abdin, seeking asylum mainly in Europe. A small faction decided that the only way to prevent the complete eradication of their community was to take up arms. They called themselves *Tukoso Dawronoyo Mothonoyo d'Bethnahrain*, or the Patriotic Revolutionary Organization of Bethnahrain. They initially received some support from the PKK, but by 1995 the Dawronoyo had their own distinct organization and network.[38]

In the spring of 2012, Dawronoyo's Syrian affiliate, the Syriac Union Party (SUP), which had been founded in 2005, declared their opposition to the Assad regime during the Syriac Akitu celebration. Several activists were quickly arrested and tortured, and a demonstration to protest the arrests was violently disbanded. In Sweden, Syriac activists stormed the Syrian embassy and released a press statement condemning "the terrorist regime of Al-Assad."

In further defiance of the regime, a group of Syriacs declared they were taking up arms. The formation of the Mawtbo Fulhoyo Suryoyo (MFS) or Syriac Military Council was announced in an online video released on January 27, 2013. Speaking the ancient Aramaic language, the men in the video proclaimed that the Syriac people were living in a "dark chapter of injustice" and that they were forced to "defend the survival of our people." They also proclaimed to believe in the Syrian revolution and that they would fight in the same trenches as their partners to "overthrow the Baath regime." Everyone in the video was wearing a mask so as to conceal their identity.[39] Soon guerrilla veterans from the 1990s were brought in from Iraq, Turkey, and Europe to train locals to fight.

Despite such radical declarations in opposition to the Assad regime, as a small minority, they would need allies in order to take action. In the summer of 2013, about half a year after they were formed, the MFS began actively cooperating with the YPG. What led to their cooperation was the fact that Jabhat al-Nusra was rapidly advancing on their region. Abjar Dawud, a Spokesperson for the MFS told me, "In one day, Nusra gained 70 km—so we had to coordinate with the YPG."[40] The decision to cooperate with their former allies was apparently not difficult. At the time of the merger, Jacob Mirza was in the leadership of the Bethnahrain National Council (Mawtbo Umthoyo d'Bethnahrain; MUB). He had been part of the movement since 1994 and had experienced the previous falling out with the PKK around the year 2000. But reconciliation was apparently an easy task: "We did not really need to discuss or decide anything new."[41]

The difficulty for the diverse Christian minority to agree on a single name and identity—whether Syriac, Assyrian, Aramaean, Chaldean, or something else—has proven more challenging than the decision to cooperate with the YPG. The lack of a common identity or even an agreed-upon term of reference is related to the lack of a modern state that could have created a unifying national identity. Class differences and divisions between urban and rural areas further compound the problem. The Christians in the Jazira region around Qamishli tend to refer to themselves as Syriacs, while Christians in the more rural Khabur region closer to Tel Tamer consider themselves Assyrians. There is also an Armenian and Chaldean community. Kino Gabriel was a founding member of the MFS and later went on to become SDF Spokesperson. He explained the divisions within the Christian minority as follows: "There are different names: Syriac, Assyrian, Chaldean, Aramaean. The political parties couldn't reach an agreement on which name to use. It's not just a matter of name—the names of the churches are related, and historic kingdoms, it's a huge debate and so far we couldn't reach an agreement."[42]

The Khabur Guards were formed around the same time in early 2013, after the Syrian regime lost control of the area around the Khabur Valley, where some thirty-three Assyrian villages are located. Although the two areas were not far apart, the Assyrians in the Khabur region insisted on maintaining a distinct unit, separate from the MFS. The idea of unifying the Khabur Guards and the MFS was first discussed in 2014, but didn't happen, in part because of the lack of a common identity but also due to the rapidly changing battlefield of the Syrian civil war. This lack of a unified command structure proved to be a fatal mistake when ISIS launched an assault on the Assyrian villages in the Khabur valley in February 2015. According to Assyrian news outlets, ISIS abducted 253 Assyrians from the Khabur Valley, including women and children, and destroyed eleven churches. Some 3,000 locals fled the area to escape the Islamic State.[43]

I first met the Syriac Military Council in February 2019 when I visited several of their bases between Qamishli and Derik (Figure 3.3). From their outpost one could easily see the snow-covered Judi Mountain in Turkey. They were predominantly Christians, including Syriacs and Armenians, but included some Syrian Kurds and Arabs as well. Their base was about 10 km away from the Turkish

Figure 3.3 Field survey at an outpost of the Syriac Military Council in northern Syria, near the border to Turkey.

border. Many of them had crosses or the word Jesus tattooed on their arms or neck (Figure 3.4).

While the Khabur Guards are focused on defending the region along the Khabur River, the Syriac Military Council deployed alongside other units of

Figure 3.4 Syriac Military Council with tattoos

the SDF to liberate cities that are inhabited predominantly by Muslims. One young man I spoke to at the Syriac Military Council in Qamishli had lost both his brothers: one was killed in Raqqa and the other in Al-Hasakah.

Bethnahrin Women Protection Forces (HSNB)

Where there is a woman there is a change. If there is not a woman, there can't be a change. I don't believe that society can only be changed by men. Men have been ruling everything until now, and we didn't get anything from it.
—Ashurina, commander of the HSNB[44]

On August 30, 2015 the Bethnahrain Women's Protection Forces (HSNB) was formed. Just as the YPJ is the women's branch of the YPG, the HSNB can be considered the women's branch of the MFS. The press release was announced in Rutan, a Syriac village near a city known by three different names, reflecting the linguistic diversity of the region: Al-Qahtaniya in Arabic, Tirbespî in Kurdish, and Qabre Hewore in Aramaic. The first HSNB academy was also established in the same city. Similar to the YPG/YPJ, the HSNB women view themselves not only as a military force to defeat ISIS, but as a political movement that aims to radically uproot the trinity of pan-Arabism, authoritarianism, and patriarchy. The HSNB, MFS, and the Sutoro internal security forces together form the armed wing of the Syriac Union Party (SUP). As explained earlier, the party itself was initially founded in 2005 to represent the interests of the Christian minority, but had to work underground like all other opposition movements at the time.

I met the HSNB for the first time on March 5, 2019, and visited them several times afterward as well. I vividly recall that first meeting in early March, when I spent about five hours speaking with their commander, who is an Assyrian-Syriac woman. She preferred to not tell me her real name, and so I've given her the code name Ashurina. Very early in my conversation with her, she readily referred to the YPJ as a "role model." The base where I met them was a small building with three rooms: a meeting room, a sleeping room, and a kitchen. The "shower" in the bathroom was a faucet with a bucket that could be filled with water and dumped over one's head. To call their living arrangements spartan would be an understatement. They did, however, have a monitor attached to the wall in the entryway that allowed one to see their outpost from multiple directions at the same time, and who was coming or going. The Turkish border was just a few miles to the north.

Ashurina explained to me that the HSNB was located in small bases spanning the region from Derik in the east to Tel Tamer in the west, which included Khabur and Al-Hasakah. Women who identify as both Assyrian and Syriac were part of the HSNB. She emphasized that the HSNB and MFS believe that Syriacs, Assyrians, and Chaldeans are all the same people, and prefer to focus on their commonalities.

The first battle the HSNB took part in was the Al Hol Operation, just a month after the HSNB were created. At first some of the men in the MFS were not sure their female comrades were up to the task. In the hours before the HSNB left for the operation, one of the MFS commanders said to Ashurina, "There could be airstrikes, there could be duschka. Are you ready for this?"

Although the Dowronoye movement had a history of armed struggle, and although the very first female Peshmerga in Iraqi Kurdistan was an Assyrian woman, the movement as a whole had never recruited women on the same scale as their Kurdish counterparts. Ashurina said: "In the Syriac community it has never been accepted, they never thought that the women of this community would carry a weapon."[45] Although many in the Syriac community were reluctant to accept women as fighters, the HSNB joined the fight in defiance of them. The commander explained that they would not have been able to convince them just by talking. It was necessary to actually take part in the fight to convince them. They later went on to take part in the Raqqa and Shaddadi operations as well.

"There has been a struggle inside the struggle for us to take part in high commands, and still it is a struggle."[46] Although their male comrades in the MFS seem to now accept the HSNB, they still maintain their operational autonomy. During military operations they coordinate as part of the SDF, but the HSNB makes their own decisions regarding the education and training they provide. Their training includes encouraging women to make their own decisions and other ways of empowering women to be independent of their families. This arrangement appears to be similar to how the YPJ also has operational autonomy from the YPG. The commander explained:

> We are independent of the Syriac Military Council, we coordinate together when it is about operations, or common work, we cooperate with different forces, especially with the Syriac Military Council, they are from our people, we have the same goals. We also cooperate with YPG/YPJ, but we are independent. We take our own decisions we make our own plans. The Syriac Military Council cannot give us orders about what to do and what not to do; they can't tell us to go fight in Deir Ezzor.[47]

The units coordinate within the unified command structure of the SDF, and yet also have more autonomy than is the case in the US military. For the male fighters I spoke to, the reasons for their insisting on autonomy was often related to their ethnic or religious identity, even when they belonged to the same faith. For example, the Arabs in the Sanadeed Forces opted not to fight in Arab-majority Deir Ezzor. Assyrians in the Khabur Guards didn't want to take orders from Syriacs in Qamishli. Hence for the time being, the small Christian minority remains divided in four different units within the SDF. Female members of the SDF often articulated their desire to maintain autonomy due to gender-specific reasons, rather than based on their religious or ethnic identity. For Kurdish, Yezidi, Arab, and Christian women I spoke to, it was their way of maintaining their independence from men.

. I heard the same feminist "we don't take orders from men" sentiment in 2016 in Iraq when I stayed with Kurdish and Yezidi women at a YBS outpost perched on top of Mount Sinjar, when Da'esh was still controlling territory not far away. And I heard it again in 2019 in northern Syria when I spoke to Assyrian and Syriac women at the HSNB base, when Da'esh was still fighting to the south of them in Baghouz and the Turkish military amassing troops to the north. I admired their independent spirit, but I was also worried.

Even though the MFS now accepts the HSNB, the women still have to convince the larger Christian minority. She lamented the fact that, in her view, the Syriac-Assyrian people have not been able to sufficiently organize or defend themselves. She put the predicament in stark terms:

> The people are living but they are dead. Now we want to do something for our people, but trying to make them speak is hard. For the women it is harder, they are not only controlled by other regimes, they are now controlled within their families or by their society. She has to come to this world to find a man and get children, and to do anything different is a struggle. It's hard to get women to live a life of freedom, this is what we want to show her and to give her.[48]

Here again I was struck by how similar her comments were to what I had heard over and over again from Kurdish women, ever since my first visit to Kobani in June 2015. Their ambitions go far beyond the mere defeat of ISIS, which in and of itself was a historic achievement. This Assyrian commander sees the HSNB as part of the fight to destroy the patriarchal structures that she believes restrict women's freedom. I asked her whether the HSNB allows their members to get married or have boyfriends. She said there was no such prohibition on getting married, but that it was definitely preferable for women to be single so they can focus on their work. She said they try to explain "what a marriage can do," as she put it. She said:

> It is our job to give them an alternative life. Everybody can do something, even if you're a grandmother and have children and grandchildren, you can still come sometimes.[49]

She further explained that the civilian structures of the Autonomous Administration were also a crucial part of the transformation of society:

> The idea of the self-administration and the democracy that we want to create is that women should play as much a role as men in the area. If she does not, the society will be handicapped. You cannot be a democracy

or reach freedom if the society you live in only has a patriarchal system that is only seen from the eyes of the men.[50]

The village where the base was located had a church that was undergoing construction. Because the HSNB base was located at the entrance to the village, these women, including both HSNB and Sutoro, were essentially the guardians of the village and hence of the new church. I asked if they got any support from the church. One of the HSNB women told me, "I didn't see any support from the church. We didn't see any support from them as a women's force—maybe the men's units got support, but not us." I then asked if they ever go and talk to the priests, she laughed and said no.

Clearly, the MFS/HSNB and YPG/YPJ have much in common. They share similar ideas, although they follow different leaders. Instead of posters of Öcalan, the HSNB and MFS outposts featured posters of Haro Mikhail, who was serving as president of the Bethnahrain National Council. While some analysts have claimed that the YPG indoctrinates others, it was pretty clear to me that the MFS and HSNB were not acting as puppets who had been brainwashed by a foreign ideology, but as members of a Christian community who had been persecuted since the time of the Ottoman Empire, decades before the PKK was even founded. My survey data from the spring and summer of 2019—prior to the Turkish intervention in October—showed strikingly similar levels of threat perceptions among rank-and-file Kurds and Christians in the SDF. I added this question to the survey because as the territorial ISIS caliphate was crumbling, then defeated in March 2019, I wanted to understand what SDF members believed was now the biggest threat to the region. It was an open-ended question so as not to lead the respondents. The survey data showed that the majority of SDF respondents ($N = 182$) believed that Turkey was the greatest threat to the region—a bigger threat than ISIS or the Assad regime. In terms of the ethnic breakdown of the respondents, 78% of Kurdish SDF respondents and 75% of Christian SDF respondents believed Turkey was the biggest threat, compared to 45% of Arab respondents.[51]

Furthermore, the HSNB seems to share the feminist principles of the YPJ, and shared many of their experiences of fighting a "struggle within the struggle" against their male comrades. By contrast, the Sanadid Forces, many of whom were recruited from the Shammar tribe, to this day does not have any women fighters, although they too, like MFS and HSNB, have been an ally of the YPG since 2013. To them we turn next.

Al Sanadid Forces of the Shammar Tribe

Throughout the course of the Syrian civil war, the Kurdish-led YPG cooperated with Arab-majority armed groups. The YPG began to actively recruit Arabs just months after regime forces withdrew from the north, or at least since late 2012. By 2019, the

SDF had incorporated Arabs from all of the major tribes in northern Syria. Arab respondents to my survey identified as belonging to 46 different tribes or clans.

The Shammar tribe's Al-Sanadid Forces led by Bandar al-Humaydi was one of the first to cooperate with the YPG, starting in 2013. In July 2019 I visited Sheikh Humaydi Daham al-Hadi, the leader of the Shammar tribe, and his son, Bandar, who was the commander of the Sanadid Forces. The Sanadid forces seemed to control a large expanse of territory, overlapping with the tribal lands of the Shammar. Sheikh Humaydi claimed the tribe consisted of some ten million members. While this is difficult to verify, the Shammar are recognized as one of the largest tribal confederations in the region, with members in both Syria and Iraq. While the HSNB outpost was ramshackle and spartan, the Sheikh and his family lived in a huge villa. When I entered his palatial villa, he welcomed us in a large and imposing reception hall. The rectangular room was so expansive, it took what seemed like a long time to just walk from the entrance to the end where he was seated, like a dignitary. I felt like I was entering a palace, albeit one whose days of glory were perhaps receding into the past. The Sheikh spoke at length about the history of the Shammar, and how his father had been arrested by the British in 1940 and kept in prison for four years, then later becoming a member of parliament after he was released.

According to Sheikh Humaydi, the Sanadid Forces were formed in 1997. However, they were primarily a political force, not active as a militia. At that time, the Sheikh explained that he "made a tour of the Arab world." The purpose of his tour was to convince the various Arab leaders that "the current system of Arab nationalism would fail, and that afterwards it would be replaced by religion, which would ruin the region."[52] He claimed that the only person who seemed to agree with him at the time was the prince of Qatar. He also put forth the idea of creating a tribal parliament in London in which all tribes would be represented. The Sheikh's ideas seemed both novel and forward-looking, but also intended to preserve the influence not only of his tribe, the Shammar, but of all tribes—perhaps even as an alternative to political parties. I had the distinct impression that he took a dim view of political parties, in general. He explained how the Shammar had historically protected the Kurds, as a people, "not as a political party." He claimed to also have good relations with the Barzanis in Iraqi Kurdistan.

Sheikh Humaydi referred to the YPG as "our friend." But he also indicated some displeasure because his traditional title of "sheikh" was less frequently used than in the past. In an attempt to undo tribal hierarchies, administration officials are encouraging people to use the term al-raey, which means shepherd.[53]

At some point, other members of his tribe and locals from Tel Alo entered the reception hall. We were served lunch on huge platters, a delicious meal of lamb with rice. Over the course of more than six hours, I toured the expansive grounds and met several dozen people, but did not encounter a single woman.

After lunch, we drove a few miles to the office of his son, Bandar, the commander of the Sanadid Forces. He was wearing an olive green galabeya and a

Figure 3.5 "Freedom Portrait by Shervan Derwish and Jack Shahine. Liberation of western countryside of Tel Abyad from ISIS. June 2015."

baseball cap. Bandar explained how the area used to be under the control of ISIS, including his headquarters where we were standing. It took about eight months of fighting, he said, to liberate the area. The first battle that the Sanadid Forces shared with the US-led Coalition was Tel Hamis in February 2015, soon after the liberation of Kobani.[54] Coordination continued between the YPG, the Sanadid, the Syriac Military Council, and the Khabur Guards in battles in Tel Brak and the area around Ras al-Ayn. By the end of May 2015, ISIS militants had been expelled from more than 230 towns and villages (Figure 3.5).[55]

Even before ISIS, they had been attacked by other forces, so they established local units which they called Jaish al-Karama, because Bandar said "you should protect your dignity."

In October 2015, when the SDF was then formed, Bandar took part as a representative of the Sanadid Forces alongside General Mazloum, the commander-in-chief of the SDF, and others. He complained, however, that the US-led Coalition provides support to the SDF, and not directly to the Sanadid. This was a complaint I had heard from the MFS, HSNB, and other units as well. Many felt that they were somehow disadvantaged because the Coalition did not supply them directly with weapons or equipment, but rather through the SDF, who then redistributed everything to the various components of the SDF. In other words, such complaints or grievances against the SDF were in reality complaints about the Coalition's policy and need to maintain oversight over the distribution of weapons.

The Sanadid Forces are organized into four groups: one controls the border, another is responsible for internal security and checkpoints, a third group consists of those who fight in combat, and the fourth group consist of what they call "Special Forces."[56] Furthermore, the Sanadid Forces claim to attract Arabs from other tribes as well, not just from the Shammar. However, there are no women in any of these four groups. Bandar explained to me:

> In our culture and tradition, the lady has their own rights and respect. But we don't expose her to violence. Even in the old history, the ladies were not fighting. The people who let the lady fight with them, they say they give her rights. But we respect the lady, it is a mistake to let her fight and expose her to violence.[57]

The contrast to the HSNB and YPJ was stark. The Sanadid Forces did not allow women to fight in combat, and clearly did not agree with those who did.

The Manbij Military Council (MMC): The SDF's Partner West of the Euphrates

We were proud that the US-led coalition helped us. They are our right hand, they are helping us, without our right hand we cannot do anything.
—Sheiko, Turkman member of Manbij Military Council[58]

Not all Syrian Arabs refused to allow women to fight in combat. While the Sandid Forces did not include any women, the Manbij Military Council created a separate unit for women, following the model of the YPG/YPJ and MFS/HSNB. Gulay, the young woman in charge of social media for the MMC, told me they would even proudly announce on Twitter every time an individual woman would join them. Sometimes, however, she said that members of a woman's family or tribe would complain, and so they would have to delete the posts. Such profound differences between the MMC and the Sanadid Forces, although both Arab-majority forces and important components of the SDF, illustrate that the recruitment of women as combatants is entirely voluntary and dependent on local customs and traditions. In particular, these differences would appear to be due to the varying histories of organizing around women's rights in these two regions of northern Syria.

After the regime withdrew from Manbij in the summer of 2012, local councils were established to run the city. A 600-member Trustee Council was created with representatives from various tribes as well as the Kurdish community—but did not include a single woman. According to Yasser Munif, a Syrian-American scholar who conducted fieldwork in Manbij in the summer of 2013 and again in December of 2013, women activists were "campaigning to get representation" but had not yet succeeded.[59] In January 2014, the city was taken over by the Islamic State. After

Manbij was liberated from Da'esh and incorporated into the structures of the Autonomous Administration, women were represented in high levels of the city administration. When I met representatives of the Manbij Civil Council in February 2019, a co-chair system was in place and two of the four leaders were women.[60]

Manbij is strategically located between Aleppo, Idlib, and the countryside of Raqqa. For years, the city straddled areas controlled by the Syrian regime, Turkey, Al Qaeda-linked groups in Idlib, and the US-backed SDF. While Arabs constitute a majority of the population, the city also includes Kurdish, Turkmen and Circassian minorities. Located on the western banks of the Euphrates and close to multiple competing hostile forces, it is not where one would have expected the Kurdish-led project of local governance to flourish. Yet that is precisely what happened.

Manbij became one of the Arab-majority areas where the ideas and structures of the Autonomous Administration were perhaps most successfully implemented. To be fair, this could be because the city had suffered so much under ISIS, Ahrar al Sham, and Jebhat al Nusra, that anything would be welcomed as an improvement. Chapter 4 elaborates on what it was like, especially for women, to live under the Caliphate. But it was not just women or non-Muslim minorities who suffered. Mohammed Kheir, an Arab man who was Co-President of the Executive Council in Manbij when I met him, told me he knew people who had been beheaded just for having internet illegally. He described the differences between rule by the FSA, ISIS, and the Autonomous Administration as follows:

> When FSA was here—there was looting, properties were confiscated, there were no services provided to the people. During ISIS we were terrorized. But now there is a big difference, like between the ground and the sky.[61]

According to Hadeel el-Saidawi, after living under ISIS for almost three years, "a majority of inhabitants welcomed the stability provided by PYD rule."[62] Founded on April 2, 2016, the MMC gained the respect of Western analysts of the Syrian conflict. In the assessment of Nicholas Heras, the MMC was "one of the most active, decorated and bloodied constituent, Arab-majority groups mobilized under the SDF banner."[63]

Because the city of Manbij was still under the control of ISIS, the MMC was founded outside the city at the Tishreen Dam, after it had been captured by the YPG. The local armed groups that merged to form the MMC included Shams al-Shamal, Jund al-Harmein, and Thuwar Manbij. Just three days later, on April 5, a local civil council was established in Sarrin, with the intent of administering the city of Manbij after it was liberated from ISIS.

The operation to liberate Arab-majority Manbij was a considerable undertaking, and necessitated implementing conscription in Kurdish-majority Kobani.[64] Even Asayîş forces from Kobani and Al-Hasakah, who were normally not supposed to be engaged in combat at all, also fought in Manbij.

Despite the immense suffering of the people, the campaign to free Manbij had to be delayed for months, because Turkish officials refused that the YPG take part.[65] In an attempt to mediate, American officials set up a meeting between Turkey and the MMC. Many locations were suggested, but they ultimately decided to meet at the Incirlik Airbase in Turkey.[66] Abu Jasim, Abu Leila, and Sheikh Ibrahim Elbenawi, head of Jind el Harameen battalion, took part in the meeting representing the MMC.

In the summer of 2016, the Obama administration authorized the SDF to cross onto the western bank of the Euphrates and capture the city from the stranglehold of Da'esh. At the time, then-Vice President Joe Biden famously promised Turkish leaders that all YPG fighters would subsequently withdraw from Manbij and return to the eastern bank of the Euphrates River.

On August 15, 2016, a little over three months after the Manbij military and civil councils had been formed at the Tishreen Dam, the city of Manbij was finally liberated from ISIS. After living under ISIS for almost three years, many people rejoiced.

While the residents of Manbij were euphoric, Turkish President Erdoğan was enraged. The liberation of Manbij from ISIS also meant, in the eyes of the Turkish leadership, the looming prospect of the SDF establishing control over a contiguous corridor along the Turkish border. This is what prompted Turkey to launch the Euphrates Shield operation in 2016. Since then, the Kurds' dream of establishing a contiguous Kurdish zone in northern Syria has been upended.

In his fury at the expansion of SDF-held territories, President Erdoğan even threatened to kill Americans in Manbij. Although unprecedented and unusual for a NATO ally to threaten to kill US service members, the tactic was effective. American diplomats felt compelled to travel to Ankara to mend relations.[67]

The conundrum for the United States was far more complex than just balancing between two allies who happened to be adversaries. Nicholas Heras summed up the predicament as follows:

> There is no quick and easy way for the U.S.-led Coalition to address this question because by backing the SDF—and simultaneously asking the SDF to govern in the wake of the Islamic State—the Coalition is also backing the implementation of the DFNS and the system of democratic confederal governance.[68]

The result of the dilemma was the "Manbij Roadmap," declared in June 2018.

To appease Turkey, the MMC did not officially become part of the SDF. There were around 6,000 YPG fighters who helped the newly established MMC. After the city was liberated, the YPG officially withdrew. Turkish officials also demanded that restrictions be imposed on the YPG to visit Manbij—even if they were natives of Manbij. In other words, Kurds who were born in Manbij, raised in Manbij, who fought bravely and risked their lives to liberate their own city from ISIS—were not allowed to then visit Manbij after it was finally free of Da'esh—all for the sake of appeasing Erdoğan. I met one Kurdish man who was a member of the MMC in Ain Issa, because he was not allowed to return to his own hometown. He related how Turkish officials did not even want him to call his father on the phone, who lived in Manbij.[69]

So, even though the MMC was, in a technical sense, not part of the SDF, the city was governed by the Autonomous Administration. However, not all of the laws were implemented in a uniform manner. For example, military conscription in Manbij was only implemented for men between the ages of 18 and 30, whereas in Kobani the age range was from 18 to 35.[70] Polygamy was still allowed in Manbij.

When I visited Manbij in early 2019, the city was still being governed by the Autonomous Administration, despite Turkish objections. The challenges they faced were enormous just in terms of providing basic services to the growing population. The size of the city had mushroomed with the influx of IDPs, from around 200,000 people in 2013 to 650,000 to around 1,200,000—another indication that many people preferred to live in Manbij than other parts of Syria controlled by the regime or other nonstate actors.

On a cold day in February 2019, I met Shervan Derwish, Abu Adel, and Abu Ali in their headquarters at the MMC. They were co-located with American forces on the same base. The three men had all grown up in Manbij, and had known each other for some twenty years. As childhood friends, they used to play on the same soccer team, which was organized, they said, by Shervan Derwish's father. They had been through a lot together. Two of their former commanders had been killed in battle. Abu Layla was shot in the head by an ISIS sniper during the Manbij campaign, and Abu Amjad was martyred in the Raqqa campaign.

Shervan Derwisch and Abu Adel are both Kurds, while Abu Ali is an Arab. Together, the three of them acted as commanders of the battalion. All three of them had fought previously in various Free Syrian Army (FSA) groups. Muhammad Mustafa Ali, known by his nom de guerre "Abu Adel" had previously been commander of Liwa Ahrar Syria from 2012 to 2014, then was part of the Shams el Shamal (Northern Sun Battallion).

Abu Adel recounted to me how his FSA battalion started to clash with ISIS in December 2013. He described how some of the Islamist-leaning FSA groups began to reidentify as the Islamic State. "About seven people who said they were from Al Nusra took an office [in Manbij] and they identified themselves as a group of rebel forces fighting the regime. A week later they started to call themselves Al Dawla Islameya in Manbij. The first group that brought Islamic thinking to the FSA was Ahrar al Sham."[71]

As the YPG began to gain in strength, Islamist FSA groups began to perceive them as a threat. Abu Adel explained: "We were fighting the regime. But Turkey told us: 'Stop now, fight the YPG instead.' All the battalions were told that the regime was in Kobani, so they should attack Kobani." The FSA groups that Abu Adel and Shervan Derwish belonged to declared that they would not fight against Kobani, because it was not true that the regime was in Kobani, as they had already withdrawn. And they didn't want to fight against Kurds. Their decision to refuse to attack the YPG, and later even join forces with them, came at a cost. Abu Adel summed it up as follows: "From 2012 to 2014 all the support we got was from Turkey, when we were FSA and fighting the regime. They gave us weapons, ammunition, financial support. And now they call us terrorists."[72]

When I visited in February 2019, the Turkish-backed Euphrates Shield forces were about 15–20 km away. They told me that around 50% of the budget of the MMC was being paid by the Coalition. Similar to other units in the SDF, they earned between $150 to $250 per month, the maximum being $300 per month. The other part of their budget was covered by customs that they levied at checkpoints. However, while many of the Turkish-backed rebel groups allegedly imposed many different fees, the Autonomous Administration imposed a single customs fee to enter their area. In other words, the MMC did not charge their own taxes separate from the AANES. They said, "If you travel from here to Azaz—you pay 18 times at checkpoints. If you come to here, you pay once to enter Manbij and can go all the way to Derik."[73] The three men also claimed that the commanders of the Euphrates Shield area have their families live in the Manbij area rather than in the Euphrates Shield area under their control, because Manbij was safer.

I asked if they ever considered officially joining the YPG. They replied simply by saying, "we're from Manbij, we have our own beliefs." I had actually expected that the question may cause some tension, but the opposite happened. Abu Adel said: "The YPG are very disciplined. They have to wake up at 6am and start exercise; I could come here at 10am, so they have different ethical codes." The three of them laughed and told him to stop tarnishing their reputation. Abu Adel pointed to Shervan and said, "If he was YPG, he could not wear civilian clothes, the YPG always wear uniforms." Again, they all laughed. Wearing a disheveled sweater, jacket, and gray pants, Shervan Derwish was sitting slumped on the couch, not disciplined like a YPG fighter. Abu Adel then declared that "if there was no war, I would be a civilian, I want to go back to my civilian life," something a cadre would never say or openly admit to. Finally, they offered this comparison: "The YPG are more ideological—they have *perwerde* (ideological training). We just have an academy."[74] The two academies of the MMC were located on the banks of the Tishreen Dam. The setting was definitely more idyllic than other YPG academies I had visited, with an expansive view of the large reservoir. But from the inside, the academies were similarly spartan and decorated with posters of the many martyrs.

Unlike cadres, all three of them were married and had kids. Abu Ali had ten kids; Abu Adel had seven, and Shervan Derwish had five children. However, they do not usually accept women into the MMC who have children, because, Abu Adel claimed, "she has commitments, it would be difficult." So they prefer to only admit single women, or married women without kids. When I visited, I was told that there were approximately 600 women in the MMC, most of whom were Arabs. I spent two whole days interviewing both the men and women. We talked late into the night and as it was too late to return to the city, I ended up spending the night in one of their academies. When I woke up early the next morning, I watched from the balcony as the men practiced their drills. The sun had just come up over the Tishreen Dam.

The Martyr Nubar Ozanyan Brigade

On the anniversary of the Armenian genocide in April 2019, a new tabur was announced: the Martyr Nubar Ozanyan Brigade. The members of the unit are mainly Armenians, whose families fled to northern Syria to escape persecution a century earlier, and include both Christians and those whose ancestors converted to Islam. The commanders of the unit agreed to allow the rank-and-file members to take a break from their military training and take my survey. They put down their weapons and took up the pens I provided. In addition to explaining where they were born, their age, which tribe they belonged to, and other basic demographic information, some of them scribbled additional details about their family history. One Armenian Muslim from Ras Al-Ayn described how his ancestors had survived the genocide by being adopted by the Harb tribe. Another Armenian Muslim from Al Hasakah said his grandfather had been adopted by Kurds (Figure 3.2). The outposts of the Nubar Ozanyan Brigade were just as spartanic as those of the HSNB, with rickety chairs and barely functioning water faucets. The walls of their small meeting room were adorned with photographs of an assortment of prominent Armenians throughout history. Two of the women were Sose Mayrig (nee Vartanian) born in 1868 who fought in self-defense units known as *fedayi* to defend Armenians from persecution during the late Ottoman Empire, and Zabel Yesayan, a novelist and professor of literature born in 1878.

The unit was named after Nubar Ozanyan, the nom de guerre of Fermun Çırak, an Armenian from Turkey born in 1956. Ozanyan was killed in combat in August 2017 while fighting alongside the SDF to liberate Raqqa from the Islamic State. He was sixty-one years old at the time.[75]

When the Martyr Nubar Ozanyan Brigade was officially announced in April 2019, they issued a statement explaining the reason for their formation. The following is an excerpt of the statement:

As children of the Armenian people, who were massacred and exiled in the genocide, today we came together to defend Rojava [...] We wanted to take a step to make April 24 not just a memorial for the genocide, but a day of resistance against the current representatives of the fascist Union and Progress Committee who carried out the genocide. The Armenian people won't just condemn the genocide and remember the lost. We want to spread the hope that they will also fight for them. Burdened by the knowledge that the genocide that happened 104 years ago continues today in different guises, we formed our self-defense force against all oppression, tyranny, massacres and assimilation attacks.[76]

In addition to military training, the members of the unit are also taught the language and history of Armenia. I watched them perform several drills where they spoke Armenian instead of Arabic. Although the Martyr Nubar Ozanyan Brigade was formed to fight ISIS, since Turkey occupied another swath of Syrian land during its intervention in October 2019, the unit now finds itself on the frontlines of the area occupied by Turkey and its militias. With the Turkish-backed armed groups less than ten miles away from their outposts, the descendants of Armenian genocide survivors are now training to defend their region from Turkey.

Conclusion

I met General Mazloum Abdi for the first time in September 2020, just over five years after I had first visited Rojava. In the span of a few years, he had grown in prominence and popularity both within the territory he controlled and in the outside world. He was the commander-in-chief of the second largest armed force in Syria, which he had led to victory against the most horrific terrorist organization in modern history (Table 3.4). And yet he remained humble. In other parts of the region, military commanders with such a track record could have easily set themselves up to be dictators. He could have used the external patronage to enrich himself. He could have issued orders to establish military dominance over the civilian institutions. He could have followed in the path of Gamal Abdel Nasser of Egypt, or Bouteflika of Algeria, and used his popularity, prestige, and control of resources to his personal benefit. As a Syrian man living in Syria, he could have legally married four wives. But as a former PKK cadre, he had renounced marriage and personal wealth. He owned no property, and had very few personal belongings at all.

I met General Mazloum in a small nondescript room on a base in Al-Hasakah. He was wearing his SDF uniform and sat across from me. Famously calm, he was introspective and open. He had never lied about his past as a PKK cadre. His forthrightness was appreciated by US officials who interacted with him, so I was told. When I met him for the first time in September 2020, Turkey had carved out another chunk of Syrian territory and was occupying the regions between Tel Abyad and Ras al-Ayn/Serêkani. Still, he was optimistic. He told me, "Turkey doesn't have any sustainable future in Syria. They will withdraw. Their forces don't belong to this region. We won't forget our history—1935 when Iskenderun was taken by Turkey."[77]

The fight with the Islamic State was over, but the SDF kept growing. I told him I had spoken to members of the Northern Democratic Brigade, and that one of them told me there were many members of the SNA (former FSA) who wanted to join the SDF. General Mazloum replied, saying,

> Yes it's true many of them want to join us. Those fighters are disappointed [with the SNA] because they don't see any progress there—we have hundreds of them that are with us already. Even some top commanders are working with us. Liwa Shimal are FSA originally. Abu Omar El Idlibly, Abu Ali Baered, Abu Issa—Raqqa Revolutionary Brigade—those are well-known. Half of our Arab commanders are former FSA.[78]

Arab commanders and rank-and-file soldiers in the SDF were key to liberating Arab-majority areas from the Islamic State such as Raqqa, Manbij, and Deir Ezzor. General Mazloum went on to say that even the Americans were surprised at the speed with which the SDF was able to maneuver in what was previously enemy territory:

> Soon after the Raqqa operation—the US brought their task force commanders to Raqqa and asked, 'How can you coordinate and handle all this?' They were shocked that we could move so freely in the recently liberated regions, that just one month earlier were under ISIS control."[79]

Finally, I asked General Mazloum about his vision for the future, their relations with the regime, and if the SDF would ever consider integrating into a larger Syrian armed force. He confirmed, as expected, that they were committed to the territorial integrity of Syria, and went on to say "We want to be part of the future Syrian army, but not the current one." Their control of territory and especially the oil resources gave them leverage over Damascus. As General Mazloum put it: "We can live without the regime, but they can't live without us."[80]

* * *

In March 2023, I met General Mazloum a second time, together with YPJ Commander Nowruz Ahmed (Figure 3.6). He was as calm as I remembered him being before, even though he had survived several recent assassination attempts. In November 2022, a Turkish drone struck inside a joint US-SDF base in Al-Hasakah,

Figure 3.6 General Mazloum Abdi and General Nowruz, commanders of the Syrian Democratic Forces.

the same base where I had met him previously and conducted numerous interviews. The Pentagon issued a public statement, saying the drone strike put American troops and personnel at risk.[81] I asked General Mazloum how the strike on the base in November had impacted him. He replied saying the SDF's intelligence unit had received or intercepted warning messages from Turkey to the effect that "in three days we will kill Mazloum." I asked if the Syrian regime had offered any promises to protect them from the Turkish drone attacks or potential ground operation. He laughed and said "no need to promise, we know they will flee. They are already fleeing." On April 7, about a week after our meeting, there was another apparent attempt to assassinate the SDF commander-in-chief. This time the attack occurred in the Kurdistan Region of Iraq, when General Mazloum was traveling in a convoy along with three American military personnel at the airport in Sulaymaniyah. The Turkish government did not claim responsibility for the drone strike, but a few days later, Foreign Minister Cavusoglu stated publicly that the Turkish government would continue to carry out operations against "terrorists" in both Iraq and Syria—even though the PKK had officially declared a unilateral ceasefire.[82] A day after the strike in Sulaymaniyah, a video circulated on social media of General Mazloum playing the saz.[83]

Life under ISIS

A War of Women against Women

Women clothed yet naked, inclined to evil and to entice to evil, their heads like the humps of a camel inclined to one side.[1]
—Excerpt from fatwa issued by the Islamic State in
Jarablus, November 2013

Samantha Sally from Indiana and Kayla Mueller from Arizona both lived in Syria under the reign of the Islamic State Caliphate. Their stories illustrate the global ambitions of Daesh and also encapsulate the dark spectrum of women's experiences under the Islamic State of Iraq and al-Sham (ISIS).

Samantha became a slave owner—while Kayla became a slave.

How did these two American women end up in Syria, and on opposite ends of the exploitation spectrum? How was it possible for the Islamic State to institutionalize the enslavement of women in the twenty-first century? Why did some women actively participate in the enslavement of other women? Once the Syrian Democratic Forces (SDF) had liberated territory from ISIS, how did they deal with a population who had lived through hell? How did they determine who was guilty, and who was innocent?

Kayla Mueller had traveled to Syria as a humanitarian aid worker. Upon leaving a hospital in Aleppo in 2013, she was kidnapped. She was later held captive in the home of a high-ranking ISIS emir, Abu Sayyaf. He was one of the top financiers of the Islamic State. Abu Sayyaf and his wife, Umm Sayyaf, held Kayla as a slave in their home, along with a number of Yezidi girls. Kayla was later killed in an air strike, but one of the enslaved Yezidi girls managed to escape on foot. She made it all the way to Iraqi Kurdistan, to freedom. It is from her that we know fragments of Kayla's story.

"Umm Sayyaf showed no solidarity with her fellow females. She locked them in a room, instigated their beatings and put makeup on them to 'prepare' them

Statelet of Survivors. Amy Austin Holmes, Oxford University Press. © Oxford University Press 2024.
DOI: 10.1093/oso/9780197621035.003.0004

for rape,"[2] explained Amal Clooney, a barrister specializing in human rights who represents some of the Yezidi survivors.

The story of Samantha El Hassani (a.k.a. Samantha Sally) is in some ways even more shocking. According to court documents, in November 2014 her husband Moussa El Hassani, informed her that he and his brother wanted to join ISIS. Between November 2014 and April 2015, she assisted the two men with joining ISIS by traveling multiple times to Hong Kong and transporting more than $30,000 in cash and gold. She is believed to have entered Syria via Turkey sometime around June 2015.[3] The El Hassanis settled in Raqqa, the capital of the Syrian Caliphate. They raised their kids there. One day the married couple went shopping at Raqqa's slave market. They bought three Yezidis: two teenage girls and one boy. Samantha's husband then serially raped the girls in their home. Ms. El Hassani's lawyers claim that she tried to offer the Yezidis protection, but could not prevent him from raping them or using her own son in an ISIS propaganda video.[4]

How could the Islamic State govern with such brutality?

The stories of Samantha and Kayla are exceptional in some ways, both of them being American women who wound up in Syria under very different circumstances. But their disparate fates do illustrate precisely how the Islamic State governed: by weaponizing women. In order to rule over such a large expanse of territory, *ISIS used women as weapons against other women.*

The crimes committed by ISIS—and their treatment of women in particular—sent shockwaves around the world. The list of atrocities they committed is long: forced religious conversion, mass displacement, kidnapping, torture, beheadings, and the sexual enslavement of non-Muslim women and girls. Former Secretary of State John Kerry said that these "grotesque and targeted acts of violence bear all the warning signs and hallmarks of genocide."[5]

If Yezidi women are unequivocally recognized as victims, the status of Muslim women who fell under their sway is more ambiguous. The policies of the Islamic State toward Muslim women living inside their self-proclaimed Caliphate were contradictory. ISIS emirs did not want to enslave Muslim women per se, but they did want essentially full control over them. Women who tried to resist were punished. Women were made prisoners in their own homes. They were not permitted to go outside without a male guardian. ISIS fatwas attempted to micromanage female behavior, even inside their own homes. Girls as young as nine years old could be married off. Nelly Lahoud compares governance under the ISIS Caliphate to a Hobbesian state of war. In her assessment, it was a "war of women against women, wives against other wives, wives against sex slaves."[6] Building off her insights, I contend that one of the primary objectives of the Islamic State was to bring about the subjugation of Muslim women so they in turn could police, punish, and even enslave other women.

Because ISIS governance entailed a *war of women against women*, this meant that while some women were victims, others became perpetrators of heinous crimes. The misogynistic ideology of the Islamic State—including the sexual enslavement of women—was embraced by some women. Female believers in jihad actively spread ISIS propaganda online and in person, and may have even helped shape some of their doctrines. Women were encouraged to join the *Hisbah*, or Morality Police, where they were paid a salary to spy on other women and punish anyone they considered delinquent. Women who were caught breastfeeding by women organized in the *Hisbah* would have their breasts bitten with metal teeth, an instrument of torture, and left to bleed to death on the streets.[7] In her memoirs, *The Last Girl*, Nadia Murad noted that ISIS women were often even more cruel than the men.[8]

As the case of Samantha Sally illustrates, it was not just local Syrians who engaged in brutality. Even after the defeat of the Islamic State as a physical Caliphate, a Filipino woman who had traveled all the way to Syria publicly defended the practice of enslaving Yezidis by claiming they were not actually slaves but just the "property" of the men who captured them.[9] In March 2020, Umaima Abdi, a German citizen, was charged with crimes against humanity, membership in a terrorist organization, and the enslavement of a 13-year-old Yezidi girl.[10]

And yet both Samantha Sally and Umaima Abdi initially claimed they were not perpetrators—despite owning slaves—but rather victims. It was their husbands, they say, who tricked and manipulated them.[11] Other women who are detained by the SDF make similar claims. At the time of writing, some 52,000 children, women, and men, including several thousand foreign citizens, are being held in the Al Hol and Al Roj camps.

In order to begin to address these larger questions of international justice and complicity, it is necessary to have a nuanced understanding of a seemingly simple question: What was it like to live inside the Islamic State Caliphate? Not all Muslim women who lived under the Caliphate were perpetrators of crimes. Many of them fell under the sway of ISIS simply by accident of geography: they happened to live in Raqqa or Deir Ezzor or some other city where Daesh hoisted their black flag, and were unable to escape. My analysis in this chapter is centered not around perpetrators of crimes or high-ranking ISIS leaders, but rather around the experiences of ordinary people, in particular the contradictory role of Muslim women.

The focus will be on the *Syrian* Caliphate. Much of what we know about ISIS, including how it operated and the conditions that led to its rise, is still often based on an analysis of Iraq, not Syria.[12] There is a general consensus that there were two primary grievances among Sunnis in Iraq that led to the creation of ISIS. These included the US-led invasion and occupation of Iraq that featured mistreatment and humiliation, especially in detention facilities such as Abu

Ghraib, and the subsequent De-Baathification policies that threatened many people's livelihoods, in particular military officers under Saddam Hussein. And, of course, ISIS grew out of Al Qaeda in Iraq (AQI), founded by Abu Musab al-Zarqawi.[13] While these may be convincing to explain the rise of ISIS in Iraq, how can we account for the rise of and expansion of the Islamic State on the Syrian side of the border? It is presumably not a coincidence that many of the top ISIS emirs including Abu Bakr al-Baghdadi, Abu Ibrahim al-Qurashi, Abu Muhammad al-Shimali, Abu Ahmad al-Alwani, and others were Iraqis—not Syrians. Furthermore, once the Islamic State took control of territory, the Sunni population in Iraq had less reason and fewer opportunities to defect, while their counterparts in Syria had more opportunities to defect. In Syria, Sunnis could either defect to other Sunni militant groups like the Free Syrian Army (FSA) in the opposition, or to the SDF, which was openly incorporating Arabs, in contrast to the Kurdish Peshmerga in Iraq. In short, the dynamics in Syria were quite different from those in Iraq, and yet many analysts still refer to the Islamic State as if the conditions on both sides of the Iraqi and Syrian border were largely similar. But they were not. The conditions in each of these countries were and still are unique, and I will not assume that Iraqi history can entirely account for the Syrian trajectory, even as ISIS emirs strived to maintain a unified message and outward image.

The analysis will be based on official documents issued by the Islamic State including fatwas, public announcements, permission slips, an online video, a manifesto on women, and other documents that are publicly available. The Islamic State became a global phenomenon, with branches in numerous countries around the world. The documents were all issued by ISIS in regions that they controlled in Iraq and Syria and were published between 2013 and 2018.

The chapter is divided into three parts. The first part describes the "philosophy" of the Islamic State toward women, based on an analysis of documents such as "Women of the Islamic State: A Manifesto on Women by the Al-Khanssaa Brigade," which was published at the height of their power in January 2015. I argue that one of the *primary objectives* of the Islamic State was to bring about the subjugation of the female sex by creating a war of women against women. The second part of the chapter shows *how the Islamic State strived to achieve their overall objectives* in three ways: restrictions on women's freedom of movement, restrictions on women's clothing and eyesight, and restrictions on women's ability to interact with men. There were numerous other restrictions placed on women, but due to space limitations I will focus on these three. The final section includes an analysis of *why the Islamic State suddenly reversed course and called women to wage jihad* in the fall of 2017.

Based on my analysis of these documents, I will make four interrelated arguments. First, I argue that the Islamic State intended to destroy the independence of Muslim women, and render them fully dependent on their fathers, husbands, or male guardians. Women who were educated, unmarried, unveiled, or traveled solo were deemed a threat to the new order they were trying to establish in the Caliphate. Destroying women's independence was not a second-order objective, but constituted the core of the Caliphate's raison d'être. ISIS placed a high priority on the subjugation of women. Issuing fatwas directed at women was one of the first things that IS militants did after they seized a swath of territory, even before they had achieved full control over a city or region.

Second, I show that ISIS was particularly concerned with subjugating women who were considered young or old enough to get married and give birth. Women who were considered "elderly"—sometimes defined as women above the age of 50—were allowed to travel without a mahram and were not pressured to wear a hijab.

Third, I show how, after issuing initial fatwas that placed major restrictions on women, questions were submitted to clarify certain issues. The *Bahuth w Ifta* (Research and Fitna) Committee, or *Hisbah* (Morality) Committee, was charged with finding answers that conformed to Daesh's interpretation of Islam. In the cases I have examined, the committees' responses invariably entailed placing even greater restrictions on women. This does not mean, however, that those women who succumbed to their rule were entirely victims. Some women embraced the ideology of the Islamic State, and took it upon themselves to spread its propaganda, as I will demonstrate in the next section of the paper.

Finally, I offer an explanation for why ISIS suddenly seems to have reversed course and called women to wage jihad. This happened in October 2017, after Raqqa was liberated by the SDF with support of the US-led Coalition. The sudden decision to call women to take part in combat would seem to illustrate the opportunism or hypocrisy of jihadist ideology. However, major questions remain around this issue. It is unclear how many women actually heeded their call and took part in combat, although anecdotal evidence suggests their numbers increased.[14] Some scholars even doubt that the infamous propaganda video purporting to show a woman in combat was, in fact, a woman. The figure clad in a long black *abaya* could just as well have been a man. What is important is that this is yet one more example of how IS men instrumentalized women. Finally, it reveals the misogyny which is at the heart of jihadist thinking: women were expected to serve as cannon fodder when it was clear that they were fighting a losing battle. Women's lives were expendable.

Those readers whose main interest is to understand the political system set up by the Autonomous Administration may feel tempted to skip over this chapter, seeing it as unnecessary to understand the present. Or perhaps others simply prefer not to dwell on past horrors. However, as the SDF assumed control of territory they liberated from ISIS, they were not facing tabula rasa, but rather a population who had suffered under both ISIS and the Assad regime. In some cases that meant caring for victims of atrocities, and in other cases rehabilitating those who were affiliated with the Islamic State. It was no easy task.

Part I: Destroying Women's Independence Inside the Caliphate

The abuses carried out by the Islamic State toward women are well-known. However, in order to recruit women, ISIS had to present itself as offering something to women that would be an improvement over their status in the West or in other Middle Eastern countries. In this section I will briefly describe what the Islamic State claimed to offer Muslim women. A document by the Al Khanssaa Brigade offers an insight into their core beliefs about women. The timing of its publication is significant. Released on January 23, 2015—the same day King Abdullah of Saudi Arabia died—it was a propaganda document intended to recruit women, especially from Saudi Arabia. It was also arguably the height of the Islamic State's power, having captured Mosul seven months earlier after dealing the Iraqi army an embarrassing defeat. The manifesto offers a glimpse into the psyche of female jihadists.

The main thesis of the treatise is that women's entire purpose in life is to serve her husband and children. As a servant of men, women are expected to remain at home to live a life of "sedentariness, stillness and stability." Because women were expected to devote themselves to their husbands and children and to abide by the ISIS interpretation of the Quran, the document concedes that women could not perform these tasks if they were illiterate or ignorant. The treatise suggests that girls should receive an education limited to religious studies—especially relating to issues of marriage and divorce, Quranic Arabic, and skills including knitting, textiles, cooking, and childrearing. Education for girls would ideally only be between the ages of 7 and 15. Marriage could begin for girls as young as 9 years old.

The manifesto identified two issues that were responsible for society's problems: the emasculation of men and the education of women. Emasculation was defined as a situation in which men were serving women or being supported by women, rather than women serving men. This can be illustrated in the following three passages from the manifesto:

> The problem today is that women are not fulfilling their fundamental roles, the role that is consistent with their deepest nature, for an important reason, that women are not presented with a true picture of man

and, because of the rise in the number of emasculated men who do not shoulder the responsibility allocated to them towards their ummah, religion or people, and not even towards their houses or their sons, who are being supported by their wives. [...] *Because men are serving women like themselves, men cannot distinguish themselves from them* according to the two features referred to by God: "Men are in charge of women by [right of] what God has given over the other and what they spend [for maintenance] from their wealth" (Quran 4:34). [emphasis added][15]

This is the great Right for husbands—"If I was to order anybody to prostrate to another person I would have commanded the woman to prostrate to her husband"—but there are few women like this, these days—generally—unfortunately, except those of the mercy of God. If men were men, then women would be women.[16]

Hence, while Islam gives man dominance, it bestows upon women the honour of implementation (executive). This is an equilibrium agreed upon from the birth of all humans and something that we have gotten used to—a commander who oversees and is capable, and others under his leadership who obey him and carry out his requests. *This is how humanity has operated for a long time and this is how it always was, even in "liberal" states and for today's "free" societies.*[17] [emphasis added]

These passages illustrate how the Islamic State tried to frame their intentions not as an attempt to subjugate women, but rather to elevate them. Only ISIS would allow women to pursue their true calling as females. This document was a propaganda tool intended for the recruitment of women. Other publications that were not intended for a female audience struck a different tone.

Propaganda Meets Reality

It appears that at least some ISIS emirs realized that not everything they were doing would appeal to women. Sexual enslavement of women and polygamy are a case in point. In order to recruit women to join the Islamic State Caliphate, certain issues were simply omitted from their propaganda directed to women. Nelly Lahoud has conducted a systematic comparison of materials produced by the Islamic State in three languages: Arabic, French, and English. In her assessment, the English and French monthly magazines (*Dabiq* and *Dar al-Islam*) were oriented toward recruiting women from outside the Levant, while the weekly Arabic (*Al-Naba'*) was intended for an Arabic-speaking audience. Lahoud highlighted how these publications employed distinct gender messaging. In her view, *Al-Naba'* went beyond merely propagating stereotypical gender roles, and used "derogatory" language that portrayed women as "inherently unequal," which may potentially offend "even those women who support ISIL."[18]

Indeed, any comparison of the documents intended for recruitment purposes and fatwas issued inside the Caliphate reveal a gaping chasm between propaganda and reality. The fatwas issued by ISIS in the territory they controlled often referred to women in extremely derogatory language, of which there are countless examples. One fatwa issued in Jarablus, Syria in November 2013 is particularly striking for its combination of brevity, irrationality, and misogynistic language. The fatwa absurdly claimed that women were naked even when they were clothed [sic] and that women were "inclined to evil and to entice to evil." In the very same sentence, women are demeaned even further, and suddenly compared to camels, as if they were subhuman.

> Women clothed yet naked, inclined to evil and to entice to evil,
> their heads like the humps of a camel inclined to one side.[19]

These passages illustrate that the Islamic State was attempting to construct a form of jihadist hegemonic masculinity, not unlike that which Osama Bin Laden had propagated.[20]

How could an organization that exuded such hatred of women recruit women to join them? One strategy appears to have been to simply omit any reference to topics such as polygamy or sexual slavery in their public-facing propaganda directed to women.

A second tactic was to focus on how—according to the Islamic State—both the West and Gulf countries (in particular Saudi Arabia) had failed women. The section entitled "The Failure of the Western Model for Women" begins as follows:

> The model preferred by infidels in the West failed the minute that women were "liberated" from their cell in the house. [. . .] Here, we are not going to present a list of the negatives that are caused in communities from the "women's emancipation" narrative. These are apparent, unhidden from the distant observer, let alone the close observer. Rather, women have this Heavenly secret in sedentariness, stillness and stability, and men its opposite, movement and flux, that which is the nature of man, created in him. [emphasis added]

As becomes clear in this passage, the main goal of the Islamic State was to banish women to the private sphere—to force them to be "sedentary." This entailed making women prisoners in their own homes. Women were only permitted to leave their homes in three circumstances. Young girls between the ages of seven and fifteen were allowed to attend school to obtain a rudimentary education in religious studies. After reaching adulthood, women were only permitted to leave the home if they were needed as doctors or teachers, as long as they strictly followed the Sharia guidelines. Finally, referencing the "blessed women of Iraq and Chechnya," women were also permitted to leave their homes to wage jihad "if the enemy is attacking her country and the men are not enough to protect it and the imams give a fatwa for it."[21]

Clearly, the goal of the Islamic State was to make women completely dependent on men, and in so doing, destroy their independence. Women were expected to be servants who could not exist independently of their fathers, husbands, or mahram.

One point worth highlighting is that polygamy was not mentioned a single time in this treatise, an interesting omission given that it was a propaganda tool directed particularly toward women from Saudi Arabia. The issue of sexual slavery of women is also not mentioned a single time.

By contrast, other documents, presumably intended for a male audience, provide lengthy justifications for the practice of sexual slavery. In one document produced by the Diwan al-Ifta wa al-Buhuth (Fatwa Issuing and Research Department), the enslavement of non-Muslim women is presented as an act of charity. The document was seized when US Special Operations Forces carried out a raid that killed ISIS financial official Abu Sayyaf in Syria in May 2015.[22] The document itself appears to be from October 2014 (a few months after the genocide against the Yezidis in Sinjar) and is entitled "From Creator's Rulings on Capturing Prisoners and Enslavement."

> Therefore we find that the most useful means to protect these women from waste, desolation and poverty, and the way to guarantee a stable life for them: making captives of them and enslaving them. [. . .] Because the master and possessor is entrusted by law to . . . spend money on her and provide her with food, drink and residence, while keeping her from the forbidden practices. . . . We find that there has come in the Shari'a allowance to enjoy sabaya (slave girls) and lie carnally with them.[23]

In an issue of *Dabiq* from September/October 2014, the enslaving of Yezidis was recounted in an article entitled "The Revival of Slavery Before the Hour."[24]

The Islamic State's use of slavery served several purposes. First, it promised male fighters access to a potentially unlimited number of women who they could rape. Men who lived in the Caliphate need not suffice themselves with just four wives. Slaves, or *sabaya*, would become their property, thus increasing the number of women who they could (force) to have sex with them. While Al

Qaeda encouraged their fighters to marry up to four wives, they did not permit sexual relations outside the institution of (polygamous) marriage.

The importance of allowing men lawful access to sex should not be underestimated as a recruiting tool—for men. But how could ISIS recruit women to join an institution that promoted slavery? Why would a woman join ISIS knowing that her husband would not just have three other wives in addition to herself—but potentially any number of sex slaves as well?

According to Lahoud, the Islamic State's messaging on enslavement, including sexual slavery, "seeks to manage women's reactions to the practice by grounding it in 'law' and religion, at the same time as recruiting men to join ISIL's ranks. The messaging is designed to convince women that sex slavery is not prostitution, while also appealing to men, promising them many sexual partners if they fight for ISIL."

Yet another example of the gap between propaganda and reality pertains to how quickly women were remarried after their husband was killed. Instead of allowing women to observe the traditional period of mourning or waiting known as *Iddah*, after their husband dies, women were often forced to remarry another ISIS fighter within a short span of time. Furthermore, since she had been previously married, she would be considered less pure and therefore of lesser value and hence often remarried to a man of lower-ranking status.[25]

By contrast, child marriage was praised in the manifesto, with girls as young as nine years old considered able to marry.

Part II: "Reprehensible Acts of Women Traveling without a Mahram"
Restrictions on Women's Clothing, Eyesight, Mobility, and Social Interactions

If destroying Muslim women's independence was the ultimate end goal of the Caliphate, what means did they use to achieve this? This is the question that will be addressed in this section. The subjugation of women was a high priority for the Islamic State. Even in the pre-Caliphate era, before the Islamic State was a state, IS militants would issue fatwas that entailed major restrictions on women's freedoms. For example, one of the first things that the Islamic State did once they had taken control of an area was to issue a fatwa that required women to wear the veil and forbade the wearing of trousers or jeans. For example, in December 2013, the "Virtue and Vice Committee" in Tel Abyad issued a fatwa. This was even before the town had come under the sole control of IS. The Islamic State first established a presence in Tel Abyad in the spring of 2013, but shared control with other factions including Ahrar al-Sham battalions. This was around the time that the local Jabhat al-Nusra faction defected and joined the Islamic State after Abu Bakr Baghdadi had called for them to merge.[26] The "Virtue and Vice Committee" is a predecessor to the *Diwan al-Hisbah and Diwan al-Qaḍa* which developed in areas that were under the sole control of ISIS.

The following statement is from a document issued by the Islamic Court in Tel Abyad in December 2013.[27]

Beginning from next Saturday, 11 Safr 1435 AH/14 December 2013, there will be a complete ban on unveiling, as well as the wearing of tight trousers and cloaks, and the adorning of oneself and imitation of kafir [disbelieving] women. And any woman who contravenes this statement for distribution will expose herself to the severest consequences.

Similar fatwas were issued in Jarablus around the same time that required women to wear the hijab and to refrain from wearing perfume or any kind of adornment. Women were given one week in order to comply with the Sharia hijab (Figure 4.1).

Imposition of Hijab Sharia on Women, Jarablus, November 2013

The Islamic State in Iraq and al-Sham announces

The obligation for women to wear the Shari'a hijab, which should be wide and fluttering, not tight, transparent, and not attractive for the eyes with adornment or perfume, and in that regard.

God has said: " . . . And do not display yourselves as in the prior time of Jahiliya . . ." al-Ahzab 33 [Qur'an 33:33]

The Prophet said: ". . . Women clothed yet naked, inclined to evil and to entice to evil, their heads like the humps of a camel inclined to one side. They do not enter paradise or smell its odour, when its odour can be smelt from so-and-so distance."

Notice: The Islamic State gives a deadline of one week from the date of this statement to comply with the Shari'a hijab, and any violation of that will expose the woman and the guardian of her affairs to Shari'a trial/court.

There are several indications that women often refused to comply by the Sharia dress code for as long as possible. For example, although ISIS began to establish control of Raqqa already in the spring of 2013, even by the fall most women

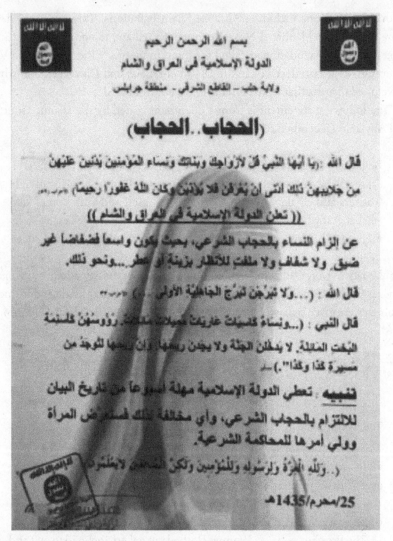

Figure 4.1 ISIS Fatwa restricting women's eyesight 'Imposition of Hijab Sharia on Women, Jarablus, November 2013'

were not wearing the niqab. It was not until ISIS declared that Raqqa was under its full control in January 2014 that women were forced to obey their dress code and hence wear the niqab.[28]

This document is noteworthy because it reveals the existence of Sharia courts run by the Islamic State already in November 2013. It also indicates that not only the woman in question will be punished, but also her male guardian. Some scholars have incorrectly claimed that women were not punished by ISIS because they were not considered "subjects of the law" and that only their male guardians were punished. In reality, women were also punished. In fact, women were often punished *by other women* who were organized in the *Hisbah* or Morality Police.[29] One woman in an IDP camp in Mosul described how she was more afraid of the women loyal to ISIS than the men: "The women would beat you for the smallest thing—how you looked or how you wore your headscarf . . . They used whips and metal sticks." Women who joined the Morality Police have confirmed that they took part in beatings of women even for minor infractions of the ISIS dress code or other forms of misconduct.[30] ISIS governance was not merely a war of men against women—but of women against other women.

Restricting Women's Eyesight

After this fatwa was issued that made it illegal for women to wear trousers or appear unveiled, questions arose about what to do if—even though a woman was veiled—some small part of her skin would show? The Research and Fitna Committee set about to find an answer. In a fatwa issued in December 2014, the committee replied:[31]

Fatwa on revealing of women's eyes

Question: What is the ruling on revealing the women's eyes whereby some of its side/cheek appears?

Answer: The Almighty has said: "Oh Prophet, tell your wives, daughters and the women of the believers to bring down over themselves some of their outer garments. That is more suitable so that they will be known and not abused. And God is forgiving, merciful." al-Ahzab 59 [Qur'an 33:59].

Ibn Abbas—may God be pleased with him—said: "Women are to cover their faces from above their heads with the jilbabs, leaving only one eye showing."

And Muhammad ibn Sirin said: "I asked Obeida al-Suleimani about the words of God—'to bring down over themselves some of their outer garments'—so he covered his face and head and exposed his left eye."

And it is not concealed that revealing of the two eyes contains a particular source of fitna if the edges of the eyelids are covered with kohl. The same applies when part of its side/cheek appears. So it is necessary for her to cover her two eyes even if with something delicate, far removed from fitna.

In Mosul, Iraq's second largest city, shopkeepers were ordered to cover the faces of mannequins after ISIS took control of the city.[32] As these examples make clear, Islamic State militants seemed to believe that even inanimate objects—mannequins in a store—could entice men to do sinful things. This suggests that the purpose of the restrictions on women's clothing was perhaps less about women than about men. Women were forced to wear a veil that covered their eyes because of men. Women were forbidden from wearing trousers because of men. And even mannequins in a store were a source of enticement—for men. This points to one of the many hypocrisies of IS "thought." If men were deemed unable to control themselves even when confronted with a mundane object such as a mannequin, why were men considered superior to women? Why should a man unable to control his desire in the face of a mannequin be given so much responsibility and even guardianship over other human beings?

Restricting Women's Freedom of Movement

It was not enough to force women to wear the hijab, which restricted their ability to see; women also lost their freedom of movement. In the realms controlled by the Islamic State, women were not allowed to travel or move about in public on their own. Similar to the male guardianship system in Saudi Arabia, women were only allowed to leave their homes if they were accompanied by a close male relative, known as a mahram. Women who traveled on their own were considered "reprehensible (Figure 4.2)."

The decision to restrict women's freedom of movement highlights another contradiction within Islamic State policies toward women. As highlighted earlier, a number of documents and videos were produced and translated to English and French with the specific intention of convincing women living outside the Levant to give up their previous lives and join the Islamic State. Of course, this would entail the necessity of traveling from abroad to Iraq or Syria, usually via Turkey. Ideally such women would be accompanied by a mahram. However, if necessary, ISIS ideologues decided that it would be permissible for women to travel *alone*—without a male guardian—in order to join the Islamic State.[33] Some women traveled long distances by themselves, including from the United States, Canada, Europe, and Central Asia, to join ISIS.

The inherent contradiction is clear: ISIS was calling upon women to *exercise their agency and autonomy as individuals* and travel unaccompanied across international borders, to then *surrender their agency* upon arrival inside the Caliphate. In order to join ISIS, women were permitted to travel thousands of miles by themselves if necessary. But once they arrived in the lands of the Caliphate, they were not allowed to even take a stroll in their own neighborhood by themselves. How did the jihadis explain such double standards?

Figure 4.2 ISIS Fatwa requiring women to be accompanied by a mahram (male guardian) at all times. 'On Movement of Women and the Garages: Raqqa Province.'

In justifying the severe restrictions on women's freedom of movement, Islamic State authorities claimed they did so out of concern for women's safety. However, women older than 50 were permitted to travel without a mahram. Hence, if the true reason for these restrictions was for women's safety, the restrictions would have surely been applied to all women, regardless of their age. The fact that women over 50 were exempt from the mahram requirement would seem to indicate that the real reason for the restriction, as I have suggested, was because of a desire to curtail women's freedom and destroy their independence. Solo women travelers were considered *haram*, particularly women who were deemed marriageable by the Islamic State.

On Movement of Women and the Garages: Raqqa Province

Indeed it is from the door of cooperation on the basis of piety and awareness of God and by which God has ordered us to safeguard the safety of the religion of the women and cultivate their religious and worldly interests, and it is for the abundance of inquiries about some of the reprehensible acts and manner of dealing with them especially on the issue of women travelling without a mahram [close male relative], and after the holding of a meeting by the supervisor of Hisbah in the center of the city with the amir of Hisbah in Wilayat al-Raqqa and with the Shari'a supervisor and by the agreement of the amir of the city, especially on some of the reprehensible acts on the issue of women travelling without a mahram, we publicize the following:

- Women may not leave the province without a mahram unless they have a transit document from Hisbah and an ID photo with seal of approval from the Hisbah office in Karajat.
- It is absolutely forbidden for women to travel to the land of kufr [disbelief]- except for serious medical conditions and by decision of the general hospital with seal of approval from the amir of the hospital.
- Women aged 50 and above are allowed to travel to the lands of the Islamic State without a mahram.
- Women younger than 50 are allowed to travel to the lands of the Islamic State with a mahram.
- Elderly women are not pressured on the issue of the hijab.
- If the travelling woman has her son with her, of competent, distinguished mind, he can be considered a mahram for her.

A question arose as to whether a mahram was required to travel with a woman. What if a man or young boy did not want to accompany his female relative when she needed to leave the house? In December 2014, the Research and Fitna Committee issued Fatwa Number 45, proclaiming that a mahram was not compelled to go out if he did not want to do so:

Fatwa on Women's Travel: Al-Buhuth wa al-Eftaa' Committee

Question: What is the ruling on a woman travelling without a mahram (and her mahram is present with her and does not go out with her)?

Answer: A woman may not travel without a mahram because Bukhari narrated from a hadith on the authority of Ibn Abbas (may God be pleased with him): "He said: The Prophet [PBUH] said: 'The woman is not to travel without the mahram.'" And is the mahram compelled to go out? In this there is disagreement and the right response: He is not compelled and God knows best.

Restricting Women's Interactions with Men

Finally, in addition to curtailing women's mobility, eyesight, and freedom to wear what they wanted, IS also enforced a kind of *purdah,* or separation of the sexes. This entailed forbidding women from interacting with men who were not close male relatives. Even during major festivals such as Eid al-Adha, where in the past it was common for people to gather together in public places, the Islamic State issued fatwas that forbade women from mingling with men or shaking hands with men. This becomes clear in the following fatwa issued in Hasakah Province of Syria in October 2014.[34]

Warning against certain customs on Eid al-Adha: Hasakah Province (October 2014)

6. Mixing of women with men: note the words of the Prophet (PBUH): "A man and woman are not to be left together unless she also has her mahram with her." In the same way the abundance of women wearing perfume who go out on this day, the Prophet (PBUH) said: "When a woman seeks to apply perfume to herself and thus goes out among the people so they may find in her such and such," of any whore/adulterer. And women shaking hands with men especially what happens among relatives among the sons of the general populace, the Prophet (PBUH) said: "Whoever touches the palm of a woman and is not from her is on the path of placing on his palm the ember of the Day of Judgment."

Part III: The Islamic State Calls
Women to Wage Jihad

In October 2017, the Islamic State called on women to wage jihad. Their Arabic-language newspaper proclaimed: "Today, in the context of the war against the Islamic State, it has become necessary for female Muslims to fulfil their duties on all fronts in supporting the mujahedeen in this battle." The sudden shift in their gender politics was justified by claiming that women had fought during the time of the Islamic Golden Age. This represented a dramatic rupture from their previous policy of confining women to their homes. Why did ISIS suddenly change course? What happened to glorifying women's "heavenly secret" of "sedentariness and stillness"? It just so happened that during the month of October, Raqqa had been liberated from the Islamic State by the SDF and Coalition forces. At that point the Coalition estimated that there were fewer than 2,000 ISIS men left in Raqqa. ISIS, however, denied that their shift to using women fighters was because they lacked male fighters. In July in an article allegedly written by a female ISIS member, women were called to "rise with courage and sacrifice in this war . . . not because of the small number of men but rather, due to their love for jihad."[35] Whether the article was indeed written by a woman is difficult to verify.

Then on February 7, 2018, ISIS released a propaganda video purporting to show women fighting for the first time.[36] Fully veiled women appear sitting in the back of a pickup truck being driven to battle, a jihadi woman shooting an assault rifle (Figure 4.3), and a brief clip of a woman running with a weapon alongside men. The voice of the male narrator says: "The chaste *mujhad* woman journeying to her lord with garments of purity and faith seeking revenge for her religion and for the honor of her sisters imprisoned by the apostate Kurds."[37]

The decision to send ISIS women into combat raises all kinds of questions. Were they allowed to go to war without a mahram by their side? How much training did they receive? How could they even see to shoot with the hijab they

Figure 4.3 ISIS propaganda video purporting to show female jihadis fighting in combat for the first time. The identity of the person in the video is unknown.

were required to wear? How many ISIS women actually heeded the call to jihad and took up arms is still unclear.

Several analysts have pointed out that the inclusion of women fighters indicated that the Islamic State had shifted from offensive jihad to a defensive one.[38] It was only after the Islamic State had lost Raqqa, the capital of its Caliphate in Syria, that the IS men decided to allow women into the ranks of their fighters. In other words, it was a sign of desperation. They didn't have enough men to defend their crumbling Caliphate, so they decided to call upon women.

Two additional points are worth highlighting. First, it is clear that women were instrumentalized by the Islamic State. IS decided to recruit women as fighters only when it suited their purposes to maintain power. If the Islamic State had truly wanted to recruit women as fighters, they would have done so at the height of their power, not when they were being driven out of their strongholds. Their inclusion of women was not a sign that men had recognized that women were just as capable as men, but that men were willing to use women as cannon fodder.

Second, the decision to use women as fighters could just as easily have resulted from the belief that women are expendable. In other words, rather than stemming from a recognition that women are equal to men, or just as able to learn the techniques of combat as men, the decision to allow women to fight—when the Caliphate was clearly in demise—more likely stems from the belief that women's lives are worth less than men's lives. Finally, this raises the question whether ISIS would have been more successful if they had recruited women earlier as combatants instead of confining them as prisoners in their own homes. Could it be that it was the Islamic State's own doctrine that brought about their downfall? In a book published in 2010, Nelly Lahoud argued presciently that jihadist doctrines carry within themselves the seeds of their own destruction.[39]

Concluding Remarks on the Caliphate

In this chapter I have argued that the subjugation of women was one of the raisons d'être of the Islamic State. Governance in the Caliphate amounted to a war of women, against women. The sexual enslavement of non-Muslim women was used as a recruitment tool for men, and justified on religious grounds, while this topic was often omitted in order to recruit women. While Christian and Yezidi women could be enslaved, Kurdish women could be brutally murdered, as they were considered to be apostates and collaborators. Any Muslim who did not submit to the authority of the Islamic State would be deemed a nonbeliever and could be "excommunicated" and killed. Finally, Sunni Muslim women living outside the Levant were encouraged to exercise their agency and travel from afar—alone if necessary—to live in the lands of the Caliphate. Upon arrival, they were expected to immediately surrender their agency. Destroying the independence of Muslim women was one of the primary objectives of their model of governance. As soon as ISIS got the chance, they imposed regulations that gave men full control over women. Even in the pre-Caliphate era and before they were the sole authorities over a given territory, IS militants would issue fatwas to enforce veiling, prohibit the wearing of trousers, prohibit women from traveling without a mahram and prohibit women from interacting with men who were not close male relatives. Subjugating women was a top priority.

When questions arose as to how to implement specific fatwas the Morality or Research and Fitna Committees replied by *increasing* rather than relaxing restrictions on women. For example, if a mahram did not wish to accompany a woman, he was not required to do so, which meant that women's freedom of movement was entirely dependent on the whims of men. This not only gave men control over women—it also in many cases gave male *children* control over *adult* women. This inverted the normal relationship between parents and children. Traditionally, even in patriarchal households where women bore the brunt of household labor, mothers could make decisions regarding their children. However, the Islamic State gave male children decision-making power over their own mothers.

In the case of women's clothing, after the ban on wearing trousers was issued and women were required to wear a veil, a question arose about what the ruling was if a part of the skin next to her eye was revealed? And here again, the answer that was provided required women to cover both their eyes with a film. In both cases after the questions were submitted, the answers that were provided increased the restrictions on women, rather than decreasing them. Both rulings enforced greater control on women—by giving the mahram essentially veto power over women's movements, and by forcing women to cover both their eyes, making it difficult to carry out any activities that require the use of her eyesight. In other words, when in doubt, decisions were made to *increase* the control that men and boys could exercise over women.

Even more pernicious than these manifold restrictions were their policies on education and underage marriage. By allowing teenagers or even girls as young as nine years old to be married, ISIS men were ensuring that girls would be transferred from the authority of their fathers to the authority of their husbands, without a moment of freedom. Daesh did not want girls to receive an education beyond the age of 15. Educated women and emasculated men were, according to them, the source of society's ills. Uneducated women and girls would be unable to challenge male authority.

By the fall of 2017 and early 2018, it had become clear that the Islamic State was fighting a losing war. Those who went to the frontlines would in all likelihood be killed defending something that was already lost. It was at this point that ISIS decided to call women to wage jihad. Sending women into combat at this point in the war did not stem from a sudden recognition of their abilities, but from the belief that women's purpose in life was to serve men. First ISIS destroyed the freedom of Muslim women living inside the Caliphate, then they asked them to throw their life away for a lost cause.

Until now, calls for an international tribunal akin to the Nuremberg Trials for the genocidaires of ISIS have been ignored. To have any chance of achieving justice, it will be necessary to understand the complex role of women inside the Caliphate, and also to discern between the motivations of local Syrians who fell under their rule and citizens of other countries who traveled from afar to join ISIS. Are not Americans, Europeans, or anyone who traveled great distances and joined ISIS of their own free will—at least as guilty if not more—than ordinary Syrians who may have been trapped by circumstances? And yet although the foreigners may carry a greater burden of guilt than the local Syrians, many countries, including in Europe, are refusing to take back their own citizens who joined ISIS. The international community's decision to largely wash their hands of responsibility, will place the burden of achieving justice on the Autonomous Administration. If the international community refuses to set up an international tribunal or hybrid tribunal to try ISIS detainees, does this not create all the more incentive for the Autonomous Administration to do so? The fact is that this will only reinforce the state-like institutions in North and East Syria. No one recognizes the Autonomous Administration as a legitimate governing body, and no one wants to support the creation of a statelet in the Northeast, with autonomy from Damascus. And yet the international community is, inadvertently, doing exactly that.

The Women's Revolution in Rojava and Beyond

We have the same ideas in Bakur and Rojava, but the systems are different. This doesn't mean we are related in everything. This revolution belongs to Syria.
—Ilham Amar, co-founder of the Women's House in Qamishli[1]

The rest of the world may have seen the fight against ISIS or Assad as the meta narrative of the Syrian conflict, the arc that explained a gruesome decade of war. But for the Kurdish women's movement those battles were just one episode of their larger struggle against the domination of men—including within their own community.

When outside observers did take note of what Kurdish women were up to, it was often to report about the young Kalashnikov-toting YPJ women who fought so bravely to defeat the Islamic State. But everything else they were doing to dismantle patriarchy went virtually unnoticed.

Yet Kurdish women were actively working to protect and promote women—even before ISIS emerged on the scene. They did this by creating new institutions of governance in each new piece of territory they wrested from the Assad regime or the Islamic State. One liberated region at a time, Syrian Kurds worked not to directly topple the Assad regime, but rather replace it by effectively building a shadow government, or what I've called a statelet of survivors.

Celebrated now as the beginning of the Rojava Revolution, July 19, 2012 marks the day when the Assad regime began its withdrawal from Kobani and other parts of northern Syria. As soon as the regime was gone, new institutions were set up to protect women. Laws were passed that bestowed rights on women unheard of elsewhere in Syria. Already in December 2012, less than six months after the withdrawal of regime forces, some of the very first laws passed by the People's Council of Western Kurdistan (MRGK) included basic

Statelet of Survivors. Amy Austin Holmes, Oxford University Press. © Oxford University Press 2024.
DOI: 10.1093/oso/9780197621035.003.0005

protections for women on personal status issues. Once the YPG/YPJ moved into a swath of land, after setting up checkpoints and flying their yellow and green flags to signpost their newly gained territory, women's shelters were often among the first institutions to be established. A simple chronology of when women's shelters were established in liberated cities—whether from the Assad regime or ISIS—illustrates that protecting women was a priority. See Table 5.5. But the advancement of women's rights was by no means a linear process. When ISIS militants rampaged across Iraq and Syria, declaring a caliphate in 2014, they aimed to obliviate women's independent existence. Yezidi women were enslaved, then bought and sold on public squares. Assyrian women were captured and held hostage for over a year, until their church paid a ransom to secure their release. Muslim women were forbidden to step outside their homes without a male chaperone known as a mahram. The Islamic State committed a long list of atrocities against women: sexual enslavement, rape, forced marriage, severely limiting the education provided to women and girls, massively restricting their interactions with members of the opposite sex, and even making it impossible to walk in public on their own. Chapter 4 delves into this in far more detail.

By contrast, the Syrian Kurds have tried to not only emancipate women from the conditions of slavery and subjugation, but to give women real power—and not just temporarily or as a tactical strategy to defeat ISIS. Furthermore, their goal is to reach *all* women, not just Kurdish women. Once the SDF liberated territory from the Islamic State, they quickly set up structures that were intended to protect women from the horrific violence they had experienced, educate them, give them (again) the freedom of movement, provide economic opportunities, protect them from child marriage and polygamy, and offer them the possibility to join the YPJ as fighters or to join the civilian administration. Thus, women of all backgrounds were offered new possibilities of political participation in their fledgling statelet in North and East Syria.

How were they able to achieve this? After all, many radical movements that emerged from armed conflicts in different parts of the world have claimed to be fighting for the liberation of both men and women. But most have fallen short of this aspiration. Indeed, some scholars have shown that armed struggle, or the militarization of any form of political contention more generally, often leads to the marginalization of women. This is because it is usually men who take up arms, thereby making women even more dependent on men and increasing their potential for violence and domination.[2] History is rife with examples—from the United States during the World War II to Algeria's war of independence from France—where women were mobilized temporarily during wartime to then be told during peacetime to return to their more "traditional" roles. In Algeria, even resistance fighters such as Zohra Drif who were celebrated as national icons of the anticolonial struggle, were unable to prevent feminist gains from being rolled back in subsequent years.[3]

Powerful institutions like the United Nations that have proclaimed their commitment to women's equality have often failed to achieve their own goals. On October 31, 2000, the UN Security Council adopted Resolution 1325, which recognized the crucial role that women play in conflict prevention, conflict resolution, peace negotiations, peacekeeping, and postconflict recovery. This landmark resolution also urged "all actors to increase the participation of women and incorporate gender perspectives in all United Nations peace and security efforts."[4] More than two decades later, only minimal progress has been made. In 2015, only 3% of UN military peacekeepers and 10% of UN police personnel were women, considerably lower than even the modest UN target of 20%.[5] That same year, an estimated 30% of the SDF were women.

Until now, women in Northeast Syria have avoided being marginalized, as so often happens in other postconflict scenarios. They have even surpassed the benchmarks for gender equality established by the United Nations. How could a small nonstate actor surrounded by enemies achieve what other movements and even powerful institutions like the UN could not?

That is the paradox this chapter seeks to explain. I make four arguments. First, I contend that the empowerment of women was possible precisely because women and their male allies built a statelet where they were able to make their own laws, institutions, and promote women into positions of power. The result has been to elevate women as de facto rulers of the very cities where Daesh had sold women in slave markets. The radical promotion and protection of women has resulted in a revolution in women's status—where women make decisions and partake in all levels of governance, a level of participation that is unheard of in parts of Syria controlled by the Assad regime, jihadist groups in Idlib, or the areas occupied by Turkey. Women shaped the statelet from the beginning.

Some of these ideas including the co-chair system of leadership (known in Kurmanci as *Hevserok*), where power is shared between a co-chairman and a co-chairwoman, were established in Turkey beginning in 2005, after the Democratic Society Party or (Demokratik Toplum Partisi—DTP), the predecessor of the People's Democratic Party (Halkların Demokratik Partisi—HDP) won some municipal elections. The Kurdish movement in Bakur had done far more than just win seats in the elections, but was in the process of building autonomous structures "inside the shell of the old society."[6] This included democratic confederal assemblies that were supposedly organized in a bottom-up manner: beginning at the level of the neighborhood, to the city, to the province, all the way up to the national level. Some of these "assemblies" or "committees" took on state-like authorities such as mediating disputes in lieu of the official Turkish judiciary.

The existence of such autonomous Kurdish-led structures alongside the official Turkish state structures constituted, according to who you ask, a kind of shadow government-in-the-making. In some regions of southeastern Turkey, such as Hakkâri and Şırnak, the democratic confederal structures may have even been more widely accepted among local Kurds, if not necessarily more powerful than the official Turkish institutions. Be that as it may, in Bakur such democratic confederal structures may have indeed operated with some autonomy from the state for a limited period of time, possibly because state officials ignored them or tolerated their existence, as long as they did not cross certain red lines. Many of the activists involved in setting up these structures were then rounded up and arrested, especially after the peace talks between the Turkish government and the PKK collapsed in 2015 and then the failed coup attempt in 2016. However, they were never able to really replace the Turkish state institutions.

By contrast, the central government in Syria was far weaker than in Turkey, and then lost control of territory in the north, as the large antigovernment protests spiraled into a full-blown civil war. Rojava was the first time Kurds could implement their ideas in a power vacuum—and hence begin building a statelet. The historical experience of organizing autonomous structures in Bakur, although in a very different context, also helps explain why PYD-affiliated Kurds were better organized than many other opposition groups in Syria. Each chapter in the book covers one aspect of the statelet-in-formation in North and East Syria, as outlined in the introduction.

Second, I illustrate that one of the primary reasons why the Rojava Revolution was able to expand beyond the Kurdish heartland of Rojava, was because many Arab, Assyrian, Armenian, Yezidi, and Turkmen women joined both civilian and military institutions of the Autonomous Administration. As the SDF gained control of territory in Raqqa, Tabqa, Manbij, Deir Ezzor, and Shaddadi, it was local women in these areas who helped ensure that the newly established institutions of governance could take root. The creation of salaried positions within the Autonomous Administration benefited both men and women. But for women, the AANES created not just the opportunity, but the *expectation* that women would participate in all levels of governance: from the highest ranking co-chair positions down to neighborhood communes.

Third, I trace the history of how these ideas originated within the PKK, and evolved over time through internecine power struggles. The collapse of the Soviet Union, the US wars in Iraq, and the creation of a no-fly zone, which led to a nascent de facto autonomous Kurdish region, caused the PKK to reevaluate both its ideology and relations with the great powers. In contrast to other national liberation movements, the PKK had never seen the United States as enemy number one, or even number two or three. And as I discovered during years of fieldwork in Turkey, in contrast to Turkish leftist militant groups, such as the Turkish People's Liberation Party-Front (THKP-C), the PKK had never launched any notable attacks on the American military bases scattered across Turkey—including those in the Kurdish regions in the southeast.[7] Although difficult to verify, some PKK defectors I spoke with even claim a meeting was held between Pentagon officials and certain PKK members to discuss the post-Saddam situation in Iraq.[8]

In addition to reevaluating its external relations, the PKK's ideology also underwent a paradigm shift. Instead of an independent Kurdish state, the PKK began advocating for the creation of decentralized autonomous structures at the local level based on the principles of "Democratic Confederalism" of which gender egalitarianism was a key component, alongside environmentalism and a cooperative economy. This sea change is often attributed to the influence of Murray Bookchin, a libertarian socialist whose books Öcalan began devouring once he was imprisoned in 1999. However, I argue that the shift was already well underway before that—and was being led by women. Or rather, that Öcalan was following the lead of women. The process was fraught with internal conflicts. Kurdish women mutinied against male leaders within the PKK, and won the right to create their own autonomous women's military units and civilian associations, without having to answer to men. In short, both the ideological and organizational transformation of the PKK happened, in part, as a result of struggles led by women.

Fourth, although the idea of gender equality was pioneered by female cadres within the PKK, my survey data of the SDF—carried out between 2015 and 2020—shows that the commitment to gender equality is no longer evident just within the small circle of cadre, but is shared within the rank-and-file, including both men and women. Furthermore, my observations during years of fieldwork have led me to believe their commitment is genuine. It is not mere rhetoric. It is not a calculated tactic to curry favor with the West. Their dedication to gender equality permeates every aspect of their lives. According to my survey data, many members ranked gender equality as more important to them than other goals, such as economic equality or ecological sustainability—as will be discussed in more detail in the following sections.

The PKK and Women's Liberation: A Very Brief History

The founding of the Turkish Republic out of the remnants of the Ottoman Empire, which had been multilinguistic, multicultural, and multiethnic, entailed an attempt to eradicate this diversity in favor of a new entity in which a single language, culture, and ethnicity—that of the Turks—would prevail over all others. As described in Chapter 2, this led to a series of no less than 20 officially recognized anti-government uprisings, including the Sheikh Saïd, Ararat, and Dersim rebellions. In the analysis of Hamit Bozarslan and other scholars, these revolts represented the single biggest threat to the new Turkish Republic. One indication of how threatening they were, is what was spent to repress them: between 1925 and 1926, an estimated 35 percent of the annual state budget was allocated to the suppression of the Sheikh Said rebellion.[9] To crush the Ararat rebellion, which was led by Kurds and survivors of the Armenian genocide, the government in Ankara found it necessary to acquire an air force. In the many decades that followed, the new Turkish Air Force was deployed for essentially a single purpose: to repress internal Kurdish-led rebellions.[10]

What is important for this chapter is to highlight that the double oppression of Kurdish women in Turkey dates to the founding of the Turkish Republic. While Atatürk's "modernization" policies offered important rights to Turkish women, Kurdish women were faced with violent assimilation. As Metin Yüksel noted, "The roots of the oppression and subordination of Kurdish women in Turkey can best be grasped at this dual juncture: the interwoven dismantling of Kurdish ethnic identity with the 'emancipation' of 'Turkish' women."[11] As he and other scholars have highlighted, for many decades both Turkish feminists and Kurdish (male) nationalists did little to address the particular forms of disenfranchisement that Kurdish women suffered. In an article published in 2006, Yüksel argued, "Kurdish women have been the victims of common oblivion of nationalism in Turkey, no matter whether Turkish or Kurdish."[12]

Like other Kurdish nationalist movements, the PKK was initially seemingly oblivious to the unique situation of Kurdish women. Founded in 1978, the PKK started a guerrilla war against the Turkish military in 1984, with the goal of achieving an independent Kurdistan. From the very beginning of the war, Kurdish women fought alongside men. But gaining real influence within the movement or even recognition was an uphill battle. At the outset women were marginalized, not taken seriously by many of their own male comrades, and ignored by the outside world.

The commitment to gender equality is now a guiding principle that permeates both political parties and the military units affiliated to this radical wing of the Kurdish struggle. It is even embraced by the rank-and-file, as my survey data illustrates. By aggressively promoting women within both political and military units, the Kurds have already upended the status quo. Less well understood, or even acknowledged by the outside world, is that their emancipatory project goes farther than just training women to fight in combat. They aim to completely change the relationship between men and women. One of the women who deserves most credit for initiating this transformation of the PKK is Sakine Cansiz.

The Forgotten Armenian Heritage of PKK Co-Founder Sakine Cansiz

Since its founding in the late 1970s, the PKK has undergone several transformations in terms of its gender politics. At the beginning, women were few in number. Sakine Cansiz was one of only two women who participated in the founding conference of the PKK in 1978. Born in Dersim, she was known by her nom de guerre, Sara, which was her Armenian grandmother's name. The second woman in attendance was Kesire Yildirim, whose code name was Fatma, and who at the time was married to Abdullah Öcalan. Yildirim later divorced Öcalan around 1987 and left the PKK, while Cansiz dedicated her entire life to the cause, eventually rising through the ranks to become one of the most powerful women in the Kurdish freedom movement.

Sakine Cansiz initiated the recruitment and education of women in the movement, waging internal battles against the male leadership to establish what would eventually become an autonomous women's movement within the PKK. At the time she was assassinated with a bullet to the head in January 2013, she was an iconic figure with a large following both inside and outside the PKK. The two other women who were killed at the same time in the office of the Kurdish Information Center in Paris, Leyla Şöylemez and Fidan Doğan, were also active in the Kurdish freedom movement. The circumstances surrounding their murders remain unsolved until this day.

The triple assassination occurred at the same time the Turkish government was holding peace talks with Abdullah Öcalan, leading some to blame elements within the Turkish state who wanted to sabotage the talks. Turkish intelligence officials, however, deny responsibility and instead have suggested their murders were related to internal disputes within the PKK.[13] Cansiz and other women did encounter pushback from powerful men within the PKK who were opposed to the creation of an autonomous women's movement. Some reports suggested Cansiz had even been relieved of her official duties after a falling out with some of the male leadership.[14] However, this was likely just a temporary mechanism. At one point or another, virtually all of the high-ranking PKK members have been relieved of their duties or transferred from one portfolio to another, as an internal mechanism meant to prevent corruption or the amassing of power in the hands of a single person. Declassified cables illustrate that in 2006 US and Turkish officials had designated Cansiz as "a priority PKK leader to bring to justice."[15] Those familiar with the movement have confirmed that being assigned to manage operations in Europe was one of the five most important portfolios within the PKK, which would suggest that she was indeed still a powerful figure at the time of her assassination. That said, how much persecution she and other women suffered internally within the PKK, we may never know. Described as "a

Figure 5.1 Funeral of Sakine Cansiz, Co-Founder of the PKK, assassinated in Paris in January 2013. ©Sadik Gulec / Shutterstock

legend" in the Kurdish movement, huge crowds gathered to attend her funeral (Figure 5.1), chanting in both Turkish and Kurdish *"Hepimiz Sakine'yiz"* (We are all Sakine) and *"Şehîd namirin"* (Martyrs never die).

And yet, Sara's Armenian roots are often omitted from the countless narratives about her life. In a speech delivered in Berlin in May 2014, historian Khatchig Mouradian highlighted this omission, saying,

> As we approach the centennial of the Armenian Genocide, let our minds, together, wander from Dersim, to Diyarbakir, to Ankara. Many of you here know that Sakine Cansiz was from Dersim, and that her *nom de guerre*, Sara, was her *Armenian* grandmother's name. Hundreds of thousands gathered to pay their respect to Sakine Cansiz in January last year. But that respect has not been paid to Sakine's grandmother, and the million and a half who perished during the genocide.
>
> That respect has not been paid to my grandparents. So let hundreds of thousands gather in Diyarbakir on April 24, 2015, to commemorate the genocide of the Armenians, Assyrians, and Pontic Greeks. And to make the voice of justice stronger.[16]

Unbeknown to Mouradian, some members of Sakine Cansiz's family were in the audience. While some individuals in the audience walked out during his speech, other members of her family thanked him afterward for his comments—indicating the level of controversy surrounding her Armenian heritage that continues until the present.

In her memoirs, Cansiz described the founding conference of the PKK in 1978 in Lice, a small town north of Diyarbakir. At the conference, she showed Kesire Yildirim, the only other woman in attendance, a pamphlet she had privately written about the need for women's units: "The Place and the Significance of Women in the National Liberation Struggle." Knowing that there were women's units in Vietnam and Bulgaria, Cansiz believed there were already enough women involved in Dersim, Elazığ, Bingöl, and Diyarbakir (Amed) to establish women's units. Although she shared the pamphlet with Kesire, she hesitated to speak about the idea with their male comrades.

> Most of the male friends were leading cadres who dominated the discussion. I couldn't compete with them. *These friends have a great responsibility*, I told myself. *They know what they're talking about, and their assessments are appropriately complete and multilayered. I've nothing important to contribute, so I must say nothing.* But the contents of the discussion would affect all of us ultimately, so I thought I had to speak up.[17]

When the PKK began to train in Lebanon in the late 1970s and early 1980s, there were just 17 women who made the journey to the Bekaa valley.[18] One of those women who were among the first to train for combat, Hanim Yaverkaya, later went on to command a mixed-gender unit in 1984, after the male commander of the unit was killed.[19]

Although Cansiz had already written about establishing all-women's units in her pamphlet in 1978, her ideas were not put into practice until the early to mid-1990s. The delay in implementation was due to many reasons. Cansiz herself was arrested around the time of the 1980 military coup in Turkey, and spent the next decade in prison in Diyarbakir. She was not released until 1991. At least 34 inmates were killed under torture in the Diyarbakir prison alone, during the time Cansiz was imprisoned there. The rampant torture of political prisoners in the Diyarbakir prison was one of the main reasons contributing to the radicalization of the PKK and the turn to armed struggle, according to former inmates.[20]

However, the traditional nature of Kurdish society in the 1980s was also a barrier to women joining the PKK. According to interviews with Kurdish women who remember the earlier years: "It was hard for men to imagine that women could engage in combat—or even carry a heavy load on their backs."[21] In *Blood and Belief: The PKK and the Kurdish Fight for Independence*, Aliza Marcus points out that in the 1980s, young Kurdish women often were not allowed to leave their homes by themselves, making it difficult to meet anyone, let alone PKK militants.[22]

The military coup in 1980 and detention of tens of thousands of Kurdish men, forced many women into the public sphere. This was the case with Leyla Zana, the first woman to be elected for the Kurdish party in the parliament. She had been married off in 1975 when she was 15 years old to an older cousin. The arrest of her husband, however, forced her to become the primary breadwinner for her two young children, and to learn Turkish. She began to take part in protests, which led to her arrest and torture, an experience that only further politicized her and strengthened her convictions.[23]

Once these barriers to women's participation in politics began to break down, and women began to join the PKK in larger numbers, it was difficult, if not impossible to reverse this trend, even among traditional Kurdish families that otherwise sheltered their daughters. As Marcus writes:

> A Kurdish father could block his daughter from working, from walking to the store alone, from going to high school, or even from wearing pants, but it was not easy to criticize her decision to fight for Kurdish freedom.[24]

By the early 1990s, an estimated one-third of all PKK members were women.[25] The entry of women into the PKK did not, however, automatically alter the prevailing gender norms.

The PKK did not always reject the institution of marriage as an instrument of patriarchal oppression. As mentioned earlier, Abdullah Öcalan himself was married to Kesire Yildirim between approximately 1976 and 1986.[26]

Their separation in 1986 coincided with Öcalan's proclamation of the introduction of "revolutionary comradely relations" between men and women within the PKK: *özgür eş yaşam* (co-equal life). The same year the Kurdistan People's Liberation Army was announced, known in Kurdish as Artêşa Rizgariya Gelê Kurdistan (ARGK). The institution of marriage and all forms of sexual relationships between men and women were to be replaced by relationships that were based on camaraderie and equality.[27] This meant that PKK fighters would not be allowed to marry or engage in any kind of intimate relationships, whether hetero- or homosexual.

The PKK's Prohibition on Marriage and Sex

When the PKK began to recruit women fighters in the 1980s, cultural norms especially in the rural parts of Kurdistan, as in many largely agrarian communities around the world, were still quite patriarchal. The only way conservative Kurdish families could be convinced to allow their daughters to join the PKK was to assure them that their honor would be protected. As the PKK recruited more and more people from rural areas, the influence of more traditional elements in society grew as well. In other words, the PKK initially became more conservative as it grew in size.[28] After the Cuban revolution, many Latin American guerilla movements shifted from the foco (small group) strategy to a strategy of mass mobilization—which led to the incorporation of women.[29] The PKK, in a sense, underwent a similar shift. However, while at least some of the Latin American guerilla movements such as the Columbian FARC allow their male and female combatants to form relationships, marry, and even have children, the PKK does not.

While the prohibition on sexual relations may be viewed critically by outsiders, for many Kurdish women it was nothing new. In traditional or rural areas of Kurdistan in the 1980s, women were expected to abstain from sexual relations until marriage. While the practice has become less common, there are still cases of women and girls being murdered, often by their fathers, brothers, or husbands in what are known as honor killings.

What this means is that the PKK initially adopted and strictly enforced a notion of "honor" that was not entirely unlike the patriarchal society that they claimed to be trying to overcome. The best way to preserve the "honor" of women was to live separately from men. As the years went by, however, the movement's definition of honor began to be associated with defending Kurdistan.[30] Later still, the notion that honor entailed male control over women's behavior was rejected entirely, and the movement instead advocated for freedom for women. This is perhaps best symbolized in the slogan "*Jin, Jiyan, Azadi*" meaning Women, Life, Freedom.

The 1990s: Women Develop an Independent Power Base within the PKK

The decade of the 1990s witnessed several major developments within the Kurdish movement as a whole and the women's movement in particular. It was during this decade that Kurdish women in Bakur began to establish their own autonomous organizations—separate from both Kurdish men in the Kurdish movement and Turkish women in the feminist movement.

In parallel to the expansion of Kurdish women's civilian associations that operated in the (limited but expanding) legal space available to them in the early 1990s, there was also an increase in the number of women fighters. But they were not always welcomed, even by their own male comrades. Şemdin Sakık, the PKK commander in Diyarbakir, allegedly refused to accept women in his unit and turned them away, reportedly saying "women spoil men" and that "war is a man's business."[31] Abdullah Öcalan later became an advocate for women—but he too was initially opposed to women organizing independently. In 1992 the PKK held a Women's Congress. However, Abdullah Öcalan reportedly announced subsequently that all of the decisions made there were null and void.[32]

Osman Öcalan, the younger brother of Abdullah Öcalan, spent almost 30 years in the PKK and has been described as a "longtime leader" of the PKK.[33] Among other duties, he served as a commander in the ARGK (now known as the HPG) in northern Iraq. In an interview in his home in Erbil, Osman Öcalan described to me how he helped establish the very first military camp for women in the early 1990s.[34] The camp was located in Zeli, near the border of Iraq and Iran. Sakine Cansiz was reportedly part of his unit and commander of the women's guerilla movement in northern Iraq. Osman Öcalan also claims to have been involved in helping to organize the first Women's Congress. His brother, affectionately referred to as Apo by his followers, was in Damascus at the time. According to Osman, his brother the *Serok* was allegedly not involved in the establishment of either the women's camp or the women's congress. In Zeli, Osman Öcalan explained, "We elected leaders of the women's movement in the Congress, prepared the program for the women's movement, and plans and strategies for them. Then we sent all the elected committee members to meet Apo in Damascus. He suggested we revise the name, that was all."[35]

In February 1995, a PKK court sentenced Osman to jail, including hard labor. According to his version of events, he was allegedly even told that he would be sentenced to death unless he changed his mind. He was accused, among other things, of helping with the establishment of a women's movement within the PKK. Almost two years later, in January 1997, the death sentence was commuted, and he was allowed to return to the High Council (*mekteb siyasi*) of the PKK. After his brother's capture in 1999, he was even part of the Presidential Council named to act on behalf of the imprisoned Öcalan.

By the mid-1990s, however, Abdullah Öcalan's position appears to have changed—in part due to the increasing number of women who engaged in suicide bombings. Öcalan began to praise the heroism of women such as Zilan (Zeynep Kınacı), who blew herself up in Dersim in June 1996. When Öcalan read Zilan's farewell letter, he allegedly said, "Zilan is my commander."[36]

Beritan is another female guerrilla whose self-sacrifice contributed to the new paradigm within the PKK. She was the commander of a PKK unit during the war in the early 1990s, fighting against both the Turkish army and KDP Peshmerga. When she was cornered, instead of surrendering, she threw herself from a mountain. A member of the women's movement who I interviewed in the fall of 2016 claimed that the incident had a profound impact not just on the PKK but on some of the KDP Peshmerga who saw Beritan jump from the mountain. One Peshmerga fighter allegedly put down his weapons and refused to ever fight again.[37]

As women were gaining in prominence within the military wing of the PKK, they were also organizing in the civilian wing as well. The first women's organization in the party was the Union of Patriotic Women of Kurdistan (Yekitiya Jinên Welatperezên Kurdistan, YJWK), founded in exile in Germany in 1987. It was the first official women's organization within the PKK that was entirely separate from men—and Syrian women from Rojava took part in it.[38]

In 1993, the decision was taken to form autonomous women's guerilla units, which then materialized in 1995 with the formation of the Kurdistan Free Women's Union (Yekitiya Azadiya Jinên Kurdistan, YJAK). Five years later, in 1999, a women's political party was formed that was autonomous from the PKK, adopting the name Women Workers' Party of Kurdistan (Partiya Jinên Kerkaran Kurdistan, PJKK).[39] In 2000, the name changed again to Free Women's Party (PJA) and in 2004 to the Kurdistan Women's Freedom Party (Partiya Azadiya Jin a Kurdistan, PAJK).[40]

As women were advancing their feminist agenda within the PKK, men were often recalcitrant. Abdullah Öcalan began to see men as the biggest problem. In an interview with a journalist in 1996, Öcalan used the expression "killing the dominant male" to explain what needed to happen to achieve true gender equality. However, it was not easy to convince men to change their behavior:

> Our men do not approach themselves with the intention of self-analysis. Since the men don't seem to feel this need, women must develop goddess-like attributes. What is meant by this? Woman must become will-power, consciousness, in fact, a force of creation and construction. Unless women like this emerge, it will be difficult to expect our men to pull themselves together.[41]

On March 8, 1998, the "Ideology of Women's Liberation" was put forward. This was meant to be an outline of the principles that women should abide by in the struggle for freedom. It stressed the need for complete autonomy from men and self-organization. To be truly liberated, women had to break free from centuries-old traditions and the mindset that justified them, and from political, social, and economic reliance on men altogether. Below are excerpts from an article published in 2021 summarizing the women's liberation ideology initially developed in 1998, which it says is "still valid today."

> The basic principles of the Women's Liberation Ideology are welatparêzî; living on the basis of free thoughts and a free will; self-organization; the determination to struggle, and ethics and aesthetics.

> *The principle of* **Welatparêzî** is seen as the principle that links women's ideology to the land, production and culture. Against nationalism and colonisation, the love for one's land is brought to the fore. . . .

The *principle of **Free Thought and Free Will*** is a notion developed to overcome the patriarchal control of women's minds. A woman who is deprived of her own will cannot be expected to play a determining role in overcoming a patriarchal society. Having free will is dependent on having knowledge, and hence, to obtain free will women first have to obtain self-knowledge and self-consciousness. . . .

The principle of ***Organizing*** is a basic necessity for every thought to be able to survive and to realise visions. Without it, no vision can become reality. . . .

The *principle of **Struggle*** is also one of the main tenets of the women's liberation ideology. Because women need to fight against the patriarchal system, in order to be able to gain knowledge and self-will to form a powerful force. . . .

The *principle of **Ethics and Aesthetics*** has also been considered as a tenet of a free life. . . . Beauty is taken beyond the notion of appearing attractive for the man, to be synonymous with freedom, cultural and ethical values. [emphasis in original].[42]

Andrea Novellis summarizes the rapid-fire evolution of the PKK's position on women within the span of a few years between 1996 and 1999:

Soon after the creation of the YJAK (1996), the PKK formulated the theory of rupture (1997), elevated Zilan as symbol of the Kurdish struggle (1998), embraced the feminist Ishtar Myth (1998), and made women the revolutionary subject (1999).[43]

In 2005, the High Women's Council (KJB) was founded, reflecting the shift from a Marxist party model to a democratic confederalist confederation model. Its constituent organizations included the PAJK, the YJA-STAR, the Union of Free Women (YJA), and the Young Women's Committee.

Öcalan's endorsement of women's equality did not just benefit women. One woman who had been active in the PKK for many years, and who now lives in the diaspora, explained to me that Öcalan introduced women into the PKK as a mechanism to solidify his own power. By prohibiting marriage, he ensured that women (and men) would not have to choose between loyalty to their spouse or loyalty to him. Since he has been imprisoned, he has written numerous letters addressed "to my women." By separating women from their male partners, Öcalan may have hoped to win their complete devotion.[44]

Öcalan's Imprisonment increases Power Struggles within the PKK—and Women Win

Regardless of why Öcalan advocated for women, whether to solidify his own power or out of a real commitment to feminism, the fact of the matter is that by the end of the millennium, women within the PKK had moved from being marginal figures to celebrated as quasi-divine. The new revolutionary subject was no longer the Kurds as an ethnic group, or the disenfranchised or subaltern, but Kurdish women. All oppression was seen as emanating from the oppression of women.

Just as women had reached goddess-like status within the PKK, their primary male champion—Abdullah Öcalan—was expelled from Syria and then captured and imprisoned in Turkey. For those men who were unhappy with the rise of autonomous women's organizations within the PKK, they saw this as a golden opportunity to bring them back under the leadership of the party. In the early 2000s, with the *Serok* in solitary confinement, a group emerged that challenged women's independent organizing capacity, and was led by none other than Osman Öcalan, the younger brother of Abdullah.

> A tendency emerged saying "The leadership is imprisoned in Imrali and the women's movement is now left to our mercy, so from now on you have to get our approval for all decisions you take." Of course, the women's movement did not accept this. There was an uprising. We made a now famous uprising. Whatever happens, no way will men make decisions about us. Our uprising was about this. All the women cut their hair. . . . It was a way to show that we did not accept [what was happening]. It created a shock: "What's happening within the PKK movement?" This was the beginning of an insurgency. If the women do this today, other things may happen tomorrow.[45]

At the PKK Congress in 2003 Osman Öcalan led a group that proposed to lift the prohibition on marriage.[46] In prior years he had allegedly tried to insist that women fighters under his command should cover their hair, a policy that women refused to implement. Other senior male leaders tried to demand that every autonomous women's institution should be brought back under their command. However, these attempts to destroy women's organizational autonomy were successfully defeated. Not only did women pushback, but they were able to mainstream their position, by using the symbolic leadership of the *Serok* to empower themselves.

In June 2004, after almost 30 years, Osman Öcalan left the PKK for good. He was one of many defectors, but exact numbers are hard to ascertain. Somewhere between 1,000 and 2,500 people left the PKK around the same time, while an estimated 3,000 militants remained loyal to Abdullah Öcalan.[47] Some people left because they wanted to marry or live openly as a couple, while others left because they believed the PKK should continue to fight for an independent Kurdistan. Nizamettin Taş, one of the highest ranking military commanders before he defected, accused Abdullah Öcalan of being a Kemalist for propagating the idea that Kurds could live inside the Turkish nation.[48] Osman Öcalan went on to marry a woman from Erbil and opened a bakery in Koya. When I spoke to him at his home in Erbil, he told me in reference to his brother Abdullah: "We were like Moses and Aaron. I made everything and prepared everything, but Moses was the prophet. Apo can take anything and put it under his command."[49]

Women and State Building in Rojava

Kongra Star: The Congress of the Women's Movement

The first autonomous civilian institution to be established after the paradigm shift was Kongra Star, which is best understood as a kind of umbrella organization of the women's movement in North and East Syria. It means "Star Congress" in reference to the ancient Mesopotamian goddess Ishtar and was originally founded in 2004–2005 as Yekitiya Star (Star Union). Many women active in Yekitiya Star had been arrested during the crackdown that followed the 2004 uprising that spread from Qamishli across Rojava.[50]

The goal of Kongra Star is "to develop a free Rojava, a democratic Syria, and a democratic Middle East by promoting women's freedom and the concept of the democratic nation."[51] When Kongra Star was first formed, they consisted of a few women working underground. Many of their members faced severe persecution. One of the most prominent members to be arrested was Hediya Yusuf, who was jailed in 2010 and not released until after the regime withdrew from northern Syria in July 2012.[52] After 2012, Kongra Star was able to operate openly and began to gain a mass following.

In mid-March 2018, as Turkey was seizing control of Afrin in the northwest, I met with Evin Sued, the Kongra Star spokeswoman in her office in Qamishli. At the time, she had two assistants and oversaw ten committees. Born in 1981, she had a degree in economics from Aleppo University. After graduating, she taught math between 2007 and 2014 in a school near Qamishli.

Ms. Sued was cheerful, confident, and clearly had a rather large skill set. I asked her why she changed careers from teaching math to working for Kongra Star. Her answer was straightforward: it was because she had met Öcalan while he lived in

Rojava. When she was just 9 or 10 years old, she traveled with her parents as part of a delegation to Lebanon. The occasion for the trip was to celebrate the anniversary of the beginning of armed struggle, or what she referred to as the August 15 revolution against Turkey. A child at the time, Ms. Sued mainly remembered Öcalan's thick black eyebrows and penetrating eyes. But when she became older, she became influenced by his ideas, saying: "when women are free, you can free your country."

I asked more about her family history. Evin told me that her maternal grandmother was named Mariam, and was a Syriac Christian. As a young girl, Mariam and her brother escaped from persecution in Turkey as fugitives. Her brother and parents were killed, but Mariam survived and was raised by a Kurdish family. She later married a Kurdish man from the Gabar tribe, whose family also had roots on the Turkish side of the border.[53]

Turning back to the present, she explained that Kongra Star organized its work through numerous committees, including: Diplomatic Relations, Participation, Media, Education, Municipalities and Environment, Justice, Culture and Art, Social Affairs, Political Affairs, and Women's Collective Self-Defense Forces.

The Culture and Art committee was responsible for reviving the Kurdish and Syriac-Assyrian culture that had been repressed during regime times. This included reviving traditional dances and folklore. The Political Affairs committee, I was told, contained eight political parties at the time: the Green Party (Keske), the Change Party (Taghrir), the Assembly Party (Tagammu), Liberal Party, Peace Party (Salam), Left Party, PYD Party, and the Syrian Kurdish Democratic Party.

However, of all these committees, the most important, she underscored, was the education committee. Because it was important for women to be educated, and to know their own history and culture.

Although pioneered by Kurdish women, their structures and promotion of women benefit women of all backgrounds. Arab, Turkmen, Syriac-Assyrian, and Armenian women have joined the YPJ, alongside their Kurdish sisters. The women's shelters that were pioneered by Kurdish women were adopted by Assyrian women. Already in October 2013 a Syriac Women's Center was opened in Al-Hasakah, and later shelters were opened for Assyrian women in both Al-Hasakah and Qamishli.[54]

The Constitutions of the Statelet-in-Formation Enshrine Women's Rights

Kurdish women in Syria had fought for equality for decades. After the withdrawal of the Assad regime, they had a chance to mainstream their ideas, even enshrine them in their social contract.

Fauzia Youssef had studied at Aleppo University, but gave up her studies to pursue activism full-time, later becoming a leading politician in Northeast Syria. She was one of the women who led the fight to enshrine women's rights in the social contracts that govern the area under their jurisdiction. She had been in Kongra Star back in 2012, then served in Tev-Dem, then became Co-Chair of the Federation of Northeast Syria. I had first met her in the summer of 2019 when she was sitting in the front row of the three-day ISIS Forum, an international conference that brought together hundreds of people from Syria as well as experts from numerous countries. Understandably, she was quite busy at the time. I had the chance to interview her in the fall of 2020, when she had stepped down from her position as Co-Chair and was taking part in the intra-Kurdish dialogue as a PYD member.

I wanted to understand if they were following a specific model in establishing their system of governance. Knowing that they were often asked about the PKK, I decided to ask about another Kurdish-led autonomous region. I realized it may be a provocative question, but she didn't bat an eye.

Me:	*What model are you following? Do you see, for example, the 1946 Mahabad Republic in Iran as a model? Or something else?*
Fauzia Youssef:	*We don't have a specific example in mind. But we have our own view to build up our system. In 2004 the objective circumstances did not allow us to build what was in our mind. This changed in 2011 with the revolution. After the 2004 uprising, the regime became more repressive towards Kurds. There was more torture, and detention.*
Me:	*What did you do after 2011?*
Fauzia Youssef:	*The first step was to found the Council of West Kurdistan, then after that Tev-Dem was established, because the population was already organized. Tev-Dem then converted institutions of the regime to serve the population.*
Me:	*How did you convert the institutions of the Assad regime to serve the people?*
Fauzia Youssef:	*For example, the Mala Gel (People's House) and Mala Jin (Women's House) were created. There was a committee for reconciliation, and a committee for dealing with domestic violence, and then other committees. In Kobani, there were protests against a police station, it was taken over by people with their own weapons. They also took over a bank. They counted the money in the bank and said, this money belongs to the people, so it would not be stolen.*[55]

In *Daughters of Kobani*, Gayle Tzemmach Lemon writes that Fauzia Youssef was inspired by the example of Tunisia. After the fall of Ben Ali, the new Tunisian constitution stipulated that women were "equal before the law."[56] Regardless of what exactly their model or frame of reference was, it is clear that guaranteeing gender equality was of paramount importance.

Tables 5.1 and 5.2 highlight how women's rights were enshrined in the two social contracts that govern the semi-autonomous regions. The first was issued in 2014 when the territory was controlled by the YPG/YPJ prior to the creation of the SDF. The second was then finalized in December 2016 but not issued until 2017, after the creation of the SDF and about four months after the liberation of Manbij.

As the SDF took control of more and more territory, Fauzia Youssef and her fellow activists were often warned that they should "slow down" their campaign for women's rights. They faced pressure both from Kurds as well as non-Kurdish communities. But instead of slowing down or forfeiting, they more than doubled the number of gender-specific articles in the second constitution in 2017. The number of provisions in the social contract that guaranteed women's equality had risen from four in 2014 to nine in 2017.

By contrast, one area where Kurds did compromise was the decision to drop the term "Rojava" from the official name of the entity they governed. While the decision angered some Kurdish nationalists, it also reflected the reality that the majority of people under their jurisdiction were no longer Kurds. Even the Jazira canton in the northeast, which Kurds referred to as part of Rojava, is also part of the traditional Assyrian homeland and is called Gozarto by Syriacs and Assyrians. Hence, in the 2017 constitution the official name of the governing entity became Democratic Federation of Northern Syria (DFNS). In September

Table 5.1 **Gender-Sensitive Provisions in the Social Contract of the Rojava Cantons (2014)**

Article 23(a): Everyone has the right to express their ethnic, cultural, linguistic and gender rights.

Article 27: Women have the inviolable right to participate in political, social, economic and cultural life.

Article 28: Men and women are equal in the eyes of the law. The Charter guarantees the effective realization of equality of women and mandates public institutions to work towards the elimination of gender discrimination.

Article 87: All governing bodies, institutions and committees shall be made up of at least forty percent (40%) of either sex.

Table 5.2 **Gender-Sensitive Provisions in the Social Contract of the Democratic Federation of Northern Syria (2017)**

Article 2: The democratic federal system of northern Syria adopts the ecological and democratic system and women's freedom.
Article 11: The Democratic Federation of Northern Syria is based on the principle of making the land, water, and resources publicly owned; it adopts ecological industry and social economy; it does not allow exploitation, monopoly, and the objectification of women; it shall realize health and social insurance for all individuals.
Article 13: Women's freedom and rights and gender equality shall be guaranteed in society.
Article 14: Women shall enjoy free will in the democratic family, which is based on mutual and equal life.
Article 25: Using violence, manipulation, and discrimination against women shall be considered a crime punished by law.
Article 26: Women shall have the right to equal participation in all fields of life (political, social, cultural, economic, administrative, and others) and take decisions relevant to their affairs.
Article 67: The democratic justice system solves the problems related to justice and social rights through peoples' participation and self-organization. The vision of justice is based on the moral principles of the democratic society. It aims at building a society which adopts a democratic approach and vision and ecology that believes in freedom of women and societal life and organizes itself on the basis of a democratic society. Services of justice are conducted through social participation and the organization of democratically formed local units.
Article 68 (6): Special feminine organizations and equal representation of women are the basis in the field of justice and its institutional activities. Women-related decisions are dealt with by feminine justice systems.
Article 69 (6): Women's justice council in the Democratic Federation of Northern Syria deals with all issues and affairs related to women and family. It has the right to monitor and coordinate with the cantons' judicial councils.

2018, the name was changed again to Autonomous Administration of North and East Syria (AANES).

The additional gender-specific provisions in the 2017 social contract appear to reflect the experience of living under the brutal reign of ISIS. Article 11 prohibits the exploitation and objectification of women, while Articles 67, 68, and 69 emphasize the need to achieve justice and accountability through special justice councils specifically for women.

Women in Military and Security Structures:
The YPJ and Asayîş

After the beginning of the Rojava Revolution in 2012, hundreds of women from other parts of Kurdistan, some of whom had fought with the YJA Star for decades, traveled to Northeast Syria to help set up the YPJ. Already in 2015, when the Syrian Democratic Forces (SDF) were founded, women represented an estimated 30 percent of the rank-and-file. Organized in separate women's units known by the Kurdish acronym YPJ, women fought in combat on the frontlines against ISIS (Figure 5.2). Nowruz Ahmed and Rojda Felat are just two of the women commanders who led some of the key battles that brought down the Caliphate, including the liberation of Raqqa, the former capital of the Islamic State in Syria.

Although pioneered by the Kurdish-led PYD political party, the commitment to gender equality has benefited women of all ethnic and religious backgrounds in Northeast Syria. Some of the many women I met during my fieldwork in Syria include Helin, who belongs to the Syrian Turkmen minority, is a member of the

Figure 5.2 Two YPJ women hugging each other after liberation of Tel Abyad in 2015

YPJ, and an outspoken defender of women's rights. Zanobia belongs to the Syriac Christian minority and is currently the commander of the Bethnahrin Women Protection Forces (HSNB).[57] When the SDF was first formed in 2015, most of the leadership positions were held by Kurdish women and men. But this is also slowly changing. Lelwy Abdullah, an Arab woman from Deir Ezzor, joined the SDF in 2016 and went on to assume an important position in the Deir Ezzor Military Council. She has survived multiple assassination attempts.[58]

My survey data shows that the commitment to gender equality is no longer embraced by just a small circle of female cadres, but is accepted among the rank-and-file of the SDF, including both men and women. One question on the survey asked respondents to rank which of the following three things was most important to them personally: equality between men and women/gender equality, equality between rich and poor/income equality, or ecological sustainability/environmentalism. Out of 380 respondents, 62 percent ranked gender equality as their top priority. Of the 380 responses, 277 were men and 103 were women. While 85 percent of women ranked gender equality as their top priority, 54 percent of men ranked it as their top priority (Table 5.3).

These findings are significant, because it shows that it is not just the leadership of the movement who espouse these ideas—but that average rank-and-file members do as well. Compared to other armed groups in Syria, this is no small achievement. While ISIS was the most extreme, with their enslavement of women, many of the other armed "opposition" groups held fast to their deeply patriarchal beliefs. The Syrian Democratic Forces are the only armed group in Syria that does not discriminate on the basis of religion, gender, race, or ethnicity.

Table 5.3 **How Important is Gender Equality for Men and Women in the SDF? By Number of Responses and (%)**

Gender	First Priority	Second Priority	Third Priority	Total Number of Responses
Male	149 (54%)	95 (34%)	33 (12%)	277
Female	88 (85%)	10 (10%)	5 (5%)	103
Total	237 (62%)	105 (28%)	38 (10%)	380

The question on the survey asked the respondent to rank the following in order of importance:
(1 = First Priority, 2 = Second Priority, 3 = Third Priority)
• Equality Between Men and Women
• Equality Between Rich and Poor
• Ecological Sustainability

Table 5.4 **Reasons for Joining SDF**

Gender	Defend Homeland / People	Women's Liberation
	Why did you join the SDF? (Open-ended survey question) By number of responses and (%)	
Male	284 (97.3%)	8 (3%)
Female	46 (47.4%)	51 (52.6%)
Total	330	59

Another question on the survey asked why they joined the SDF. It was an open-ended question, allowing respondents to write anything they wanted. I found that their responses fell largely into two categories: those who said they wanted to protect their land or country from ISIS, and those who mentioned a gender-specific reason for joining. My survey data shows that women were more likely to enlist in the SDF because of the desire to protect women from violence, or as a means to emancipate women. Men were more likely to enlist in the SDF due to the desire to protect their homeland (Table 5.4).

Chapter 3 is dedicated to analyzing the YPG/YPJ and SDF and includes sections on other women's units such as the Manbij Military Council and the Bethnahrain Women's Protection Units.

Women in the Civilian Structures of the Autonomous Administration

Women also occupy important leadership positions in all levels of the civilian administration. At the highest levels are Ilham Ahmed, a Kurdish woman from Afrin, who is currently Co-President of the Executive Committee of the Syrian Democratic Council (SDC) and Elizabeth Gawria, a Syriac woman from Qamishli, who serves as Deputy Co-Chair on the Executive Committee. They have both represented the Autonomous Administration in diplomatic visits in Washington, DC, Moscow, and numerous European capitals.

Below that, at the level of the governorates or provinces, women also serve in important positions. Layla Moustafa is a Kurdish woman from Raqqa trained as a civil engineer, who served as co-president of the Raqqa Civil Council, the city that was once the capital of the Islamic State caliphate in Syria. She is one of many new officials who symbolize the triumph of women over those who once sought to enslave them.

In Deir Ezzour, even as the last campaign to defeat the Islamic State was still being waged, the civil council was co-headed by Laila Hassan. Like Raqqa, Deir Ezzour was also ravaged by ISIS. It is also the second-largest governorate in all of Syria, with a population of just over 2 million, including internally displaced people.

These women illustrate how the Self-Administration is striving to be inclusive of the ethnically diverse population. Moustafa is a Kurd, Hassan is an Arab, and Gawyria is a Syriac Christian. I had the privilege of meeting all three of them during my various trips to Syria, some of them multiple times.

When I met Layla Moustafa in her office in Raqqa, she was wearing a black leather jacket, black skinny jeans and her hair in a bun. Layla Hassan in Deir Ezzor was wearing a traditional dress, bright green with gold embroidery and a scarf. She complained that under ISIS she had to wear a black niqab all of the time. Now, she told me, she wanted to wear colors. Gawyria proudly wore a necklace bearing a cross around her neck when I interviewed her.[59]

All the women face daunting challenges of overseeing the rebuilding of cities that lay in ruins with little to no help from the international community. Hassan explained the dire situation in Deir Ezzor because of the lack of basic medical facilities. For a population of 2 million, at the time they had just one single incubator. She told me "If two babies are born that require an incubator, one of them will die."

Only two nongovernmental organizations (NGOs) were reportedly operating in Deir Ezzor during my visit in March 2019. In addition to the battle in the last ISIS stronghold of Baghouz, former President Trump's repeated withdrawal announcements and the uncertainty of the continued American presence had discouraged NGOs from setting up shop.

The Self-Administration is working to improve the lives of women and girls who have been traumatized by years of rule by extremists who put women in cages and sold them on the market. They have also passed progressive legislation on women's rights, bringing their part of Northeast Syria into the community of nations that prohibits polygamy and child marriage.

In the territory controlled by Damascus, the Syrian Personal Status Law regulates issues of marriage and is based on Islamic Sharia and Hanafi jurisprudence. Polygamy is permitted, and the legal age of marriage for women is set at 16. However, girls may be married much younger.

The Autonomous Administration has set the legal age for marriage at 18 and outlawed polygamy. However, the ban on polygamy was not immediately implemented in all areas under AANES jurisdiction. In an interview with Lelwy Abdullah, an Arab woman from Deir Ezzor, I asked why the AANES could not yet implement the ban on polygamy:

> Regarding the issue of polygamy, of course we are not able to implement those laws fully in Raqqa and Deir Ezzor because of the prevalent

mentality there. However, when it comes to early-child marriage, we are controlling the situation—we have been able to prevent this for the most part. Polygamy it is more challenging. Sometimes men who don't have four wives will be excluded from social gatherings, because they are seen as "not a real man." Polygamy is a real problem in Deir Ezzor. Once there was a woman with a Tunisian accent; she was fully covered, wearing a *niqab*. We thought she was an ISIS woman, so we arrested her. But it turns out she was one of the wives of someone from the Sheitat tribe, who he married when he traveled to Tunisia. So of course, we released her. But what can we do? We cannot break up polygamous marriages.[60]

During a follow-up visit to Syria in September 2021, I visited Manbij, where the women in the Zenobiya Association explained how the AANES was beginning to enforce the ban on polygamy. They explained that if a man who worked for the Autonomous Administration enters into a polygamous marriage by taking a second wife, that he would be fired from his position. If his second wife also works for the Administration, she too would be fired. His first wife, however, would not be punished.[61]

Turkey is famously opposed to the Autonomous Administration, claiming they are implementing PKK ideology, which it views as an existential threat to Turkey's national security. In fact, the Woman's Law passed by the AANES is similar to Turkey's own Civil Code, which also outlaws child marriage and polygamy. In reality it is unlikely the ideology which the current AKP government sees as problematic, but the mere existence of a Kurdish-led self-governing entity. However, in the areas that Turkey occupies in Syria, many of these advancements in women's rights have been rolled back. In October 2021, it was reported that a "Polygamy Bureau" was opened in Azaz, a city occupied by the Turkish military after the 2016 intervention.[62]

The assistant chief of the UK General Staff, Major-General Rupert Jones, praised Layla Moustafa in a tweet, describing her as "a hugely impressive woman who has been at the helm of the civil council since it set up in early 2017." He added, "working with Kurds and Arabs, she has always worked bravely for the good of the population."[63]

During her visits to Washington, DC, Ilham Ahmed, co-president of the Self-Administration, was received warmly by many members of Congress. However, while praising the SDF and Kurds in particular for their bravery and fighting prowess, US officials have been hesitant to offer overt praise for their political project, presumably out of fear that any political recognition or praise would be interpreted by Turkey as a type of provocation.

Even more disturbing than the unwillingness to publicly praise the advancement of provisions that protect and promote women is the fact that the brutal assassination of Hevrin Khalaf, a civilian politician who was known for her work on behalf of women, was not immediately condemned by the U.S. State Department.[64]

Aborîya Jin/El Iktisad el Marra: The Women's Economy

Perhaps even more important than the promotion of individual women into leadership positions are the institutions that strive to lift hundreds of thousands of women out of poverty, or provide shelter to women fleeing domestic violence. In 2015, the AANES launched an ambitious plan to create a "Women's Economy" known in Kurdish as *Aborîya Jin* and in Arabic as *El Iktisad el Marra*. As part of this initiative, the AANES has established both mixed-gender and all-women cooperatives. Like cooperatives elsewhere in the world, the co-ops in Northeast Syria are owned by the employees and are intended to foster cooperation rather than competition. The women's cooperatives have an additional goal: to make women financially independent of men. During one of my trips to Syria, I visited three different all-female cooperatives in the city of Qamishli: a furniture store, bakery, and clothing store. While the overall number of people participating in these co-ops remains relatively small, there are now more Arab women than Kurdish women working in the cooperative economy. Furthermore, it should be underscored how rare such feminist developmental strategies are. As of January 2020, there were only five countries worldwide that had adopted feminist foreign policies Canada, France, Mexico, Norway, and Sweden.[65] The northeastern corner of Syria may have not yet achieved their goal of fully economically empowering women, but most countries have not even really tried.

A much more detailed explanation of the history of regime-imposed underdevelopment in the Northeast, the women's economy, and the larger Autonomous Administration's economic and developmental strategies, is available in Chapter 6.

The Mala Jin/Beit el Marra—Women's Houses Provide Shelter from Domestic Violence

Belonging to the older generation of Kurdish activists, Ilham Amar did not mince words about how the revolution led her to reevaluate her own life and marriage. She had been an advocate for women's rights since the time she was a teenager, when she was first jailed by the Assad regime. Arrested in 1988 because of her covert work to identify victims of domestic violence, she was beaten so badly while in detention that she became deaf in her right ear.[66] In 2011, Amar co-founded the Women's House in Qamishli. I met her in their office in March 2018. It was a tense time, as Turkey was completing its seizure of Afrin, and many members of the YPG/YPJ had deployed to Afrin and hence were diverted from the fight against ISIS. Yet civilian officials within the Autonomous Administration continued their work.

Women's Houses were opened in many cities and towns across northern Syria after the region declared autonomy from Damascus in mid-2012. Known as *Mala Jin*, which means Women's House in the Kurmanci dialect of Kurdish, or *Beit el Marra* in Arabic, these houses serve a variety of functions. They act as shelters for women fleeing domestic violence, and also as dispute resolution centers. By mediating marriage or family disputes, they are intended to relieve some of the burden on the courts. As the war against ISIS progressed, the courts of the Autonomous Administration became more and more overwhelmed with dealing with tens of thousands of cases of ISIS detainees.

As mentioned earlier, the fact that these women's houses were opened almost immediately after the outbreak of mass protests against the Assad regime—in Qamishli, the shelter was opened the same month the uprising began in March 2011—is an indication of the high priority assigned to the protection of women. Already in September of 2011, a shelter was opened in Afrin. This was before the Assad regime had withdrawn, and well before the emergence of the Islamic State. In retrospect, it appears almost prescient: Kurdish women were setting up shelters, as if they could see on the horizon the massive violence about to be wrought upon them—before anyone had ever heard of ISIS. Women of all backgrounds have sought refuge in the shelters.

I spoke to Ilham Amar and her colleague Beheya Murad in the Women's House in Qamishli. Several other women were gathered in the room as well, but Amar did most of the speaking. Plastered on the wall was a larger-than-life poster of Abdullah Öcalan and his mother, who was wearing a white veil. Cameras outside monitored the Women's House from all sides. A video screen hung inside the meeting room, displaying on four screens every entrance to the building.

When they first opened the Women's House in March 2011, the regime's Mukhabarat had surrounded the building, they told me. Even though, according to Amar, it was not a gathering of political parties. In her view, what had alerted the regime's intelligence was the simple fact that "Only women were there. No men." Our conversation continued roughly as follows.

Amar: *The regime tried their best to destroy our ideas and our longing for democracy. Even though we are not related to any political party. We are only defending women's rights.*

Me: *How can you claim you're not related to a political party when there is a huge picture of Abdullah Öcalan on the wall?*

The question upset her. She replied vehemently.

Amar: *We put his picture here because he defended women and respects women. Unless we liberate women, we cannot liberate the minds of women. It is because of his ideology that we fought against Daesh.*

I pressed on the topic, but tried to approach it from a historical vantage point.

Me: *How did the PKK or YPG change from prohibiting marriage, to now allowing it?*

Amar: *In the mountains they cannot get married. How could they have children? They need milk for children—they cannot find these things. But here they are among families, they go back to their homes. In the mountains if a man and woman want to get married, they will leave the PKK and then get married because there are no houses there. They are fighting a guerrilla war. I am married and have children. But if I had known the ideas of the revolution, I would have never gotten married. This institution of marriage is not healthy because men oppressed us.*

I was taken aback by her candid comments, openly admitting that she personally regretted getting married. Before I thought of how to respond, the translator Mohamed interjected and gestured to me saying, *"She is not married."*

All the women in the room suddenly laughed, including me.

Table 5.5 lists some of the cities across North and East Syria where women's centers were opened, along with the date the city was liberated (from either the Assad regime or ISIS) and when the centers were opened.

Table 5.5 **Women's Houses Expand Across North and East Syria**

City/Region	Date of Liberation	First Women's House Opened
Qamishlo	July 2012 (from regime)	March 2011
Afrin	July 2012 (from regime)	September 2011
Sheikh Maqsoud (Aleppo)	March 2012 (from regime)	January 2012
Derik	July 2012 (from regime)	March 2012
Kobani	July 2012 (from regime)	May 2012
Tel Hamis	March 2015 (from ISIS)	November 2015
Tel Abyad	July 2015 (from ISIS)	October 2015
Manbij	August 2016 (from ISIS)	November 2016
Raqqa	October 2017 (from ISIS)	August 2017

Figure 5.3 Women's Shelter in the Washokani IDP camp September 2020

Such apolitical, humanitarian institutions, whose only goal is to provide a safe space for women, have also suffered from the repeated Turkish
cross-border operations. Turkey launched its fourth intervention into Syria
in October 2019, under the pretext of wanting to remove Kurdish PKK
militants from their border. However, hundreds of thousands of civilians
of all ethnic and religious groups including Arabs, Armenians, Assyrians,
Yezidis, and also Kurdish civilians were forced to flee. The displaced population was so large that a new IDP camp, known as Washokani, had to be
created to house them. When I visited the Washokani camp in September
2020, I met some of the women who had previously worked in domestic
violence shelters in Ras al-Ayn. To my amazement, they had set up a *Mala
Jin* in a tent inside the camp. They continue to do the hard work of building
cooperatives and running women's shelters—even from inside IDP camps
(Figure 5.3).

Table 5.6 illustrates how the Autonomous Administration has enshrined
women's rights in their part of North and East Syria, and how their laws diverge
from those of the Assad regime.[67]

Table 5.6 **Syrian Women under the Assad Regime and the Autonomous Administration**

	Syrian Regime	*Autonomous Administration*
Adoption of Women's Quota?	No	Yes (40 percent quota in all representative bodies)
Domestic Violence Penalized?	No	Yes (Article 25 of the 2016 Social Contract and expansion of domestic violence shelters / Women's Houses)
Polygamy Outlawed?	No	Yes (Polygamy is illegal, but enforcement is unevenly implemented.)
Integration of Women at all Levels of Military and Police Forces?	No	Yes (Women are integrated in the SDF and police forces, both rank-and-file and leadership positions.)

The Statelet of Women

It is through the creation of the Autonomous Administration that these new women-empowering policies were able to be passed and implemented. The AANES also was the vehicle through which women could be hired into paid employment. Table 5.7 summarizes the gender ratio of officials of the Autonomous Administration by province and by institution, as of 2023. The table makes clear how their commitment to gender equality is being institutionalized region by region and institution by institution. A few points are worth highlighting. The province of Jazira has by far the largest number of AANES employees (40,000). Deir Ezzor, although it is similar in size to Jazira, has a much smaller number of employees (15,541). This could reflect either the fact that the AANES was established some seven to eight years earlier in Jazira than in Deir Ezzor, or that the population of Deir Ezzor is more reluctant to join the AANES. However, 80.7% of AANES employees in Deir are women – an indication that Deiri women may be more eager to join or support the Administration (and its feminist policies) than their male counterparts.

The variation by institution in terms of gender ratio is also worth highlighting. The institutions that have the lowest percentage of female employees are the Justice Council (27.1%) and the Islamic Conference (18.3%). This is likely due to the fact that, prior to 2011, women were less likely to work as lawyers or judges than men, and also less likely to be trained as religious leaders. The historical legacy of these traditionally male-dominated fields appears to continue to shape the current reality of northern Syria. Overall, however, women now represent 52.6% of all civilian employees of the Autonomous Administration, while men represent 47.2% (see Table 5.7).

Table 5.7 **The Statelet of Women: Gender Ratio of Officials in the Autonomous Administration of North and East Syria by Province and Institution in 2023**

Gender Ratio by Province			
Province	*Total Number of Employees*	*Female Employees (Percent of total)*	*Male Employees (Percent of total)*
Jazira	40,000	55.4	44.6
Euphrates	8,272	42.5	57.7
Deir Ezzor	15,541	80.7	19.3
Raqqa	11,118	41.5	58.5
Afrin	3,879	30.4	69.6
Manbij	7,769	38.9	58.8
Tabqa	4,391	42.7	57.2
Gender Ratio by Institution			
Institution			
Executive Council	5,000	40	60
Justice Council	907	27.1	72.9
Syrian Democratic Council (SDC)	199	60.8	43.7
General Council	146	34.9	65.1
University Coordination	423	41.8	58.1
Islamic Conference	218	18.3	81.7
Total (not including Internal Security)	97,863	52.6	47.2
Internal Security Forces (Police)	35,000		
Grand Total	132,863		

Will Women in Northeast Syria Lose Everything they Gained?

These hard-won gains, both in terms of women's equality and overall stability in Northeast Syria, are already in jeopardy. The region is under attack from all sides. Syrian President Bashar al-Assad continues to try and retake control of the defiant Northeast. He has the help of Russia and Iran. Meanwhile Turkish President Erdoğan repeatedly threatens to invade and annex another chunk of Syrian territory. ISIS sleeper cells are still active, and have assassinated women who are active in the Autonomous Administration. Finally, the Kurdish National Council, a long-standing rival of the PYD, is opposed to the co-chair system and 40 percent quota for women.

In those areas of Syria already under Turkish occupation, women have often been the first targets. Turkey launched its latest operation under the moniker "Peace Spring" on October 9, 2019. Furthermore, in areas occupied by Turkey the gender-egalitarian structures created by the AANES have been systematically dismantled. Prior to the Turkish intervention, the city council in Ras al-Ayn included 21 women and 21 men. Now that Ras al-Ayn is under Turkish occupation, a new city council was created with 25 people: 24 men and one single woman.[68]

Finally, not all Kurdish political parties support the commitment to gender parity. In June 2020, historic unity talks began between rival parties, the Democratic Union Party (PYD) and Kurdish National Council (KNC). The United States, which for the first time is acting as mediator in these talks, hopes that they will lead to greater political pluralism in Northeast Syria, while also reducing tensions with Turkey and the Kurdistan Region of Iraq. One of the main obstacles during the talks is that the KNC is reportedly opposed to both the 40% quota for women and the co-chair system. It is unclear whether the KNC's opposition is due to ideological differences, or the simple fact that they do not have as many female members in their own party. During previous rounds of Kurdish unity talks in Erbil in 2012 and Duhok in 2014, the KNC was represented by an all-male delegation, while the PYD-aligned party had both men and women delegates. In an interview, one of the male KNC leaders taking part in the current unity talks described the issue of women's representation as a minor detail. There are not many women in leadership positions in the KNC, but those who are have not come out publicly against the women's quota. Perhaps because they recognize that the women's quota, although championed by the PYD, would benefit non-PYD women as well. However, because one side of the negotiating table is dominated by men, it is possible that the PYD's radical commitment to gender equality will be sacrificed on the altar of Kurdish (male) unity.

Delinking from Damascus

The Economic Underpinnings of Political Autonomy

We transformed Afrin from a consuming city to a producing city.
—Dr. Ahmed Youssef, Finance Minister of North and East Syria[1]

Historically the regions east of the Euphrates have been the most economically underdeveloped parts of Syria. Regardless of who was in power in Damascus, officials in the central government preferred to maintain the northeast as a kind of internal colony: an agrarian hinterland that produced raw materials for the rest of the country. The feudal system of land tenure inherited from the Ottoman Empire persisted until 1958, when the first Land Reform Law was introduced. Until then, 45 percent of the irrigated land was owned by just 2.5 percent of all landowners. Most of the large estates were held by absentee landlords, while 70 percent of the rural population did not own any land at all.[2] In the Jazira region in the Northeast, described by one scholar as "the main zone of the latifundia in Syria," just forty people, including Bedouin chiefs and urban notables, owned 90 percent of agricultural land. Ten of them owned 70 percent of the irrigated land. One of those ten included Sheikh Humaydi Daham al-Hadi head of the powerful Shammar tribal confederation, who would later become one of the first Arab sheikhs to partner with the YPG.[3]

In the assessment of Raymond Hinnebusch, the agrarian revolution in Syria as a whole was carried out with "reasonable success" in that it created a middle-stratum of rural landowners who were also incorporated into political life.[4] This class in particular became "the social base of Ba'athism," which imparted both stability and longevity to the regime in Damascus.[5] And yet it was in the Jazira, where land reforms were arguably needed the most, that they were the least implemented. In the Northeast, high levels of inequality persisted, as did the phenomenon of landlessness.

Statelet of Survivors. Amy Austin Holmes, Oxford University Press. © Oxford University Press 2024.
DOI: 10.1093/oso/9780197621035.003.0006

Deliberate steps were taken to prevent the development of local industry, ensuring that the region remained poor. Decree 49 of 2008 made it more difficult to transfer property or housing within 25 km of the border to Turkey without explicit permission from the central government in Damascus.[6] The construction of large new buildings in the Jazira canton was also restricted.[7] Before the conflict erupted in 2011, Al-Hasakah, Raqqa, and Deir Ezzor had the highest levels of poverty in all of Syria. Those three governorates alone accounted for half of all Syrians living in poverty.[8] The majority of people in these areas made their living as farm workers. For Kurds and Yezidis who had been deprived of their Syrian citizenship or rendered stateless, known as the *ajanib* and *maktoum*, it was impossible to own property—including the land on which they labored. Not unlike Russian serfs under the Tzar or landless peasants on haciendas in Latin America, these Kurds and Yezidis had been forced to the margins, stripped of basic political rights and trapped in poverty.

Syria, however, is a land of contradictions. In comparison to other authoritarian countries in the MENA region, the Syrian Arab Republic had made efforts to increase literacy in the decades prior to the outbreak of the conflict. This resulted in dramatically different literacy rates among different age groups. In 2004, among those in the 15–24 year old age bracket, 92.5 percent were literate (94.6 percent of men and 90.2 percent of women), while among those 65 and older, only 39 percent were literate (53 percent of men and only 23 percent of women 65 and older).[9] Central government officials, for all their autocratic transgressions, had at least placed importance on educating the population. Although here again, Kurds faced discrimination. There was not a single university in the Kurdish-majority areas, and the Kurdish language was banned. This is one of the reasons why the creation of universities under the Autonomous Administration was hailed as a major achievement by many Syrian Kurds, as explained in Chapter 7. Kurdish youth who, against all odds, strived to be upwardly mobile had no choice but to leave the region. Needless to say, the lack of industry or institutions of higher learning was detrimental to everyone in the region, not just Kurds. Instead of training locals to work in the oil industry in eastern Syria, engineers and other high-skilled employees were recruited from Damascus or outside the region. Many Syrians in the northeast believed the neglect was intentional.

Despite these inauspicious circumstances, the Autonomous Administration has managed to not only survive and provide for the basic needs of the population, but has also taken important steps to begin the process of developing their regional economy. What theory, if any, has guided the officials of the local administration as they took control of liberated areas and set up their own forms of governance? How has the semi-autonomous region survived economically throughout the course of more than a decade of conflict, the destruction of infrastructure during the war, an influx of IDPs and Iraqi refugees, followed then by US sanctions and massive devaluation of the Syrian currency? What are the economic underpinnings of their political autonomy?

In a kind of political jujitsu, the leaders of the region have tried to transform their weaknesses—the externally-imposed underdevelopment and relative lack of exposure to capitalism—to their benefit in order to establish a unique economic ecosystem. Control of oil, rich agricultural lands, important waterways such as the Tabqa Dam, and employee-run cooperatives have been key to their economic survival.

But administration officials have larger ambitions than mere survival. In what may be the first such project of its kind anywhere, a parallel "Women's Economy" is being created, with separate structures and institutions that appears to operate according to their own feminist logic, distinct from that of the general economy. As will be discussed in the section on the Women's Economy, female-run cooperatives have been established that are geared to making women financially independent. Both mixed-gender and all-women communes are intended to mobilize the population as active participants in rebuilding the economy, similar to how the SDF mobilized civilians to defeat ISIS and defend the region.

The Rojava Revolution has elements of both top-down "revolutions from above" directed by professional cadres who dedicate themselves to the movement, as well as bottom-up "revolutions from below" in which the larger population participate via civilian and military institutions such as the communes and the YPG/YPJ, and later the Syrian Democratic Forces (SDF). In other words, in the civilian sphere, the communes are the economic counterpart of local councils that do more explicitly political work, while the SDF provides security as part of the military sphere. Although the Rojava Revolution is often described as left-leaning or even Marxist in orientation, in reality, they do not fit neatly into existing categories. As Joost Jongerden has correctly highlighted: "the PKK did not see any of the countries of 'real socialism' as a guiding star: not China, not Cuba, not Albania, not the Soviet Union."[10]

I will argue that the economy of North and East Syria does not follow a single theory or praxis, but is an eclectic mix of radical feminism, a social-democratic commitment to provide a safety net for a population ravaged by war, as well as elements of capitalism that tries to promote small and medium-sized enterprises in the private sector. The lack of reliable macroeconomic data for Syria as a whole, combined with the lack of transparency regarding the data that is available, and frequent shifts in territorial control makes it difficult to assess economic indicators with quantitative precision. However, it is possible to discern broad patterns in the economic policies of the Autonomous Administration. I argue that these can be broken down into the following short-term, medium-term, and long-term strategies (Table 6.1).

Table 6.1 **AANES Strategies for the Economic: Development of North and East Syria**

	General Economy		Women's Economy	
	Goals	*Strategies*	*Goals*	*Strategies*
Short-Term	Survival Prevent mass hunger Provide shelter, food, water, and electricity to local population and more than 1.4 million IDPs and refugees from Iraq Protect population from pandemic; prevent spread of Covid19	Mixed-gender cooperatives Subsidies for basic goods Additional security forces to protect farmland from fires set by ISIS Assistance from humanitarian NGOs Lockdown and travel restrictions to prevent spread of Covid19	Survival Training and capacity-building for women Protect women from ISIS and other extremist groups Protect women from domestic violence	All-female cooperatives YPJ Academies provide military training for women Civilian Academies provide courses on *Jineology* for women Women's Houses (*Mala Jin*)
Medium-Term	De-link economy from Damascus Development of regional economy Rebuild region devasted by the war Economic growth	Confiscate state-owned land Collect taxes for the AANES and refusal to pay taxes to Damascus Seize and maintain control of oil and gas resources Crackdown on oil smuggling to regime-held territories Repair damaged oil infrastructure Promote small and medium-sized private enterprises	Make women financially independent of men	All-female cooperatives Redistribute land to all-female cooperatives All-female villages Co-chair system Women equally represented in key economic ministries Ensure equal pay for equal work Ensure women have equal inheritance
Long-Term	Diversify the economy Normalize relations with Turkey and the Kurdistan Region of Iraq	Establish trade relations with Turkey Prevent cross-border smuggling and regulate customs Export oil outside of Syria	Achieve full economic and political equality between women and men	Increase women's involvement in the private sector Cultivate women entrepreneurs

From Internal Colony to Self-Sufficiency?

Short-Term, Medium-Term, and Long-Term Economic Strategies of the AANES

Since the withdrawal of the Assad regime from the Kurdish regions in the summer of 2012, the goal of the administration was quite simply to make it on their own: to survive. This meant taking steps to avert a famine and then, beginning in early 2020, to prevent the spread of the COVID-19 pandemic. The Autonomous Administration had to ensure that food, water, and electricity was provided for the local population indigenous to the North and East of Syria, as well as the influx of more than 1.4 million internally displaced people (IDPs) from other parts of Syria, and more than 10,000 Iraqi refugees who fled from Iraq to Syria.[11] The simple task of survival was made more difficult when ISIS militants began setting fire to farmland, destroying the harvest that millions of people rely on for their food supply. When Turkey shelled the Alouk water station in 2019 during the "Peace Spring" intervention, the water supply that people in the Northeast depend on for drinking water, irrigating crops, or just washing their hands, was imperiled as well. Nothing, not even the provision of basic necessities, could be taken for granted.

In the medium-term, the goal has been to make the regional economy less dependent on the central government, or what I call "De-linking from Damascus." This does not mean that the leaders of the Autonomous Administration want to declare independence—on the contrary, they have repeatedly confirmed their commitment to the territorial integrity of Syria—but rather that they want to fundamentally change the nature of their relationship with the central government which, for decades, has treated the Northeast as a kind of internal colony, consigned to a state of economic underdevelopment.

Finally, the long-term strategies are more difficult to discern, much less predict, given the chaotic and uncertain nature of the larger Syrian conflict. How or if the regional economy will further develop depends a lot on the impact of US sanctions, and whether Russia succeeds in closing down all border crossings into the Northeast, thereby strangulating the semi-autonomous region. If the Semalka border crossing remains open and investors take advantage of the sanctions waivers announced by the U.S. Treasury in Syria General License 22, there are numerous possibilities. Several high-ranking officials in the Autonomous Administration have said both publicly and in private conversations that they hope to eventually normalize relations with Turkey, and that establishing trade relations could be one way for that to happen.

The canton of Jazira produced about 60 percent of the total grain production in Syria. In Kobani, both cotton and grain were key, while Afrin was (until the Turkish occupation) the second-largest producer of olive oil in Syria, after Idlib. After the regime withdrew from Afrin and it was run by the Autonomous Administration, it was one of the few parts of Syria that experienced economic growth, according to local media and administration officials.[12] However, the lack of access to capital and sanctions have limited their ability to move beyond self-sufficiency.

Since the withdrawal of regime forces in the summer of 2012, the Autonomous Administration has had to devote a lot of resources to mere survival. Even after the defeat of the territorial caliphate, the statelet was still forced to spend about 40 percent of their expenditures on defense, according to data from 2020. However, they have also been trying to develop the region economically. Despite significant expenditures on defense, the Autonomous Administration was able to pay salaries that were more than double those paid under the regime. Because many people are unable to travel to regime-held territories for fear of arrest, this has also forced them to be more self-reliant. In other words, if the Northeast becomes economically independent of the regime, it will be in part because the regime forced them to rely on themselves.

Despite being under embargo and under siege from all sides, the Autonomous Administration now can offer salaries to their "civil servants" that are more than double what is paid by the central government in Damascus. Those employees who work for the Autonomous Administration are known in Arabic as "muazafy al-idariya" and in Kurdish as "karmendên rêveberiyê," which roughly translates to administration employees, as opposed to "government employees," to refer to those who work for the central government.

Rojava's Theory of Economic Development

The Rojava Revolution has often been portrayed as Marxist-inspired, but in fact their theory of economic development diverges in important ways from the centrally planned economies of socialist countries. Repudiating both the logic of capitalist neoliberal economies and state socialism, the officials who were in charge of economic planning aimed to establish what they called a "social economy" (*Aboriya Civaki*) and saw cooperatives as the foundation for this. As I have argued previously, their policies on integrating women into the economy are in many ways reminiscent of National Action Plans adopted by numerous countries around the world that aim to close the gender gap.[13]

The social economy is based on the following principles: to prevent the establishment of monopolies, to integrate women into the economy, preserve the environment, and through employee-run cooperatives for workers to develop their own intrinsic values rather than having the (authoritarian or profit-maximizing) values of outsiders imposed on them.[14]

While Marxists see the relationship between workers and the bourgeoisie as the root cause of exploitation they seek to overcome, Rojavan economists see the relationship between monopolies and the community as the main problem to be overcome. Rather than abolishing private property, they believe private property should serve the community. Small and medium-sized private enterprises, in their vision, should be the engine of economic growth. Two scholars summed up the approach as follows: "Just as the national state and local autonomy are meant to co-exist peacefully, so too are capitalist and cooperative production."[15]

Dr. Ahmed Youssef was central in helping to shape the economy of Rojava. A native of Afrin, he did his PhD at Aleppo University on the role of the banking system in the economic development of Syria. He became head of the Economic Ministry when the Autonomous Administration was announced in 2014. He was also involved in helping to set up the Chamber of Industrial Trade, which had some 300 members, as well as a union for tailors, which had some 900 members. When Turkey intervened in Afrin in early 2018, he was forced to flee with his family. But being forcibly displaced from his home did not stop his work. When I met him in September 2020 in Qamishli, he had recently been appointed as Finance Minister of North and East Syria.

I asked Dr. Youssef what theory guided him, as he was at the time serving as the de facto Finance Minister of the entire semi-autonomous region. His optimistic response surprised me, given that the workshops he had helped set up, and indeed all of Afrin, was now occupied by the Turkish military. The root of his optimism is that he fundamentally believes it is possible to transform the economy, regardless of how bad the current economic situation may be. However, he said, it would take time: "maybe between ten to fifteen years." Dr. Youssef elaborated:

> We have to first understand the hierarchy dividing the community: there are rich and poor people. If you exclude anyone, you exclude the vision. The vision depends on rich people to play their role at the same level as the poor people. In the underdeveloped countries we think the rich are responsible for the suffering of the poor—but that is not entirely true, both play a role. Our vision was to remove the conflict between these two groups.[16]

This theoretical approach is reflected in practice in their policies on land ownership.

Land Ownership

Key to understanding class relations in any society is the issue of land ownership. Peasants and agricultural workers around the world have often had remarkably similar demands. From *les paysans* during the French Revolution, to sharecroppers and slaves on plantations in the American south, to the *fellaheen* in Nasser's Egypt, land reform has often been one of the foremost demands in the course of revolutions and civil wars. This was also true of Kurdish insurgents in the various parts of Kurdistan.

When the PKK was founded in Turkey in 1978, one of their first targets was not the Turkish military or other institutions of the Turkish state, but Kurdish landowners in the southeast.[17] By targeting co-ethnics who owned large tracts of land, the PKK intended to bring about a transformation of Kurdish society, which they saw as still retaining elements of feudalism. The Kurdish landowners were seen as the primary beneficiaries of the quasi-feudal social relations that still prevailed, and as having been co-opted by the Turkish state through export-oriented industrial agriculture which was not ecological and did not benefit the majority of the population in the rural southeast.[18] The PKK's decision to target Kurdish landowners, as well as rival Kurdish parties, set in motion a pattern of political polarization that soon enveloped the entire Kurdish community. Kurds were forced to choose sides; remaining neutral was not an option. This laid the groundwork for decades of fratricidal violence known in Kurdish as *brakozhi*.

In Rojava, the Kurds took a different approach to private property. Instead of confronting large landowners, Article 41 of the Social Contract stated that private ownership would be protected. However, the Social Contract also stated that private property may be appropriated for the sake of the "social interest" because the goal of the Autonomous Administration is to put private property in the service of society.[19] As of now, however, large landowners in North and East Syria have not been confronted. Nor has the Autonomous Administration attempted to redistribute land that had been taken from Kurds and given to Arabs in the context of the Arab Belt policies. After their lands had been flooded by the building of dams along the Euphrates River, some 4,000 Arab families from Aleppo and Raqqa were resettled in the Kurdish areas of Al-Hasakah. They were then given land that the central government seized from Kurdish landowners. Because their lands had been flooded, they are known colloquially as *makhmoureen*. The resettlement process happened in 1974–1975, and was based on a study produced by Lieutenant Mohamed Talab Helal in 1963. An officer in the Ministry of Interior, his study laid the groundwork for the Arab Belt policies. Lieutenant Helal's study called for

> making the northern border strip of al-Jazeera a military frontline, in which military assets are deployed with the mission of housing the Arabs and evacuating the Kurds, according to whatever plan the state formulates.[20]

Hence, some of the Arabs who had been resettled in the 1970s may have feared that once Kurds had been elevated to positions of power within the Autonomous Administration, that they would use the opportunity to take revenge. Or to somehow reappropriate the property back to the previous Kurdish landowners. Until now, however, this has not happened. A report by Amnesty International that alleged that Syrian Kurds had engaged in "ethnic cleansing" of Arab communities was refuted by the United Nations Independent Commission of Inquiry:

> Though allegations of "ethnic cleansing" continued to be received during the period under review, the Commission found no evidence to substantiate claims that YPG or SDF forces ever targeted Arab communities on the basis of ethnicity, nor that YPG cantonal authorities systematically sought to change the demographic composition of territories under their control through the commission of violations directed against any particular ethnic group.[21]

Property that belonged to the central government, however, is not protected by the Social Contract. The Autonomous Administration has confiscated Syrian state property across North and East Syria.[22] Only governmental buildings in Hasakah and Qamishli that were deemed necessary were left untouched. These include the airport in Qamishli, as well as the land registry, passport and immigration offices, and offices to register marriages, births and deaths. By the end of 2016, much of the land that belonged to the governmental farms, known in Arabic as *Mazara al-Dawla*, had been turned over to agricultural cooperatives.

Abandoned properties represented another conundrum for local officials. The Syrian conflict has displaced half of the population of the entire country: either internally as IDPs or externally as refugees. This meant that a considerable amount of real estate had simply been abandoned. In September 2015, the Legislative Council of the Jazira region issued a bill that allowed the Autonomous Administration to confiscate all assets of residents who had left the region. The bill was justified as an attempt to "protect" the property from seizure by hostile third parties, but presumably also intended to put the private property "in the service of society" as outlined in the Social Contract. Given the influx of IDPs and refugees in need of housing, local officials may have thought they could put the abandoned properties to better use than simply allowing them to stand vacant. However, after harsh criticism, especially from 16 Armenian, Assyrian, and other Christian organizations, PYD officials reversed the decision and handed the properties that belonged to Christian owners over to various churches.[23]

Post-Regime Economy

The withdrawal of Assad's security forces from the Kurdish regions in July 2012 was widely celebrated by those who were happy to see the backs of Baathist officials. But it also presented enormous challenges. Thomas Schmidinger, an Austrian academic who conducted fieldwork in northern Syria during the winter of 2013–2014, describes the situation as follows:

> The first two winters after the withdrawal of the Syrian army were very hard in all three Kurdish regions of Syria. There was hardly any fuel available, and people often queued for hours in front of the bakeries. I still remember well the sight of people chopping up their furniture for firewood. In the winter of 2013–2014, I saw chilblains on the feet of a small child from a family of internally displaced people, the first I had ever seen. Power supply was limited to just a few hours per day, and medical care was disastrous. However, by 2015, the worst of these supply problems had largely been solved. The collapse of Syria's highly centralized and state-run economy led to a war economy in which the various warring parties traded with each other even though they were enemies on the battlefield.[24]

After the regime withdrew from Afrin, local officials established several new industries and expanded existing ones, including textiles, canned foods, and olive oil products. In Afrin alone, there were some 900 different workshops that produced clothing. Most of the workshops produced civilian clothing, and not military uniforms. A new brand of jeans that were "made in Afrin" became known as a high-quality export product to other parts of the country and region. Dr. Youssef was also involved in helping to set up the Chamber of Industrial Trade, as noted before. He explained the significance of the new institutions as follows:

> Of course there were such institutions under the regime—but the people who led the institutions were pro-regime people. What made us different is we opened the door for all the people to participate, including people not linked to the regime. Half of the population of Afrin was living in Aleppo, but after we started these policies, opposite immigration started from Aleppo to Afrin. And Afrin flourished during that time.[25]

The fact that Dr. Youssef was involved in establishing both a Chamber of Industrial Trade and a workers' union is an indication that the officials of the autonomous administration often played multiple roles. It also raises questions about how independent the trade unions truly were from the oversight of the administration. However, workers are allowed to engage in strikes or other forms of collective action, just as political protests are permitted as well.

The relative stability in Afrin for more than five years, from mid-2012 until January 2018, allowed Afrin the opportunity to develop its economy. Protected by the YPG and YPJ, militants of the Islamic State were never able to extend their caliphate to the far northwestern canton. Furthermore, the location of Afrin also helped trade to flourish because of its proximity to Aleppo and Manbij. By 2016, about half of the industrial factories and workshops in Aleppo were relocated or rebuilt in Afrin due to the destruction of Aleppo. At that time in the spring of 2016, some two million jeans were produced every month in Afrin and sold across Syria.[26] Some of the goods produced in Afrin including olive oil, laurel soap, canned goods, and textiles were even exported outside of Syria: to Libya, Jordan, Yemen, Kuwait, and Iraq.[27] Administration officials say they even tried to export to Turkey, but Ankara had closed the border crossings for trade in 2012, very early in the conflict. This meant the enclave became dependent on the single border crossing into the Kurdistan Region of Iraq known as Semalka on the Syrian side and Fishkhabour on the Iraqi side.

In Afrin, the locals established a Council of Guidance of Investment (*Maglis el Tersheed El Istismarat*) in 2014. The Investment Council was the first such institution in the AANES territory; a similar council was never established in Kobani or Jazira. This is in part because the three original cantons (Afrin, Kobani, and Jazira) were not only autonomous from the regime in Damascus, but also to a certain extent, from each other. Hence, although Dr. Youssef's ideas were quite influential in shaping the local economy in Afrin, they were not implemented equally in all parts of Rojava. In his assessment, his ideas were implemented fully in Afrin, partially in Kobani, and least of all in Jazira.

At the same time, however, it should be remembered that the three cantons had somewhat different historical legacies. For example, the regime's Arabization policies were implemented in all Kurdish areas, but the measures appear to have been harsher in the Northeast. Arabization of village names happened everywhere, as did the resettlement of Arabs from other parts of Syria. During the union with Egypt from 1958 to 1961, known as the United Arab Republic, Arab families were resettled to Afrin City and the Jandaris subdistrict of Afrin canton.[28] However, Kurds in Afrin were for the most part not impacted by the survey that rendered their counterparts stateless in the Jazira canton in the northeast. These historical legacies may have contributed to the thinking of administration officials who then implemented their own policies according to the situation in the individual cantons. Furthermore, there appears to have been greater out-migration in the Jazira canton than in Afrin, which resulted in more abandoned properties. The requisitioning of abandoned properties in the Northeast led to protests. In Afrin, however, there are fewer known instances of such protests, possibly due to the fact that fewer properties were abandoned.

Cooperatives

Observers who are sympathetic to the movement in Rojava have often pointed to the establishment of cooperatives after 2011 (see Figure 6.1) as an example of democratic confederalism in practice. According to the basic tenets of democratic confederalism, the establishment of cooperatives is meant to create alternatives in the here and now, rather than wait until some point in the future when the conditions are deemed ripe. There are two basic requirements for a cooperative. First, the means of production should be owned by the members of the cooperative. Second, decisions should be decided collectively and democratically. At their core, cooperatives are about getting people to cooperate, rather than compete.

The majority of cooperatives are agricultural, while some are involved in livestock, mainly sheep, cattle, and chickens. Other cooperatives have been created in the service industry as well as several types of manufacturing: bakeries, restaurants, shops, tailoring, hairdressing, sewing, salt production and electricity.[29]

There are different accounts as to how exactly the income of cooperatives is distributed. According to some, 5 percent of the surplus goes to the union of cooperatives, 25 percent toward developing the cooperative, and 70 percent the assembly can decide themselves what to do with. Most of the time, this is paid as salaries to the members. According to others, the assembly can keep as much as 90 percent of the profit.

Ideally, cooperatives should also create a division of labor that removes the burdens imposed on women and promotes women's will. They are also meant to pave the way for women to be more involved in social and economic life. The Administration does not see cooperatives as a purely economic undertaking, but as a political project that is meant to contribute to the emancipation of women.

Women's Economy: Not Profit, but Financial Independence from Men Is the Goal

In 2015, Kongra Star launched an ambitious plan: to create an autonomous "Women's Economy," known in Kurdish as *Aboriya Jin* and in Arabic as *El Iktisad el Marra*. The idea goes far beyond even the most radical approaches to feminist economics that advocate for lifting women out of poverty through pay equity, microloans, capacity-building, or gender mainstreaming. Kongra Star does not merely want to integrate women into the existing economic structure, but aspires to establish a parallel economy for women. The idea is similar to how the YPJ is a parallel military structure for women. Rather than including women as individuals into the YPG or SDF, the YPJ has their own military academies,

Figure 6.1 Cooperatives in the Jazira canton

units, and command structure. Whether it will indeed be possible to create a parallel women's economy remains to be seen.

In September 2020, I visited the headquarters of the *Aboriya Jin* in Qamishli, where I met with Armanc Mohamed Ahmed. She was born in Serêkaniyê in 1987 to a family of farmers. She told me that before 2011, she used to have to ask her father or brothers for money if she wanted to leave the house to go grocery shopping or use public transportation. "It was hard to convince them," she said.

Ms. Ahmed was born to a family of *maktoum* or stateless Kurds, whose Syrian citizenship had been revoked in prior decades. Without any citizenship or ID papers whatsoever, her existence was unrecognized by the Syrian government. In 2007, after she finished high school, she applied to study at the Agricultural University in Al-Hasakah, but her application was rejected because she was stateless. After the uprising began in 2011, Bashar al-Assad suddenly offered to reinstate citizenship for the *maktoumeen*, but it wasn't until 2015 that Ms. Ahmed was able to actually obtain a Syrian identity card. Even then she had to pay a bribe of 500,000 Syrian pounds to the government official, just so he would register her Kurdish name (Armanc), which means struggle in Kurmanci. He initially insisted on registering her under an Arabic name, and only relented after she offered him money to register her name in Kurdish. Ms.

Ahmed now acts as director of the Women's Economy in all of North and East Syria, an indication of how the administration puts their ideas into practice, by promoting women into positions of power who previously had suffered severe discrimination.

Ms. Ahmed explained the approach of the Women's Economy to me as follows:

> We don't have a mentality of profit. If women are working there, that is a success. If they are self-financing, we will keep the shop working. Our objective is to give women a chance to be independent of men.[30]

Put simply, the goal of women-run cooperatives is not to make a profit, but to make women economically independent. In other words, while the goal of the mixed-gender cooperatives is to encourage cooperation and self-sustainability, the all-female cooperatives see themselves as having an additional agenda that entails the empowerment of women.

In Jazira, the Women's Economy has set aside around 80,000 donum (around 20,000 acres) for women. I asked Ms. Ahmed who owned the land previously. She explained that under the regime, it had been public land, mainly governmental farms. As a member of a Kurdish family in northern Syria, she explained how her own family had been impacted by the Arabization policies. Her grandfather had previously owned 800 donum in Ras al-Ayn/Serêkaniyê. But at the time of the "Arab Belt" 500 of the 800 donum were seized by the central government and given to Arabs from Raqqa (*makhmoureen*) who were resettled in Jazira on confiscated Kurdish land. As a result, her grandfather only had 300 donum left. After the uprising in 2011 began, some of the resettled Arabs were afraid that the Kurds would take advantage of the situation, and would take back their land. However, instead of reclaiming what was previously theirs, there have been few verified reports of large-scale land seizures. As Ms. Ahmed put it: "They took our lands, but despite that we are helping them."[31]

Indeed there are now reportedly more Arabs involved in the women's cooperatives than Kurds: some 60 percent of the women are Arabs, while 40 percent are Kurds.[32] Together with Armanc, I visited three women's cooperatives in Qamishli: a furniture store (Figure 6.2), a clothing store, and a bakery.

After being launched in 2015, the first conference of the Women's Economy was held in Derik in June 2017. Around 150 delegates attended the conference from Jazira, Kobani, Manbij, and Girê Sipî (Tel Abyad). Hevrin Khalaf served as Co-Chair of the Economics Committee at the time, and gave the opening speech.[33] In October 2019, she was brutally murdered during the Turkish "Peace Spring" intervention.

Figure 6.2 Photo of Mobilya – a woman-run Furniture Store and cooperative part of the Women's Economy

It is difficult to know exactly how many women actively participate in the institutions of the *Aboriya Jin*. According to local news reports, there are some 5,000 women in Raqqa who have found work in various projects established by the Raqqa Women's Committee.[34] Bakeries, dessert shops, factories to produce cheese and yogurt, and communal vegetable gardens are among the projects they have implemented. In several small towns on the outskirts of Raqqa, greenhouses were built that reportedly employ around 155 women. The city of Manbij has also witnessed the growth of women's cooperatives. Manbij was liberated from the Islamic State in August 2016. Just over a year later, the Beit al Baraka was established as an all-female agricultural cooperative in September 2017.[35] In November 2017 a Women's Economy Center was opened in Manbij, with a sign in Arabic, Kurdish, Turkish, and Circassian, reflecting the ethnic and linguistic diversity of the city.[36] In the following year a textile cooperative was founded, the

Martyr Sakine Eseliye Workshop. After the outbreak and spread of COVID-19, the workshop shifted to producing personal protective gear, including masks.

The cooperatives have some flexibility in terms of how they distribute the earnings. For example, there is an agricultural cooperative near the town of Al Qahtaniya (known as Tirbespî in Kurdish and Qabre Hewore in Aramaic) where the members decided to allocate resources according to their needs, rather than according to the number of hours worked. So a family with five children gets more than a family with two children. This shows that cooperatives have some flexibility to decide what to do as long as they stick to the basic framework.[37] One observer suggested that women's cooperatives were better run, but more influenced by the economic committee, while the general cooperatives were not as well organized but had more autonomy.[38]

However, the Turkish intervention in 2019 destroyed some of the local initiatives created by the Women's Economy. One of the largest women's cooperatives in Northeast Syria was previously located in Serêkaniyê, but has ceased to operate since falling under Turkish control. Ms. Ahmed explained that prior to the Turkish invasion of Serêkaniyê, there were an estimated 3,200 women who were actively involved in the Women's Economy. After the intervention, there are now some 2,700 women still involved.[39]

Not all mixed-gender cooperatives have women in leading roles. Indeed, despite their ambitions, the women in the cooperatives are confronted with some of the same problems that women face everywhere. In Qamishli, a group of women had opened their own restaurant which they ran as a cooperative, and although it was successful, they eventually had to close the restaurant. Working late hours at the restaurant proved to be incompatible for most of the women who were mothers with young children at home.[40] At an agricultural collective called Baxçeya Demsal (The Season Garden) a young woman described how her family did not want her to work outside the home, even though they were suffering from economic hardship. They told her that working outside the home would "corrupt her mind."[41]

Changing people's mindsets was found to be one of the biggest challenges, according to the author of a report on cooperatives. The problem was not so much individualism, but rather what the author described as a "feudal" mindset. They led a discussion with some members of the cooperative about how to prevent cooperatives from falling back into such a mindset. One of the leaders offered this analogy:

> You have to renew yourself continuously. Water that flows continuously is always clean. Water that stays in the same place and doesn't renew itself begins to rot and becomes polluted. How do we renew ourselves? Through practice and education.[42]

Taxes and Customs

One of the fundamental requirements of statehood is the need to raise revenue, or what Charles Tilly called "extraction." This is usually done in the form of raising taxes from the population one claims to protect, and collecting customs duties on imports entering the territory under one's control. As Tilly noted in his essay "War Making and State Making as Organized Crime," extraction can take a range of forms, from "outright plunder to regular tribute to bureaucratized taxation."[43]

Since the semi-autonomous region of Rojava was declared in 2012, extraction has taken a variety of forms. While their revenue-raising mechanisms have not yet reached the level of "bureaucratized taxation," they are getting close. At the same time, however, smuggling networks and customs duties on trade—including with unsavory actors—has also been a feature of extracting revenues from the population. In other words, even as the ideology of democratic confederalism purports to want to create a stateless democracy, the very act of raising taxes is a quintessential aspect of statehood.

In North and East Syria, the Finance Commission is the central institution responsible for managing the budget, but local councils are also allowed to impose taxes and raise revenue. The AANES collects income taxes, and also collects fees in order to practice a profession, register a company, or secure a building permit. However, as with many other regulations, the fees may vary from one canton to the next. For example, according to one report published in 2019, doctors in Raqqa were required to pay an annual fee of SYP 65,000 (around $100), while in Al-Hasakah doctors had to pay a fee ranging from SYP 10,000 to 25,000 ($15–$40). The varying levels of taxes may be attributed to the different needs of the canton. Raqqa was much more destroyed during the war against the Islamic State, and hence the reconstruction needs are greater than in Al-Hasakah, which could in part explain the need for higher taxes (Table 6.2).

Table 6.2 **Budget for the Autonomous Administration of North and East Syria for 2019**

Income:
Surplus from 2018: SYP1,789,722,602 ($679,409)
Income from oil and diesel sales: SYP155,989,653,035 ($72,570,763)
Other income of the Autonomous Administration: SYP 38,937,129,783 ($42,143,917)
Total income: SYP197,716,505,420 ($115,394,089)

Expenditure:
Regional salaries and budgets: SYP128,549,077,430 ($45,495,870)
Other expenses: SYP67,024,546,600 ($66,749,950)
Total disbursements: SYP195,573,624,030 ($112,245,820)
Surplus: SYP2,142,881,390 ($3,148,269)

Table 6.2 highlights a few important things about the AANES budget. First, if we subtract the surplus from 2018 from the total income, then we see that taxes and fees (listed as "other income") accounts for about 36 percent of the total AANES revenues. Income from the sale of oil and diesel accounts for about 63 percent of AANES revenues.

A large portion of AANES revenues had to be spent on defending the region. According to one estimate from 2016, as much as 70 percent of the budget was spent on defense.[44] By 2019, the amount spent on defense may have decreased to around 40 percent, but this is still a very large portion of the budget. However, the United States also covers a large part of their budget through salaries paid to the SDF.

According to one study, revolutionary states have been found to increase their defense budgets by an average of 264 percent.[45] Hence, if the AANES has managed to decrease their expenditure from 70 percent of the budget to "only" 40 percent, this in and of itself should be seen as an achievement—likely in no small measure due to the fact that the US is essentially subsidizing their defense budget. It is also, however, an indication that the AANES is attempting to shift its budget to covering the needs of the population and are not paying exorbitant salaries to the military leaders in the SDF. The customs that are imposed on "imports" to the AANES appear to vary depending on region. According to one report, 4 percent was imposed on goods from regime areas coming through Tabqa and Deir Ezzor, 5 percent on goods from opposition areas through Manbij, and between 2 and 7 percent on goods from the Kurdistan Region through Semalka.[46]

In March 2021 a new lax law was passed. Implementation of the new law, however, was delayed until January 2023. During an interview with Ra'ed Sheikhan, the Co-Chair of the Taxation Directorate of Jazira canton, he explained how from 2017 until 2023 it was only the cantons of Jazira and Manbij that were effectively paying taxes. In other words, just those two cantons were largely subsidizing the costs of running all of the cantons that belong to the Autonomous Administration. Mr Sheikhan acknowledged that people in Jazira and Manbij complained about the uneven tax burden they were carrying for all of Northeast Syria. He justified the delayed implementation as largely necessary due to the unstable security situation, especially in Raqqa and Deir Ezzor, where Islamic State cells still occasionally demand "taxes" or *zakat* from local residents. Just a few months earlier, a businessman in Raqqa reportedly was asked to pay 40,000 USD to the Islamic State after they planted an IED near his vehicle and threatened to kill him if he refused to pay.[47]

Oil

Control of Syria's oil fields changed hands several times since 2011. At one point, the Islamic State controlled most, but not all, of the oil in Syria, making it, in the assessment of the World Bank "the richest jihadist group in the world".[48] See Figure 6.3 showing a map of oil fields in Iraq and Syria as of March 2016 and ISIS control. But as the Syrian Democratic Forces defeated the Caliphate, one grueling battle at a time, so too did they increase their control over Syria's natural resources. By the time they were finished, after the Battle of Baghouz in March 2019, the Autonomous Administration had almost all of Syria's oil Table 6.3. The oil fields in Al-Hasakah had fallen under PYD control already in 2012, and were officially managed by councils that provided gasoline for cooperatives.[49]

But before the oil revenues could be used to replenish the emptied coffers of the semi-autonomous region, much of the oil infrastructure had to be repaired, as it had been damaged through years of war. Despite operating at a low capacity, and being forced to sell the oil far below its market value, the oil generated significant income for the semi-autonomous region.

The oil trade between Syria and Iraq is reported to have begun already in 2014, although some Syrian Kurdish officials have made claims to the contrary.

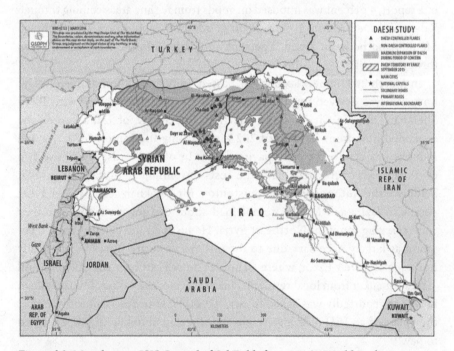

Figure 6.3 Map showing ISIS Control of Oil Fields from 2016 – World Bank Map. Source: Quy-Toan Do et al. 2017

Table 6.3 **Oil Fields under the control of the Autonomous Administration of North and East Syria, Based on territorial control after March 2019**

Al Hasakah Province	Deir Ezzor Province
Rumaylan	Al Omar
Al-Suwaydia	Al Tanak
Al Jabsa	Al Jufra
Youssoufia	Conoco

In a May 2015 interview Akram Hesso, who was Prime Minister of the Jazira canton at the time, stated that the Autonomous Administration wanted the oil to benefit all of Syria, and hence did not have the right to export oil outside of the country.

> Jazeera's oil is a strategic resource of Syria; we believe in the unity of Syria and, so, we don't have the right to export oil, to sell it outside Syria by ourselves. We will not export this oil before we have a new and democratic government in Syria. And it will be the new Syrian constitution to decide what we can do with this oil, because it is not only for us, the Jazeera region, but for the wellness of all the Syrian people.[50]

As explained earlier in the chapter, AANES officials were keen to stake out their own path of economic development, which they hoped would distinguish them from the crony capitalism of many of their neighbors. Syrian Kurdish officials have been even more eager to assuage any fears that they harbored separatist ambitions. And yet however ideologically committed they may have been to democratic confederalism, the territorial integrity of Syria, or just to the more concrete goal of using oil resources for the benefit of their own people, the lack of refining facilities in the Northeast meant that they were dependent on refineries located elsewhere. They were faced with two options: either to use refining facilities in Syrian regime territory, or to export across the border to Iraq.

The two refineries in Homs and Banias, which were under control of the Syrian regime, were in need of modernization in order to be able to process light crude. The geographical proximity of the oil fields in Al-Hasakah and Deir Ezzor to the Iraqi border, meant that exporting was an attractive option.

The cross-border trade entailed exporting crude from eastern Syria into Iraq, via the "Uday" pipeline, which was named after one of Saddam Hussein's sons. In return, the refined products would then be imported back to Syria, from both the Kurdistan Region of Iraq (KRI) as well as federal Iraq. According to a March 2020 issue of the Iraq Oil Report, North East Syria was selling oil for as little as $60 per ton (or $9 per barrel) and traders would then resell the crude to refineries in the KRI for between $240 to $260 per ton (about $35 per barrel).[51] Around the same time, Brent crude on the international market was going for almost $40 a barrel, which would indicate that the Autonomous Administration was selling the oil for about one-fourth of the market price. Despite only reaping a fraction of its market value, these exports were reportedly earning "tens of millions of dollars per month" as revenue for the Rojavan statelet.

In Iraq, the Syrian crude is known colloquially as "Mahmoudiya crude," where it is fed into "topping plants" in the Kurdistan Region. The demand for the Syrian crude increased significantly after the Kurdistan Region lost control of Kirkuk province in October 2017, including the Bai Hassan and Avana Dome oil fields. In these topping plants, the crude is refined. According to one owner of a topping plant in Kurdistan: "You don't get to ask questions such as who brings it and from where it's coming. When the time comes, your crude arrives at your doorstep."[52]

Despite the "no questions asked" policy, the cross-border oil trade could hardly go undetected. In February 2020, the Iraqi Integrity Commission charged four employees at the Rabia border crossing with helping to smuggle 1,500 tankers. Due to the inherently illicit nature of smuggling, it is difficult to know all of the smuggling routes. In addition to the Semalka/Fishkhabour and the Rabia border crossings, oil is also believed to be smuggled as far south as Abu Kamal on the Syrian side and Al Qaim on the Iraqi side of the border, and likely at points in between as well.

Delta Forces, Delta Crescent: Republican Donors and the Syria Oil Deal

The role of the United States in the Syrian oil economy remains somewhat murky. What is clear is that Trump's decision to withdraw US troops from the border with Turkey after a phone call with Erdoğan in October 2019 was quickly reversed. While the dire humanitarian consequences of the Turkish "Peace Spring" intervention and betrayal of SDF allies alarmed many, Trump explained his motives for changing course as follows: "We're keeping the oil, we have the oil, the oil is secure, we left troops behind only for the oil."[53] Trump also reiterated, "And we may have to fight for the oil. It's OK. Maybe somebody else wants the oil, in which case they have a hell of a fight."[54]

In February 2018 US forces had already clashed with Syrian regime and Russian mercenaries because they had encroached on oilfields being guarded by US Delta Forces. At the time, US Delta Forces were co-located with the SDF, when Syrian regime militias and private contractors belonging to the Wagner Group began advancing on SDF-held oil fields. No Americans were killed during what was described as a brutal four-hour battle, while the number of Syrian regime forces or private contractors who were killed remains unclear.

Despite the fact that American forces were guarding the oilfields, US sanctions law prohibited Americans from investing or trading in Syrian oil. This changed, however, after Trump's botched withdrawal fiasco. In July 2020 Senator Lindsey Graham announced that an American company had made a deal with the SDF to "modernize the oil fields" in eastern Syria. Special Envoy Joel Rayburn confirmed during a House Foreign Affairs Committee hearing the following December that a company called Delta Crescent Energy had received permission to exploit the oil. No other company had apparently been granted the special sanctions exemption by the US Treasury.

Delta Crescent Energy was founded by James Reese, a former veteran of the US Army Delta Force. His two other business partners included former diplomat James Cain and John P. Dorrier Jr., former GulfSands Petroleum executive. Cain had donated at least $30,681 to Republican causes since 2003 and previously served on the Republican National Committee. Dorrier had donated $6,947 to Republican causes since 2016.[55]

So, in sum: a US Delta Forces veteran founded Delta Crescent, which became the only company to be granted sanctions exemption by the US Treasury to exploit the oil in Northeastern Syria, where a few years earlier US Delta Forces fought back against Russian mercenaries and Syrian regime forces to prevent them from seizing control of the oil.

Despite the dubious origins of the company, administration officials hoped that it would help cement the American military presence in northern Syria, and perhaps transform the illicit cross-border oil smuggling into a legitimate export business with the Kurdistan Region of Iraq.

In the fall of 2020, Abdel Karim Malek was serving as Head of the Jazira Oil Company, after having worked in the oil fields in Rumaylan for some 40 years. I interviewed him in his office at the Jazira Oil Company. Ronahi television was playing in the background and there was a picture of Abdullah Öcalan hanging above his desk with the quote "Bê Serok Jiyan Nabe" ("No life without the leader").

Abdel Karim Malek's comments shed light on their relationship with the Assad regime, and how Administration officials try to square the circle of their ideology with the oil trade:

> We are a private company, but we take a green light from the Autonomous Administration. The company gets 25% of the profits and

the Administration gets 75%. But the costs are all on the company, so the Administration does not take any risks." He further explained: "It is not a company based on profits, the ideology of this company is not capitalist, but to serve and support the administration. Because petrol is essential for Northeast Syria.[56]

Mr. Malek explained how the company was known as the Syrian Petroleum Company under the regime, and that the Autonomous Administration founded the Jazira Oil Company in 2018. In the early years of the crisis, he said, some 60 percent of the employees, most of whom were highly skilled engineers, left the country. But everyone who did not leave were kept on by the new company. In the fall of 2020, there were some 3,000 employees who worked in the Jazira company, according to Mr. Malek. Every month, however, the regime would reportedly fire employees for no reason and without any formal charges. "They lose their salaries and their pensions—but we keep them," he explained. While at the time the regime paid at most 70,000 Syrian pounds to engineers working at the company, the Autonomous Administration were able to pay salaries of around 400,000 Syrian pounds.[57]

While priding themselves on paying higher salaries than the regime, the relationship was complicated. According to a report by the Syrian Observatory for Human Rights, oil smuggling between the Autonomous Administration and the regime takes place in two main areas: in Deir Ezzor from Shehil to Biqris on the southern bank of the Euphrates River through ferries that often operate at night or pumps or pipelines between the two banks of the river. And secondly in Tabqa, where tankers transport oil across the Euphrates dam. In the spring of 2019, the AANES imposed a fine of 2,000 USD on individuals who smuggled into regime-held areas after the regime refused to recognize the AANES in the constitution.[58] This, in turn, led to a scarcity of refined oil products which led to a sharp increase in fuel prices that sparked resentment and street protests against the administration. In other words, officials have made decisions that were actually against their economic interests in raising revenues in order to achieve their political goal of recognition for Kurdish rights.

The signing of the oil deal in July between the Autonomous Administration and the American company was viewed as "a new level of Kurdish defiance" and provoked hostile reactions from Damascus, Tehran, Ankara, and Moscow.[59] Ilham Ahmed led a delegation of the Syrian Democratic Council to Moscow, presumably in an effort to repair the damage. Delta Crescent had originally hoped to seal the deal for all of Northeast Syria, but, according to Mr. Malek they renegotiated under pressure from the regime and Russia. The contract was then limited to Al-Hasakah, and did not include the oil fields in Deir Ezzor. In early September 2020 two oil tanks at the Tel Adess Station near Rumaylan were attacked. No one claimed the attack, but Mr. Malek claimed they could tell who was behind it due to the nature of the attack, without going into details. The Spokesperson of the Global Coalition at the time, Colonel Myles Caggins, announced that there would be additional training to protect the oil facilities. Already in late October 2019, Defense Secretary Mark Esper had announced that the American forces protecting the oil fields were prepared to use "overwhelming military force" in self-defense.[60]

At some point in our conversation in his office, images of a man known by the code name Dozdar Hamo flickered on Ronahi. I recognized him as someone I had met back in the summer of 2015 in Kobani. He had allegedly been killed already in November 2019 during Turkish airstrikes in Iraqi Kurdistan, but the PKK did not confirm his death until September 2020.[61] A Syrian Kurd whose real name was Abdul Rahman Hamo, he was born in Afrin in 1969, and reportedly joined the PKK in 1990. I recalled how we sat with others in the leafy garden of the guest house in the summer of 2015 in Kobani. He spoke to me in Turkish and encouraged me to visit Afrin, saying it was beautiful there. Of course, it was impossible to get to Afrin from Kobani at the time. Some of the movement leaders I had interviewed over the years did not always like all the questions I would ask them. But Dozdar was different. Sitting on the picnic bench, I remember how he encouraged me to ask questions, even almost commanding me with the imperative of the verb to ask in Turkish: *sor*.

I tried to bring my thoughts back to the interview about oil, and asked Abdel Karim Malek what he thought about relations with Turkey. Without hesitation, he said: "If today Turkey would open the door and start to have agreements and deal with us, then tomorrow we will export oil to them."[62]

Aron Lund's research on corruption is illuminating in this context. He describes how the war impacted the nature of corruption in Syria:

> Before 2011, corruption in Syria manifested itself through politically engineered state–business partnerships and, increasingly in Bashar al-Assad's era, an untouchable caste of regime-linked private-sector tycoons. During the war, it has mutated into a many-headed hydra of armed actors running their own rent-seeking operations and trade networks. The continued need for trade and other exchanges across military front lines has given rise to a new niche for fixers and conflict traders who interpose themselves between the warring parties.[63]

While Lund is certainly right to highlight the rent-seeking nature of many of the armed actors on the Syrian battlefield, it is also true that the PYD cadres are expected to abide by a strict behavioral code that forbids them from personal enrichment, or even owning property. Not everyone, however, lives up to these expectations. One of the cadres I had met, I later discovered had secretly gotten married to a woman in the YPJ. When he was arrested, they discovered large amounts of gold jewelry he bought for his wife in their apartment.

Furthermore, the Autonomous Administration has on several occasions actually halted the oil smuggling to regime-controlled areas in an attempt to pressure Assad into making political concessions, although this of course meant a loss of revenues. Finally, the AANES launched an anticorruption campaign that was intended to prevent the misuse of revenues. At times, in my personal assessment, they overreached. After a two-week research trip in September 2020 I tried to tip the driver who had driven me around, crisscrossing parts of northern Syria on roads ridden with gaping potholes and checkpoints. Friendly to a fault, he never complained about the long hours or when my meetings would get delayed or last longer than expected. I handed him a bit of cash at the Semalka crossing, just as I was about to depart back to Iraqi Kurdistan. He at first refused, but I insisted. I was later told that because another administration official at the border had seen this, that the money I had given him as a tip was taken away from the driver. I was informed that tipping was not allowed, and that the money would be waiting for me until my next visit—whenever that may be.

Conclusion

For decades, the central government in Damascus pursued a policy of underdevelopment or even de-development vis-à-vis the northern and eastern regions of Syria, essentially treating it as an internal colony whose purpose was to produce raw materials for the rest of the country. These were the historical circumstances that the Rojavan revolutionaries sought to undo. In this chapter I've argued that the Autonomous Administration has developed short, medium, and long-term strategies to promote both economic development for their region as a whole, and to specifically empower women.

In contrast to Mubarak and other autocratic rulers in the Middle East, the Assad regime did place some importance on education and literacy. The literacy rate had slowly increased over the decades. Before ascending to the presidency, Bashar al-Assad obtained a medical degree from Damascus University and a graduate degree in ophthalmology in London. And yet whatever value the Assad dynasty may have placed on education, literacy in Arabic, and foreign language training in English or French, this did not extend to Kurds. The Kurdish language was banned, and there were no universities in Qamishli, Kobani, or Afrin, where Syrian Kurds were concentrated. In order for youth in these areas to be upwardly mobile, they had to move to Aleppo or Damascus or other larger cities.

The demand for economic development was one of the key slogans in many revolutionary movements across the region, epitomized in the chant for "bread, freedom, and social justice" (*Eish, horreya, adela igtamaya*). Internal center-periphery dynamics played out between Cairo and Upper Egypt (the *Saied*), Tunis and the interior, where the revolution began in Sidi Bouzid, and other countries that witnessed mass upheavals. And yet the Rojava Revolution emanated entirely from the periphery. They received little to no support from the capital or more economically developed regions of Syria. Due to the fight against the Islamic State, the Autonomous Administration in the north liberated regions that were just as poor and underdeveloped as they were, such as Deir Ezzor in the east. While this meant that they gained control over vital oil fields, it also meant that they owned all the associated problems of economic underdevelopment, on top of the political challenges related to establishing some level of local governance post-ISIS in a culturally conservative region.

Clearly, the Autonomous Administration had high ambitions, and not just in terms of their political, military, and security goals, but also in terms of their economic plans. They wanted to develop the North and East of Syria—a goal shared by many countries in the developing world, and a goal that is encouraged by international financial institutions such as the IMF and World Bank. Their second goal was to establish a women's economy, and thereby make women (more) financially independent from men in their families.

I argue that these AANES economic strategies—both in terms of the general economy and the women's economy—can be broken down into short-term, medium-term, and longer-term strategies. In the short term, survival was the main goal. Averting the kind of famine that has ravaged the population in Yemen was no small matter, and yet it is often taken for granted by outside observers. Nonetheless, the AANES deserves some credit for preventing mass starvation given the absolutely dire conditions. In *Daughters of Kobani*, Gayle Tzemmach Lemmon describes how the YPJ fighters on the frontlines fighting ISIS in 2015 would often eat nothing but two-day old bread for breakfast. They were also instructed by their commanders to eat canned meat, rather than the chickens that were roaming around the countryside because the chickens would feed off of the dead bodies of those who had been killed in battle.[64] Even in later years there were often shortages of basic food items such as sugar or tomatoes. Survival was not a given.

In the medium term, their goals were equally daunting: to de-link their regional economy from Damascus and to increase women's economic activities. The goal of economic development has been a shared goal of many low-income countries across the world, both communist, capitalist, and other ideologies in between. The goal of integrating women into the economy was also no small feat. According to 2020 data from the World Economic Forum that measures the gender gap in terms of economic participation and opportunity, Syria ranked 152 out of 153 countries.[65] Against this backdrop, the launching of a "Women's Economy," known in Kurdish as *Aborîya Jin* and in Arabic as *El Iktisad el Marra*, appears even more ambitious. As part of this initiative, the AANES established both mixed-gender and all-women cooperatives. It should be underscored how rare such feminist developmental strategies are. As of January 2020, you could count on one hand the number of countries worldwide that had adopted feminist foreign or developmental policies.[66]

Finally, in the long-term administration officials say they would like to diversify the economy, normalize trade relations with Turkey and the Kurdistan Region of Iraq, and achieve full economic and political equality between men and women. Whether these developmental dreams will be realized remains to be seen.

Although democratic confederalism is often held up as the political ideology guiding the AANES, I argue that the economic theory is in fact rather eclectic, and includes elements of democratic socialism, radical feminism, and capitalism. Their strategies on women are similar to the National Action Plans or feminist economic policies adopted by sovereign states.

While the Assad regime had restricted the ability of Kurds and Yezidis to own property, the AANES has used their control of territory to redistribute land. However, the redistribution has been mainly limited to taking land from what were previously governmental farms or properties, and some abandoned properties, and not from individuals, even if they owned large tracts of land. For example, Sheikh Humaydi, a large landowner in the east, has not had to parcel out his vast tracts of land. Some of this land has been used to establish either mixed-gender or all-women cooperatives, where the goal is to encourage cooperation as opposed to competition. The capitalist element of their strategy involved supporting small and medium-sized enterprises. Many factories were relocated from Aleppo to Afrin, which contributed to a flourishing regional economy that produced olive oil, soap, and textiles which were sold throughout Syria and even exported abroad. Control of oil and agriculture have been crucial, not only in terms of feeding the population and maintaining the flow of diesel, but have also increased the bargaining power of the AANES vis-à-vis the regime.

The cost of defending this statelet of survivors is high. And yet although they spend a lot on defense, they appear to have bucked the trend whereby revolutionary states on average increase their defense budgets by 264 percent, and in fact have reduced their defense budget from around 70 percent of their revenues to around 40 percent.

Although the oil deal with the American firm appears to have been hoisted upon the Autonomous Administration and was given to a previously unknown firm in a noncompetitive process, Administration officials hoped that it would help cement the American military presence in Northeast Syria, deepen trade relations with Iraqi Kurds and potentially weaken Turkish hostility to the Autonomous Administration if Turkish companies would get a cut of the profits. These are the same dynamics that allowed Iraqi Kurds to wrest greater autonomy from Baghdad. During the boom years, Iraqi Kurds gave enough oil contracts to Turkish companies with ties to the ultranationalists and also facilitated peace talks between the MIT and Öcalan. After the Biden Administration took office, they began a review of US policy to Syria and ultimately decided not to renew the OFAC license granted to Delta Crescent. At the time of writing, the American oil company is winding down its operations.

The School of Revolution

The Autonomous Administration Creates a
New Education System

> *Arabic language, Arabic culture, Arabic history, Arab society, Arab nation,*
> *Arab country, land of Arabs. As they taught it, outside Arabs, there was*
> *no other people. From our childhood till the age of 18 we didn't know that*
> *in Syria there were also Armenians, Syriacs, Circassians, Turkmens and*
> *Assyrians.*
>
> —Shirin Hemo, Co-Chair of the Education
> Committee in Jazira canton

So described Shirin Hemo what she was taught in school when the forces of
Bashar al-Assad still controlled the north of Syria.[1] Kurds and many other non-
Arabs in Syria had been rendered invisible, erased from the official textbooks in
schools across the country.[2] Kurds and Yezidis had been further disenfranchised
when the regime created arbitrary legal statuses that declared them as either
foreigners (*ajanib*) or stateless (*maktoumeen*). In 1962 Decree 93 classified
some 120,000 Kurds as foreigners, meaning they could not vote, own property,
or find employment in government jobs. The *ajanib* status was passed down
from parents to their children, so the number of "foreign" Kurds born in Syria to
Syrian parents increased year after year. The Kurds classified as *maktoumeen* were
even worse off: they had no identity documents whatsoever. It was as if the state
wanted to render them nonexistent.[3]

The Armenian and Syriac-Assyrian minorities often attended private
schools run by their respective churches, where they were permitted to learn
the Armenian and Aramaic languages. However, instruction was limited to just
a few hours per week, hardly enough to learn the language fluently, and the
schools were usually overseen by a Baath Party official appointed by the regime. So when the forces of the Assad regime withdrew from the north in the
summer of 2012, Kurds and Syriacs in particular saw it as an opportunity to

Statelet of Survivors. Amy Austin Holmes, Oxford University Press. © Oxford University Press 2024.
DOI: 10.1093/oso/9780197621035.003.0007

create a new education system that did not deny their existence or linguistic rights.

Shirin Hemo, a Kurdish woman from Jazira, went on to become Co-Chair of the Education Committee in the canton where she grew up. One of the primary goals of the Autonomous Administration was to create a new curriculum and a new education system that reflected the true ethnic and religious diversity of the region. Non-Arabs wanted to be seen and heard. They wanted their histories and cultures to be reflected in the curriculum. They wanted their own languages to be taught in school. Kurds wanted to learn Kurdish. Syriac and Assyrian Christians wanted to learn Aramaic. But undoing the legacy of decades of Baathist ideology was difficult. Creating a new school system from scratch—in the midst of a brutal war—would be even more so.

The Seven Challenges

The Autonomous Administration faced daunting challenges in establishing their own education system. First, their plan to create a new school system was opposed by virtually everyone. The Assad regime saw it as undermining rule by the central government. Islamic State militants lobbed explosive devices into school buildings even after the caliphate was defeated. The Kurdish National Council (KNC) was also bitterly opposed to it because they thought it would lead to a new generation of Democratic Union Party (PYD) supporters. Even some in the local population had their doubts. Skeptics believed that the Administration would use their school system as a tool to indoctrinate people into an ideology inspired by the founder of the Kurdistan Worker's Party (PKK), Abdullah Öcalan, and the American anarchist thinker, Murray Bookchin. From their vantage point, the ideas inherent in "democratic confederalism" were about as far removed from the mores of a conservative tribal society as one could get. How would a society accustomed to schools that taught rote memorization and obedience to Assad embrace such radical ideas? Some analysts portrayed it as nothing less than an "alien ideology."[4]

Second, the Northeast of Syria had been historically neglected by the central government in Damascus. Investing in the economic development or educational infrastructure of the region had never been a priority. The regime had never established a major university in the Kurdish regions of Syria. Those Kurds who wanted to obtain a university degree had to move outside the region, usually to Aleppo or Damascus. Undoing decades of neglect was no easy task, even in peacetime. But the Autonomous Administration didn't have the luxury of waiting until the Syrian conflict was over. The war dragged on, year after bloody year. They set up their school system while fighting against the most horrific terrorist organization the world had ever seen.

Third, when the Kurdish language was introduced, after being banned for decades under Baathist rule, some saw it as a step toward secession. For a country that for generations had been indoctrinated in Arab nationalist ideology, this was nothing short of heresy. Even more improbably, the Aramaic language was also introduced. Historians believe it is the language that was spoken by Jesus. It is still spoken by the Syriac-Assyrian Christian community in Syria today, yet teetering on the brink of extinction. UNESCO ranks it as an endangered language.

Fourth, many teachers were unwilling to teach in the new schools. When the region first gained autonomy in the summer of 2012, some civil servants, in particular teachers, preferred to keep their jobs. There were two reasons some teachers were reluctant to join the new education system. Some may have doubted that the new system would survive the war and feared retaliation by the regime. Others may have simply preferred to maintain their salaries paid by Damascus, which were initially higher than what the local authorities could offer. In either case, it is hard to run a school system if you have no qualified teachers to teach. As the war raged on, many middle-class Syrians who could leave the country did so. The exodus of the middle class meant that the Administration had to resort to training new teachers.

Fifth, under the reign of ISIS, intolerance and hatred were propagated. Illiteracy increased. Muslims were taught that Christians and Yezidis should be killed or enslaved. Even Syrian Kurds, although they were predominantly Sunni Muslim, were portrayed by ISIS as takfiri—as Muslims who had gone astray and betrayed their own kind by cooperating with infidels both local and foreign. Kurdish leaders became the key interlocutors with the Global Coalition. For this reason, ISIS subjected Syrian Kurds to collective punishment. In Raqqa, ISIS issued a fatwa forcing all Kurds to leave the city. Even Kurds who were not part of the Syrian Democratic Forces (SDF) or who did not work for the Administration were forced to flee Raqqa within 48 hours, losing their property and anything they could not carry with them. How could the Administration expect people of different religions and ethnicities, who had been taught to hate and kill each other by ISIS, to immediately forget all that and come together in a shared school system? There were also some students who had simply stopped going to school. I met numerous young people, especially girls, who told me they had dropped out of school rather than be educated by ISIS demagogues. How could youth be convinced to reenter the education system after not going to school for years?

Sixth, during the course of the war, many schools were destroyed. To give just one example, in Tabqa there were 400 schools before ISIS took over in August

2014. When I visited in 2019, they only had 140 schools. But the population had quadrupled due to the influx of people fleeing other parts of Syria. In other words, each school would have to accommodate an increase of at least 11 to 12 times more students—more than a thousand percent (1,000%) increase in students per school. Although the United States claims to support education as part of its stabilization efforts in Northeast Syria, stabilization funding was put on hold for various reasons under the Trump Administration. At one point the actual amount of funding allocated to education dropped to zero. According to a Bilateral Relations Fact Sheet of the US Department of State from May 2020, "improving and supporting the education sector to help children return to school"[5] was one of the objectives of US stabilization funding in the Northeast. However, the amount initially allocated specifically for education in 2018 had dropped from $2,810,000 to $0 according to a previous report of the Office of Inspector General.[6] In short, outside support from the United States could not necessarily be relied on.

The local authorities faced one final dilemma. When, against all odds, the Autonomous Administration managed to set up and run a school system, Bashar al-Assad had a special weapon he kept in reserve. In addition to his stockpile of chemical weapons and conventional weapons, his weapon of choice against the Administration's school system was simple: he refused to recognize them. Why would any parent send their children to a school that was not recognized by the government of their own country, much less by anyone else?

To summarize, the Autonomous Administration faced seven challenges in setting up a new education system: (1) the overall under-development of the Northeast in terms of educational infrastructure (2) the unfamiliarity of the population with the "alien ideology" of democratic confederalism; (3) suspicions that introducing the Kurdish language was a step toward secession; (4) the initial reluctance of some teachers to teach in the new schools; (5) the increase in illiteracy under ISIS and spread of extremist propaganda during the time of the Caliphate; (6) the destruction of many schools during the war; and finally (7) the refusal of the central government to recognize the degrees granted by the schools. None of this boded well for the Autonomous Administration.

Overcoming Challenges—Against All Odds

One by one, each of these obstacles was tackled. How did the Administration manage to set up a new education system—all while fighting a brutal war against ISIS that was enormously costly in terms of blood and treasure? The Autonomous Administration's ambitious education program—essentially a deradicalization or reeducation campaign—was in some ways akin to what happened in West Germany after the end of World War II. And yet unlike West Germany after 1945, the local authorities in the Northeast of Syria did not have the benefit of a massive aid program like the Marshall Plan. Nor had the war even ended. The Autonomous Administration had very little outside help and no outside recognition. How did they do it?

First, although they had no political recognition, they did control territory. And the territory they held kept expanding, thus increasing both the population and resources under their control, and thereby made the Autonomous Administration more powerful. But it also increased their potential vulnerability. In order to address this, they decided that decentralization was the best option—each canton was allowed to determine the educational system that best suited them. In Arab-majority regions of Deir Ezzor and Raqqa, the UNESCO curriculum was used. In Manbij, the regime curriculum was still in use at the time of writing, while Kurds and Syriacs in the Northeast adopted their own curriculum that they created after 2012.

Second, they made education a top priority. It was a priority in three ways. They devoted precious financial resources to rebuilding schools. Although they had to devote considerable resources to warding off existential threats from the regime, ISIS, and Turkey, they devoted a considerable portion of their budget to education. Second, as soon as areas were liberated from ISIS, they lost no time in creating makeshift schools in whatever structures were left standing. They saw it as an urgent task—not as something that could wait until some point in the future. Third, they wanted to ensure that education was made available for everyone: for boys and girls, for Christians, Muslims, Kurds, Arabs, Yezidis, Turkmen, and for civilians, but also for those who fought in the SDF.

Finally, although Syrian Kurds had no prior experience in setting up a school system, they could draw on the experience of Kurds in other parts of Kurdistan. In the early 1990s, several hundred thousand Kurds from Turkey fled to northern Iraq due to the destruction of their villages by the Turkish military. These refugees eventually settled in a camp in Makhmour located about an hour away from Erbil in the Kurdistan Region of Iraq. Because the refugees included entire families as well as children, they also set up their own education system with their own teachers and schools.[7] The language of the refugees was Kurmanci, the dialect of Kurdish spoken in Turkey, while most of the local schools in the Kurdistan Region of Iraq offered instruction in Sorani. Hence the Makhmour camp eventually acquired the means to produce their own schoolbooks in Kurmanci. Some of those books were adopted by the Autonomous Administration in Syria, because Kurmanci is also the dialect spoken by Kurds in both Syria and Turkey.

During my fieldwork, I met numerous young women in the SDF who told me that they had never been to school a day in their lives. They were illiterate. And yet after joining the SDF, they were taught how to read and write. Beyond teaching basic literacy, courses are also offered in Kurdish history as well as women's history. I've personally sat in on lectures about women's history at academies in both Syria and the Sinjar mountain region of Iraq. Kurds refer to it as *Jineology*. The term is derived from the Kurdish word for women (*Jin*). The development of *Jineology* can be traced to a historical shift within the PKK when the role of women became more prominent, as discussed in Chapter 5. The term *Jineology* was first introduced by Abdullah Öcalan in 2008, in *The Sociology of Freedom*, the third volume of his *Manifesto for a Democratic Civilization*. It has since become widespread throughout the Kurdish movement aligned with the PYD.[8] Critics see it as a form of indoctrination. Proponents of Jineology contend that it is merely an attempt to highlight women's role in Kurdish history and society. In some ways it is not unlike the introduction of gender studies curricula in schools and universities elsewhere in the world, which was often also initially met with criticism.

Whether one views this as indoctrination or not depends on one's perspective. Instead of teaching the Arab nationalist ideology of the Baathist regime, or the ideology of hatred and intolerance propagated by ISIS, the schools run by the Autonomous Administration taught principles of religious, ethnic, and gender equality. Kurds, Armenians, and Syriac-Assyrians were taught their own language, history, culture, and music.

The Language Revolution and the Empowerment of Minorities and Women: Kurdish and Aramaic Languages

In an ideal world, education should expose students to new ideas and impart new skills. It should empower young people as they prepare for the future. For ethnic and religious minorities, who were forbidden from speaking their own language, or who were never taught it in school, learning their own language and history can have a transformative impact on their sense of identity. Especially for those who suffered under the Islamic State, the impact can be even more profound.

While many Kurds in Syria were able to speak Kurmanci, they had never been taught the language in school. It was not uncommon for Syrian Kurds to be fluent in both Arabic and Kurmanci, but to only be able to write in Arabic since that was what they were taught in school.

Some members of the Christian minority in Syria were not even able to speak Aramaic. In contrast to Kurdish, which is spoken by some 30 million Kurds worldwide, the Aramaic language is on the verge of extinction. Reviving the Aramaic language would take even greater effort than what was needed to introduce Kurdish language instruction.

Although it is impossible to quantify, the impact of the new school curriculum may have also had a gendered dimension. The schools set up by the Islamic State propagated extremist views and religious indoctrination in lieu of a proper education. It was bad for everyone, but especially for young women and girls. The "education" that girls received was even more limited than what boys were taught—and then they were forced out of school altogether at a young age. Even prior to the eruption of the civil war, illiteracy was higher among females. According to World Bank data, adult literacy among men in Syria was 88 percent, but only 74 percent of women were literate.[9] The sections below on the "education" of women under the Islamic State and illiteracy in Manbij elaborate on this issue. For a more detailed analysis of ISIS rule see Chapter 4.

Already in 2011, during the very early days of the revolution in Syria, Kurds began to make preparations. According to Arshek Baravi, the founder of the Kurdish education system, teacher training centers were established in PYD-held areas of Syria and in Damascus. A conference was held in Makhmour, a refugee camp in the Kurdistan Region of Iraq that governs itself on the same democratic confederalist principles that inspired Syrian Kurds, where a committee was set up that was tasked with writing textbooks that were later used.[10]

Despite these early preparations, it was not until the fall of 2015 that the Kurdish language curriculum was introduced. The introduction of the new system was met with criticism. In November 2015, 16 Assyrian and Armenian organizations or churches issued a statement rejecting the new system, in part out of concerns that the degrees would not be recognized. However, over time, some of these conflicts were resolved.[11] The Administration allowed the private Christian schools to continue their own curriculum. Furthermore, the Autonomous Administration committed itself to allowing language instruction in all of the local languages, not just Kurdish. The official logo of the Self Administration of North and East Syria is in four languages: Arabic, Kurdish, Aramaic, and Turkish (Figure 7.2).

I visited the Olaf Taw Association in Qamishli, a language school that was dedicated to reviving the endangered Syriac-Aramaic language (Figure 7.1). Previously, the language had only been taught as a liturgical language, or a language of prayer. Now it was being taught as a language to be spoken outside of church, in everyday life. The teacher was a young man by the name of Jalinos, who himself was a member of the Syriac Christian minority. Clearly talented and with a passion for his work, Jalinos was trilingual, speaking fluent Arabic,

Figure 7.1 Syriac Reading Book Fourth Grade

English, as well as Aramaic.[12] To my surprise, a number of the students were Muslims. I had erroneously assumed that it was perhaps only the Syriac-Assyrian minority who would be interested in learning the language of their community. At least three of the female students were wearing the traditional hijab. Although some Arabs may have seen the introduction of Kurdish or Aramaic as threatening or even as a step to secession, others clearly embraced the opportunity to learn new languages, as I explain later in the chapter.

The Armenian minority has also used the space created by the Autonomous Administration to begin to reclaim their heritage. As explained in previous chapters, many Armenian children were orphaned at the time of the genocide around 1915 and were subsequently raised by Kurdish or Arab families. Because they were raised in Muslim families, or hid their identity to avoid persecution, many of these Christians came to identify as Muslims, and grew up speaking Kurdish or Arabic, leading to the phenomenon of "hidden Armenians" or "Islamized Armenians." In early 2020, the Armenian Social Council was established in Al-Hasakah, which provides Armenian language and history classes. Students include Armenians who belong to both Christian and Muslim families.[13]

Finally, Turkish language instruction has also been introduced in some parts of northern Syria under SDF control such as Tel Abyad, a town along the Syrian-Turkish border that has a Syrian Turkmen minority.[14] Despite tensions with the Turkish government, the Autonomous Administration appears dedicated

Figure 7.2 Official Logo of the Autonomous Administration in Four Languages: Arabic, Kurdish, Aramaic, and Turkish

to its commitment to offer language instruction in the native tongue of all the minority groups in their area, including the Turkmen community (Figure 7.2).

Kobani: The Classroom in a Container, June 2015

My first trip to Syria was in June 2015, when I visited Kobani a few months after the liberation of the city from ISIS. I had planned to do what I thought was a narrowly defined research project focused on the YPJ—the Kurdish women's units—in Kobani. At that point in June 2015, it was not possible to visit other cantons under PYD control. The people of Kobani were still encircled by hostile forces who wanted to kill them.

I arrived in Kobani the middle of the night. When I woke up the next morning, the first thing they wanted to show me was not the YPJ, but their new schools. Much of the city had been destroyed. Yet somehow they had acquired an aluminum container which they converted into a classroom. They lost no time in creating a make-shift classroom and getting kids to go to school—even during the hottest days of summer. They were so proud of this aluminum container that they insisted on bringing me there first. It was hard not to be impressed by the mere fact that kids were sitting in this make-shift classroom in summer, with grins on their faces. But back then, in the summer of 2015, I didn't fully appreciate the significance of what I saw. They were not just showing me kids sitting in a container-converted-to-classroom. They were showing me their new school system. Like many outsider observers, I was in awe of how this band of rebels had kicked the Islamic State out of Kobani, which was a decisive turning point in the larger war. But they had also dethroned the Baathists—at least in this corner of the far north. Now they had a chance to set up a new education system from scratch.

The enthusiasm I witnessed during the heat of the summer in 2015 was mirrored in statements by high-ranking Kurdish officials. Salih Muslim, former copresident of the PYD, emphasized the importance of education as a do-it-yourself endeavor. "You have to educate, twenty-four hours a day . . . you have to reject the idea that you have to wait for some leader to come and tell the people what to do, and instead learn to exercise self-rule as a collective practice."[15]

From a social or cultural perspective, the establishment of a new school system, even the rudimentary and improvised classroom container, was as significant as the liberation of Kobani was from a military perspective. A Human Rights Watch report from 2009 described how successive governments in Damascus had banned Kurdish publications and also forbidden the Kurdish language from being spoken even at private marriage ceremonies.

> Kurdish publications were officially banned during the presidency of Adib al-Shashakli (1951–54), and again during the years of Syria's union with Egypt (1958–61). The Ba'ath party has also enforced the ban, forcing Kurdish authors and editors to have their publications printed in Lebanon and illegally brought into Syria. Two decrees in the 1980s (nos. 1865/S/24 and 1865/S/25) also forbade the use of Kurdish in the workplace, as well as during marriage ceremonies and festivities.[16]

With the evacuation of Assad's forces from the north of Syria, Kurds could begin to speak Kurmanci at work. They made it one of the official languages of the Autonomous Administration. They could print textbooks in Kurmanci. They could teach school children the history of the Kurdish region of Syria in Kurmanci. Below is an excerpt from the school textbook "Ziman Kurdi" about Afrin (Efrîn in Kurdish) in the northwestern region of Syria that was considered to be majority Kurdish, by some estimates over 90 percent. The textbook is from 2017 (Figure 7.3). The textbook is geared for young school children to teach them Kurmanci, as well as the geography and history of Kurdish-inhabited regions. The section on Efrîn describes a conversation between three

Figure 7.3 Image of Kurdish textbook—page about the Kurdish region of Efrîn in Northwest Syria

friends Lîlav, Sîpan, and Evîn, wherein Lîlav describes his family's visit to Efrîn. He says:

> Efrîn is a colorful city in Rojava. It is like a bouquet, which is decorated with olive trees, rivers, springs, plains and roofs. Because of that, its climate is very nice and cool. In addition, there are many historical places in Afrin, such as; Seman Castle, Huriyan Castle and Eyndara are famous and historical places. Along with them, there are Sulava Meydanke and Basuta, which are very beautiful places and are like resorts.
>
> The section ends by describing how Sîpan and Evîn decide to visit the region of Efrîn with their families the following year.

In January 2018, Turkey invaded and occupied Afrin, expelling hundreds of thousands of its native inhabitants who were predominantly Kurds. The school system in Afrin and other parts of northern Syria under Turkish control has also undergone major changes. Even historical references to the Ottoman Empire have been modified in textbooks. Any history books, even those issued by the Syrian government in Damascus, that used the phrase "Ottoman occupation" have been replaced by "Ottoman rule."[17] The series of Turkish interventions in northern Syria is discussed in more detail in the concluding chapter.

In contrast to the Kurdistan Region of Iraq, the Autonomous Administration appears to be maintaining Arabic as a language of instruction. In other words, the Kurdish, Aramaic, and Armenian languages are not replacing Arabic, but have been added alongside Arabic as a language of instruction. In the Kurdistan Region of Iraq, not all schools teach Arabic, and hence Arabic has become a secondary language. It is not uncommon for the younger generation of Kurds who grew up in the Kurdistan Region of Iraq to not be able to speak Arabic fluently. When Arabs from other parts of Iraq fled to the Kurdistan Region as internally displaced people (IDPs) during the war against the Islamic State, some human-itarian organizations noted a language barrier between Kurds and Arabs as one possible reason that impeded integration of the Arab IDPs.[18]

Challenges in Arab-Majority Regions of North and East Syria

The city of Kobani was predominantly Kurdish, and the people of Kobani had fought to the death to prevent the Islamic State from taking over their town. Their heroic battle against the Islamic State catapulted Kobani to prominence and became a symbol of Kurdish resistance. For the first time, neither Islamist extremists, nor Arab nationalists, nor Baathists had any say in what happened now in Kobani. Introducing a new Kurdish curriculum was perhaps the next log-ical step. But the fact that the people of Kobani welcomed the new education system was no guarantee that this would happen elsewhere.

Over time, more and more Arab-majority cities were liberated. The SDF assumed de facto control over vast territories that extended far beyond the Kurdish region known as Rojava. Obviously the Kurdish curriculum could not be imposed on an Arab population. But developing a new curriculum that would be accepted by all was not an easy task. The challenges were many. Not least among them was the fact that many young students had been educated in schools run by the Islamic State. Hatred was propagated. Illiteracy increased. Some young people had simply dropped out of school altogether.

The "Education" of Women under the Islamic State: Indoctrination and Submission

The Islamic State caliphate established a political and social order that was de-voted to the subordination of women. In fact, ISIS demagogues believed that the education of women was responsible for what they perceived as the deca-dence and downfall of not only the West—but all societies that did not ascribe to their extremist views. ISIS ideologues believed that the education of women was in fact the primary reason men had—in their view—become emasculated. Once the Islamic State established their self-proclaimed caliphate, one of their foremost objectives was to undo the education women and girls had achieved. By attempting to indoctrinate women into submission and undo their pre-vious levels of educational attainment, the Islamic State believed that the sup-posed emasculation of men would also be undone. If women were ignorant and submissive, men would be made more masculine again. So went the perverse logic of the Islamic State.

Instead of getting an education that might empower them, women's entire purpose in life was to serve her husband and children. As a servant of men, women were expected to be banished in the home, where they were to lead a life of "sedentariness, stillness and stability." A treatise published by the Al Khanssaa Brigade in January 2015 outlines women's education in the caliphate. Because women were expected to devote themselves to their husbands and children and to abide by the ISIS interpretation of the Quran, the document concedes that women could not perform these tasks if they were illiterate or ignorant. Therefore, young girls should receive an education limited to religious studies, especially relating to issues of marriage and divorce, and Quranic Arabic. The only practical skills they were to learn were knitting, textiles, cooking, and child rearing. Education for girls was limited to the ages of between seven and fifteen. Marriage for girls could begin as early as nine years old. During the time of the Islamic State, young women and girls were taught that they must submit themselves at all times to male authority. They required a male guardian (mahram) to escort them if they wanted to leave their own homes even for a brief outing in their own neighborhood. Young women were forced out of school soon after puberty.

Manbij: Illiteracy Increases under ISIS—Even after the Defeat of ISIS, Many Girls Remain Out of School

I met numerous young women in Syria who had no interest in being educated in such a system. Instead of being indoctrinated by ISIS demagogues, they simply dropped out of school. In Manbij, I met a soft-spoken young woman named Mariam. She had grown up in Manbij, and told me she had never been to school.[19] During the beginning of the Manbij operation, her father had been standing in front of their house when he was killed by a Coalition airstrike that was meant to target ISIS, but killed her father by mistake. After the death of her father, she and her mother and sister moved to the home of her uncle. Henceforth her uncle became the de facto head of the household. As the new patriarch of the family, Mariam's uncle insisted that she should marry his son— her first cousin. She did not want to marry him, but did not have much choice in the matter. I asked how old she was at the time. She said she thought she was 17, but didn't seem very confident about her age. After remaining married for five months, she asked to get a divorce. When I asked why she got a divorce, she said simply, "because I didn't want him." Upon divorcing her cousin, Mariam then joined a unit of the YPJ that belonged to the Manbij Military Council,

Figure 7.4 Mariam, Arab member of the Manbij Military Council

which in turn works with the SDF (Figure 7.4). A more detailed description of the relationship between the Manbij Military Council (MMC) and the SDF is provided in Chapter 3.

As Mariam's story makes clear, even after the defeat of ISIS, patriarchal traditions continued. Women were still expected to be obedient to the male head of the household, even if he was not her own father. Women were expected to marry at a young age, even as young as 11 or 12. And women could still be forced to marry their own cousin. Clearly, the defeat of the Islamic State caliphate did not mean that women were automatically free to do as they wished. The authority over women was simply transferred from ISIS men to other men. Instead of being subjected to the extremist beliefs of ISIS *amirs*, women were subjected to the dominance of other men—who could still force them to obey their orders. In some ways the situation merely reverted to the way it was pre-ISIS. However, the creation of women's units within the SDF allowed women an alternative to forced or arranged marriages. The creation of new civil society organizations, such as the Zenobiya's Women's Association, allowed women a space to gather and work collectively to overcome problems they faced. And the creation of the new school system also allowed women the opportunity to receive an education.

Tabqa: The Population Quadruples in Tabqa, While Most School Buildings Are Destroyed

The Tabqa region is one of the western-most cantons under SDF control. The regime controls territory to the south and west, while Turkey currently controls

Afrin to the north. Tabqa had been liberated from the Islamic State in May 2017. Just two months later, teachers and volunteers began cleaning up schools to get them ready for the school year. Even cleaning up schools was dangerous due to the unexploded ordinances.

I met with Rawa Romy, who was Co-Head of Education in Tabqa. She described the enormous challenges they faced:

> Under ISIS reign our children reached illiteracy, 5 dark years of igno-
> rance and persecution, our children only saw blood and destruction.
> The schools during ISIS reign were prisons and detention centers. Two
> months after the liberation of Tabqa by the SDF we were able to open
> two schools with very limited resources. On August 1, 2017—teachers
> and volunteers went to different schools and started to clean them, al-
> though they were endangering their life. From the first year after liber-
> ation they were able to open 140 schools. We had 20,000 students, but
> we did not have a lot of books. So teachers relied on the information
> that they had in their brains without books.[20]

I visited Tabqa on March 3, 2019—about a year and a half after schools were first re-opened after ISIS. As mentioned above, the population of Tabqa had quadrupled. They had more than 400 schools before ISIS. A year and a half after ISIS had been defeated, they still only had 140. Ms. Romy estimated that about 25% of the students stayed at home and didn't go to school. She believed there were an estimated one thousand IDPs in the camps who did not go to school.

Deir Ezzor: Islamic State Militants
Attack Schools

The governorate of Deir Ezzor presented even greater challenges than Tabqa, and is the largest governorate under SDF control. It was also the area where the Islamic State maintained its final stronghold: Baghouz. I traveled to Deir Ezzor in early March 2019, before the caliphate had been defeated. Although large parts of Deir Ezzor had been liberated two years earlier, only one or two NGOs worked there—this meant that the majority of reconstruction and service pro-vision had to be provided by the Autonomous Administration.

I met with Layla Hassan, the Co-Head of the Deir Ezzor Civil Council in her office. An Arab woman from Deir Ezzor with a degree in Arabic literature, Ms. Hassan was wearing a long and bright green dress with gold embroidery on the day I met her. I complemented her on her beautiful dress. "Under ISIS

rule, women were forced to wear black all the time. Now I want to wear colors."
Even something as simple as wearing a colorful dress was a sign of the new era.
As I sat in her office, local male members of the Deir Ezzor Civil Council would
join us over the course of the two hours we were there. It was clear that they
respected her authority as the Co-Chair of the Council. Ms. Hassan was not
just wearing a colorful dress in defiance of the old ISIS dress code, she was now
the boss.[21]

In March 2019, Deir Ezzor had some 160,000 students and 460 schools
(compared to 20,000 students and 140 schools in Tabqa). Ms. Hassan described
the massive level of destruction in her governorate. Many schools had no win-
dows, no doors, and no desks. At that time there were some 5,400 teachers on
the payroll of the Autonomous Administration.

Ms. Hassan explained how the teachers had to teach two shifts because
they did not yet have enough school buildings or teachers. The first shift
was from 7:30 a.m. to 12:00 p.m., then the second shift was from 12:00 p.m.
to 3:30 p.m.—because there was not enough room to accommodate all the
students in the existing buildings. Even so, class sizes were still very large. Ideally,
the Administration didn't want to have more than 20 students per classroom, yet
they sometimes had between 40 and 50 students in each classroom due to sheer
lack of infrastructure. There were some schools that had been totally destroyed
during the war, and others that were partially destroyed. Nevertheless, she said,
the Administration still encourages kids to go to school.

I was able to witness their attempts to rebuild schools first-hand. Kamal
Moussa, Co-Chair of Education, took us to a school that was heated by an oil-
burning stove, with a simple chalk board. The school had no functioning toilet.
But it had already been outfitted with new desks built by the Administration.
Standing in front of the school building, he described how on the very same day,
another nearby school had been attacked by ISIS sleeper cells.[22] Fortunately, it
was a Saturday, and so no students were present in the building. But it was an indication that ISIS sleeper cells continued to target the school buildings—a clear
attempt to not only destabilize the area but to also discourage students from
attending school. Furthermore, the school that had been attacked was in the area
inhabited by the Al-Shaitat tribe. The Al-Shaitat tribe from Abu Hamam in Deir
Ezzor were openly hostile to ISIS. In the summer of 2014, between 700 and 900
tribal members were summarily executed by ISIS.[23]

Like Tabqa, Deir Ezzor had also experienced a large increase in population.
Ms. Hassan described how there were some 450,000 people who had recently
fled to Deir Ezzor from regime territory. The IDPs were also incorporated into
the schools. In Deir Ezzor, they have the same curriculum as in regime areas, "except the course on Arab nationalism and Baathist propaganda—we don't teach
that," she said.

Table 7.1 **Schools in North and East Syria run by the Central Government versus Autonomous Administration in April 2020**

Number of schools run by the Autonomous Administration	4,317
Number of schools run by the Central Government	33

Economic Incentives and Expanding Bureaucracy

By early 2020, the Autonomous Administration of North and East Syria managed some 4,317 schools (Table 7.1). There were only 33 schools on their territory still connected to the central government. The Autonomous Administration was able to offer teachers a salary that was approximately double that paid by Damascus.[24] This is one reason why those teachers who were initially skeptical of the new system began to shift their allegiance.

In January 2020, the Autonomous Administration employed more than 250,000 people in their bureaucratic apparatus. This included 70,000 SDF soldiers, 30,000 police, and 150,000 civil servants. Included in the number of civil servants are some 40,000 teachers who receive a monthly salary of between 120 and 200 USD, double the amount paid in the territory under the control of the regime. By this time, a "significant proportion" of civil servants who were previously paid by the central government in Damascus had joined the Autonomous Administration. This means they risked losing their salaries paid by the regime. Haenni and Quesnay estimated that almost 20 percent of the working population of Northeast Syria are dependent on an income that is provided either directly or indirectly by the Autonomous Administration.[25]

Setting up this new educational system entailed the creation of a sizable bureaucratic apparatus: a dozen institutions or organizations related to the new education system were created by Autonomous Administration. These range from administrative bodies, to teachers' unions, to autonomous academies that are connected to the women's movement, the Democratic Islamic Religious Academy, and a whole host of other organizations (Box 7.1).

Deradicalization after ISIS: Teaching Empathy or Indoctrination?

Critics have claimed that the AANES schools are mere instruments for indoctrination in the philosophy of Abdullah Öcalan. In her comparison of

---

Box 7.1 New Educational Institutions Created by the Autonomous Administration

1. Education Committee of the Democratic Society (Komîteya Perwerdeya Civaka Demokratîk).
2. The Department of Education and Teaching, at the canton level (Desteya Perwerde û Fêrkirinê).
3. The General Administration of Schools, led by teachers and schools (Rêveberiya Dibistan ya Giştî).
4. The Teachers Union (Yekîtiya Mamosteyan).
5. The Department of Kurdish Language (Saziya Zimanê Kurdî).
6. Various autonomous intellectual academies, connected to the women's movement, the youth movement, the Democratic Islam religious academy, for employees of the Autonomous Administration, TEV-DEM, etc. (Akademiyên Bîrdozî).
7. Department that prepares textbooks (Saziya Branşan).
8. Academy of the Kurdish and Arabic branches (Akademiya Branşên Kurdî û Erebî), that conducts research for the improvement of the education system.
9. Universities (Zanîngeh).
10. Faculty of Education Science (Peymangeha Zanistên Perwerdeyî), which trains future teachers.
11. Summer Faculties (Peymangehên Havînî) for training and improvement of teachers.
12. The Autonomous Administration "branches" (Branşên Rêveberiya Xweser) in Kurdish, Arabic and Syriac.

---

textbooks used in Turkey and Northeast Syria, Pinar Dinç found that "Unlike their Turkish counterparts, Rojava's textbooks begin with no flags, maps, national anthems, oaths, or portraits of leaders. They contain only an imprint that reads 'Democratic Autonomy' (Xweseriya Demokratik) followed by canton's name in Kurdish, Arabic, and Assyrian."[26] However, the notion of martyrdom and self-sacrifice is emphasized in the textbooks, including examples of fighters who participated in suicide bombing. The final section of *Zanisten Civaki* 4 portrays three "martyrs": Arin Mirkan, a Kurd; Temir Basil, an Arab; and Temir Behde, an Assyrian, who were all killed while fighting as part of the YPG or YPJ.

Although the section on martyrs emphasizes the sacrifices of non-Kurds, the rest of the textbook discusses Kurdish history, Kurdish geography, and Kurdish culture. However, while the three Turkish textbooks she analyzed contained many references to the nation's leader Atatürk, and images of the Turkish flag, the three Rojava textbooks only contained one reference to Öcalan, and the YPJ flag appeared only once in partial view behind the portrait of Arin Mirkan.[27]

During my own research in Syria, I tried to assess the extent to which rank-and-file members of the SDF were familiar with the ideology of democratic confederalism by conducting a survey of over 400 men and women in the SDF. There are limitations to the survey because it was only conducted among members of the SDF, and not civilians. However, I did include questions about the level of education of recruits, and about their political beliefs and plans for the future. An additional question inquired as to whether they had ever read anything by Abdullah Öcalan, the co-founder of the PKK who has written prolifically while imprisoned in Turkey, and is still influential within the Kurdish movement.

My questionnaire was not designed to assess the education system. However, I did ask respondents to rank what they considered most important in terms of political goals (equality between men and women, equality between rich and poor, and ecological sustainability).

According to my survey respondents, 47.7 percent of the SDF members had never read anything by Öcalan at all.[28] This is worth highlighting as the SDF grew out of the YPG/YPJ, the Kurdish militia. It is possible that the number of people who had not read Öcalan is even higher. As one observer put it, admitting to have not read anything by Öcalan at all is kind of like admitting "you didn't do your homework." My survey results highlight the limitations of the spread of ideology of democratic confederalism, even within the ranks of the SDF. In addition to military training, the SDF also provides ideological training, and yet a little less than half of my survey respondents admitted to having ever read anything by Öcalan.

Education Level in the SDF Based on Gender—Survey Data

Gender	No Education	Some High School	Graduated High School	Some University	Graduated University	Total
Male	28 (10%)	113 (40%)	90 (32%)	30 (10%)	22 (8%)	283 (82%)
Female	15 (24%)	24 (38%)	16 (25%)	7 (11%)	1 (2%)	63 (18%)
Total	43 (12%)	137 (40%)	106 (30%)	37 (11%)	23 (7%)	346

In the course of this research, I encountered a number of non-Kurds who expressed not just support but also enthusiasm for the new political order that was created and initially led by the Kurdish authorities. For example, in March 2019, I met a young woman named Helin, a member of the Turkmen minority who had joined the SDF. The mere fact that members of the Turkmen minority had joined the SDF was virtually unreported in the media, which tends to portray the conflict as one only between Kurds and Turkey. I asked if she had any message she would like to deliver to the outside world, and if she would like me to record her speaking. She readily agreed to allow me to film her. Standing in the dark outside of the YPJ academies and with a cold wind blowing, she spoke—without any preparation—about how Yezidi and Arab women suffered a lot under ISIS, and how schools need to be rebuilt because children had not gone to school in many years.

At the Olaf Taw Association in Qamishli, I met a number of Muslim women who were learning the Syriac-Aramaic language spoken by the Christian minority. Considering that the region of Northeast Syria was still suffering from the various convulsions caused by war and mass displacement, I was surprised that the students were gathered to learn an ancient language spoken by a small group of people. I asked the Muslim women if any of them would be willing to explain why they were learning the language. A woman named Esraa readily volunteered. Similar to Helin, she had no preparation and spoke spontaneously. Esraa wore a traditional black hijab that covered her hair and neck. She spoke about why she wanted to learn the Aramaic language spoken by the Christian minority. It was important to learn Aramaic, she said, because it was a local language of the region where she grew up, and that it was necessary to learn the languages of one's neighbors (Figure 7.5).[29]

Rojava University

The local authorities had loftier goals than abolishing illiteracy and teaching new languages. They wanted to create their own universities in the Northeast. The first university was established in Afrin in August 2015. New textbooks with the new curriculum had also been introduced in 2015, up to the eighth grade level. According to Harriet Allsopp and Wladimir van Wilgenburg, in the Afrin region "greater demographic homogeneity, absence of organized political opposition and geographic isolation allowed the education system to develop relatively quickly."[30] In Jazira Canton, a university in Qamishli was established in 2016 (Figure 7.6).

Figure 7.5 Esraa, Arab woman studying the Syriac-Aramaic language

Figure 7.6 Photo of Rojava University

Did the New Education System Create
Unity or Division?

As has become clear in this chapter, the region of North and East Syria is characterized by ethnic and religious diversity in addition to political divides. Did the implementation of a new educational system increase or decrease these divides? It is still too early to answer this question. Based on fieldwork that was carried out in Syria between 2016 and 2017, Allsopp and van Wilgenburg argued that the education system may have contributed to the fragmentation of Syria:

> The Kurdish origins of the system and the extension of its ideology into non-Kurdish areas, appeared, in many cases, to exacerbate political, ethnic and religious fissures within Syria's communities and no solution had been developed to address this. In other cases cooperation was, at least temporarily, facilitating the development of mechanisms of navigating the conflict in Syria and developing new forms of governance and representation. In the long run, however, the widespread fragmentation of education in Syria promised to deepen ideological, cultural and linguistic divides.[31]

However, their assessment may be premature. Things change quickly in Syria. At the time of writing, the UNESCO curriculum is used in Raqqa and Deir Ezzor, while in Manbij the regime curriculum is still in use. In the canton of Jazira, there are three different curriculums: one is in Kurdish with some lessons in Arabic and Aramaic; one is in Arabic with some lessons in Kurdish and Aramaic; and one is in Aramaic with some lessons in Arabic and Kurdish. The Autonomous Administration is currently working to unify the educational curriculum across all regions under SDF control—approximately one-third of Syria. Whether this will be possible remains to be seen. The new Syriac school books do not, for example, use the term "Rojava" to refer to northern Syria (Figure 7.1). Furthermore, due to the lack of recognition of their schools by the regime, even some people who work in the Autonomous Administration, or are sympathetic to it, send their children to schools run by the regime or the churches.

Conclusion

The Autonomous Administration overcame massive obstacles in establishing an educational system while also fighting an array of adversaries. Local officials made it a priority, losing no time in setting up schools after areas were liberated so that school-age children could regain a sense of normalcy. Dedicated cadres were assigned the task of setting up the new school system. Higher salaries for teachers created an economic incentive for teachers to switch loyalties to the new education system. The education law requiring mandatory school enrollment for boys and girls created an incentive for parents who may have been reluctant to send their children back to school. The education system was also decisive in empowering the youth by providing them with new skills. After illiteracy had increased under ISIS, the schools that were created postliberation aimed to root out illiteracy.

The Autonomous Administration is still working to unify the school curriculum across all regions of North and East Syria. It is still a work-in-progress. The entire region is still threatened from the north by Turkey and from the south by the Russian and Iranian-backed Syrian regime. An attack from either direction may lead to another wave of massive displacement and destruction. However, even if Assad is able to reclaim all of Syrian territory including the Northeast, it will be difficult—perhaps impossible—to revert to the pre-2011 status quo. A generation of young Syrians in the Northeast have received an education that, while imperfect and lacking recognition, teaches notions of democracy, human rights, and equality.

Finally, the creation of the new school system points to a contradiction inherent in the Kurdish-led project. Abdullah Öcalan himself professed to have given up the dream of creating a Kurdish state. Writing from his prison cell, he declared that the nation-state leads to oppression and is part of the problem, not part of the solution. At the same time, the movement assigns a high degree of importance to education. They are not content to merely recruit young people to fight against the Islamic State—they want them to be literate, to be educated, to be immersed in the values of democratic confederalism. The creation of a new education system entails creating a bureaucratic apparatus. It was not a state that the Syrian Kurds wanted, they claimed, but a stateless democracy. Yet they also wanted to speak and learn their own language, and to be educated in a school system that did not deny their existence. This desire was shared by Assyrians fighting to ensure their language does not become extinct. Their dream of a stateless democracy could only be achieved by creating a bureaucracy, a statelet-in-the-making.

Yezidis and the Statelet of Survivors

Recognition, Representation, Religious Freedom, and Protection

"Where are the Nuremberg Trials for the Yezidis?"
—Pari Ibrahim, Free Yezidi Foundation[1]

Yezidis have inhabited Greater Syria for a millennium. Due to Islamization, repeated massacres since the time of the Ottoman Empire, and genocidal atrocities committed by the Islamic State beginning in 2014, their numbers have dwindled. In a country with a rich history of ethnic and religious communities, Yezidis are a "double minority"—persecuted for both their religion and ethnicity—making them one of the most vulnerable minorities in all of Syria.

Since the beginning of the conflict in 2011, Syrians have lived under four very distinct forms of governance: the Assad regime, the Islamic State Caliphate, the Kurdish-led Autonomous Administration, and under Turkish occupation. This chapter will offer an overview and comparison of these four types of government and their impact on the Yezidi community of northern Syria.[2] Under the Assad regime, Yezidis experienced systematic denial of their identity, followed by enslavement and genocide at the hands of ISIS. The SDF fought hard and made tremendous sacrifices to defeat ISIS: more than 11,000 young men and women were killed on the battlefield. But defeating the Caliphate was only the beginning. By creating a new system of governance, the Autonomous Administration was able to officially recognize the Yezidi religion, thereby creating the conditions to allow the Yezidi culture to flourish. In this chapter I will highlight how the Autonomous Administration has strived to improve the situation of the small Yezidi community in five ways by offering (1) recognition of their existence, (2) political representation, (3) religious freedom, (4) protection from annihilation, and (5) attempts at accountability by establishing courts to try Syrian ISIS members. In so doing they have created an environment that aims to foster

Statelet of Survivors. Amy Austin Holmes, Oxford University Press. © Oxford University Press 2024.
DOI: 10.1093/oso/9780197621035.003.0008

tolerance and coexistence, quite unlike regions of Syria controlled by the Assad regime, Turkey, or the jihadists in Idlib.

However, many of these gains may be ephemeral, and some have already been rolled back in the areas now occupied by Turkey. Ensuring the mere survival of Yezidis entailed building an army and stopping a genocide. But allowing Yezidis to obtain political recognition and exercise religious freedom, entailed building a form of local governance that I've called a statelet of survivors. Decimated by waves of violence, the small surviving Yezidi community has helped build this statelet alongside Syriacs, Armenians, Assyrians, Kurds, Arabs, and others.

The Yezidi Identity

The Yezidis in Iraq and Syria belong to the same distinct ethno-religious minority. Pockets of Yezidi communities also exist in southeastern Turkey, Iran, Armenia, and the Caucasus. They are followers of the same ancient monotheistic religion. The earliest documented history of Yezidi presence in Greater Syria (known in Arabic as Bilad al-Sham) can be traced to the year 1070, when Sheikh Adi bin Musafir was born in a small village in the Bekaa Valley.[3] Yezidis have lived in Afrin, the predominantly Kurdish region in the northwest of Syria, since at least the twelfth century. Numerous ancient monuments and shrines attest to their long-standing presence in the area. According to their own accounts, the Yezidi people have suffered some 74 massacres throughout history. Yezidis have been subjected to Islamization, or encouraged to hide their identity to escape persecution. In 1935, there were around 85 Yezidi villages in Afrin, but by 2011 only 23–33 remained (Figure 8.1).[4]

Due to constant persecution over centuries, their numbers have dwindled. The best current estimates indicate there are no more than one million Yezidis left worldwide.[5] It is difficult to obtain reliable information about the precise number of Yezidis in Syria, in part because under the Baathist regime Yezidis were required to register as Muslims on their official ID cards. However, prior to the onset of the Syrian conflict in 2011, the United States Department of State estimated that there were some 80,000 Yezidis in Syria.[6] Sileman Cafer, a Yezidi leader from Afrin and author of the book Qewlen Ezdiyan (The Yezidi Texts) estimated that there were approximately 60,000 Yezidis in Afrin alone prior to 2011.[7] Sebastian Maisel believes the number is considerably lower, with perhaps no more than 15,000 Yezidis in all of Syria.[8]

Although ISIS at one point controlled almost half of Syria, they were never able to launch the kind of massive assault on any Yezidi communities in Syria as they had done in Sinjar. This is in part due to the geographic dispersion of Yezidis—but also because of the YPG's fierce determination to protect them. In contrast to the situation in Iraq, where Yezidis were historically concentrated

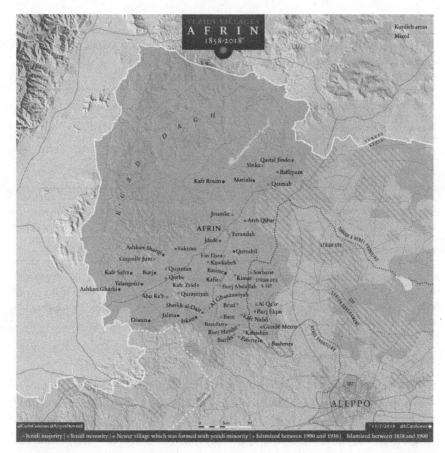

Figure 8.1 Map of Yezidi Villages in Afrin

in the region of Sinjar, in Syria the Yezidi community is dispersed across five different areas from the far northwestern canton of Afrin to Amude and Hasakah in the northeast. Table 8.1 illustrates the geographic dispersion of Yezidi settlements, meaning towns and villages with Yezidi inhabitants, and not villages that are solely inhabited by Yezidis. Syrian Yezidis are clustered in the north, in areas where the Kurdish People's Protection Units, YPG, had established de facto control since mid-2012. Under YPG protection, Yezidis in Syria were spared many of the horrific crimes that their co-religionists in Iraq suffered.

Baathist Rule: Denial of Yezidi Identity

Even before Hafez al-Assad became President in 1970, the central government in Damascus had promoted an ideology of pan-Arabism, which denied recognition

Table 8.1 **Table of Yezidi Settlements in Syria**

Five regions of northern Syria with clusters of Yezidi settlements[a] (not including IDP camps)	Number of settlements with Yezidi inhabitants	Current control of region (2023)
Afrin	33	Turkey and affiliated militias
Ras al-Ayn/Serekaniye	18	Turkey and affiliated militias
Amude	12	Syrian Democratic Forces
Hasakeh	24	Syrian Democratic Forces + some regime presence
Qahtaniyah/Tirbespi	8	Syrian Democratic Forces
Total number of Yezidi settlements in Syria	95	—

[a]In his book *Yezidis in Syria*, Sebastian Maisel identifies five distinct regions of northern Syria with traditional Yezidi settlements. He refers to one area as Wadi al-Jarrah, which is close to the city of Qahtaniyah (Tirbespi in Kurdish). I have chosen to refer to the area as Qahtaniyah/Tirbespi because these terms are more commonly used.

to many of Syria's distinct minority groups in an attempt to consolidate power over a diverse society. Yezidis were unable to identify as Yezidi on their official ID cards, but were registered as Muslims. They were not allowed to celebrate religious holidays, including major holidays such as their New Year, known as *Charshama Sor* (Red Wednesday), nor were they allowed to have Yezidi religious symbols on their gravestones. The most holy site of the Yezidi religion, Lalish, is located in Iraq. The delineation of the border between Iraq and Syria in the early twentieth century meant that it was difficult for Syrian Yezidis to make a pilgrimage to Lalish, the Mecca of the Yezidi religion. Furthermore, Yezidis were required to participate in Islamic Studies classes in public school. They had to use the Quran to have sworn testimony in court, and were bound by Islamic Sharia courts in terms of marriage, divorce, and inheritance laws—although Yezidis are not Muslims.[9]

The United Arab Republic: Union between Egypt and Syria 1958–1961

Arabization Policies Targeted both Yezidis and Kurds

The union between Syria and Nasser's Egypt, known as the United Arab Republic, was short-lived, lasting only between 1958 and 1961. The devastating legacy of the Arabization policies, however, continued even after the two countries had split up. These policies are often described as if they were only directed at the Kurdish minority, but they also impacted the Yezidis.

Two years after Syria had withdrawn from the United Arab Republic, Lieutenant Mohamed Talab Hilal produced a report in November 1963 entitled "Study of the Province of Jazira in its National, Social, and Political Aspects." It was a top-secret document meant only for internal use by the government. When parts of the report were leaked to the public, an outcry resulted—at least among non-Arabs. The authorities responded that it did not represent the Baath Party, but merely the author's opinions. However, Lieutenant Hilal was rewarded for his efforts: he was made Governor of Hama, and then Minister of Supplies from 1964 until Hafez al-Assad came to power in 1970. The two following short excerpts from his report illustrate succinctly that the Arabization policies viewed Kurds (including Yezidis) as a "tumor" which should be removed from the "Arab nation":

> Such then is the Kurdish people, a people with neither history nor civilization, neither language nor ethnic origin, with nothing but the qualities of force, destructive power and violence, qualities which are moreover inherent in all mountain peoples.[10]
>
> The Kurdish question, now that the Kurds are organizing themselves, is simply a malignant tumor which has developed and been developed in a part of the body of the Arab nation. The only remedy which we can properly apply thereto is excision (*al-batr*).[11]

Lieutenant Hilal proposed a Twelve-Point Plan which was to be implemented immediately, and in cooperation with Turkey, Iraq, and Iran. His twelve suggestions are summarized in the following list:

1. "The state must embark on an operation to transfer the population and disperse it in the interior. [...]
2. Political obscurantism: not to open schools or scientific institutions in the region [...]
3. [...] It is necessary to expel the elements whose nationality (Syrian) has not been proved and hand them over to the authorities of their country of origin. [...] what is important is to take note of the results of the latest census and then continue with the expulsion programme.
4. Stop employment: opportunities of work should be closed to Kurds, in such a way that they are no longer in a position to move but in a state in which they are prepared to leave the country at any moment. This then is the task of the agrarian reform authorities: the Kurds must be forbidden to

possess or to rent (lands), especially since Arab elements are available and, by the grace of God, numerous.

5. Unleash a vast anti-Kurd campaign among the Arabs, first of all to condition them against the Kurds, then to undermine the situation of the latter and sow in their midst the seeds of distress and insecurity.

6. The Kurdish ulemas must be deprived of their religious authority and replaced by pure Arab ulemas. [...]

7. The Kurds must be antagonized against each other.

8. Settle Arab nationalist elements in the Kurdish regions, the entire length of the borders. These elements will be our future outposts, and can at the same time supervise the Kurds until their transfer. [...]

9. Proclaim the northern belt a military zone, in the same way as the front, and station there army detachments whose task it will be to settle Arabs and expel the Kurds, according to the plans drawn up by the state.

10. Create collective farms for the Arabs who will be settled in the northern belt [...]

11. Disenfranchise all persons in these regions who do not speak Arabic of the right to elect and be elected.

12. Absolutely refrain from conferring Syrian nationality upon those who want to settle in this region, be their original nationality what it may, always excepting Arabs, etc."[12]

In 1965, Hilal's plan was adopted by the central government and the Baath Syrian Regional Leadership, creating an "Arab cordon" (hizam al-Arabi) in the Jazira along the Turkish border, a strip of land 300 kilometers in length, stretching from the Iraqi border in the east to Ras al-Ayn/Serêkaniyê in the west. This entailed deporting around 140,000 Kurds—and Yezidis—from some 332 villages. Most of those deported were peasants from rural areas.

Not all villagers submitted themselves passively to deportation. In Al Qahtaniyah/Tirbespi, on May 15, 1967, Yezidis resisted military orders to abandon their homes and be relocated in the south of the country as part of the Arab Belt policies. Their resistance became known as the Tell Khatun intifada and was organized by Osman Sabri, the leader of Kurdish Democratic Party in Syria.[13]

Such acts of resistance did not, however, put an end to the Arabization policies. In 1973 Arabs were brought from the area around Raqqa, after their land had been submerged due to the creation of the Tabqa Dam.

Statelessness: Ajanib and Maktoum

In addition to deportations, a surprise census in 1962 was used to strip many Syrian Kurds and Yezidis of their citizenship. As a result of the census, new legal

Figure 8.2 Red Identity Card for Stateless Kurds and Yezidis

categories were created. Some Syrian Kurds and Yezidis were rendered as *ajanib* (foreigners), while others were rendered *maktoum* (stateless). Instead of a passport, they were given pieces of paper that were meant to substitute for the lack of a national ID card or passport. These Kurds and Yezidis were deprived of their basic civil, political, and economic rights:

> The stateless have been deprived of all their rights, including the right to register their marriage, the right to own property, the right to education, the right to have a decent housing, the right to travel abroad, the right to travel by plane, and the right to stay at hotels as well. I have met many of them who were stripped of their nationality while showing Syrian documents they had gotten before 1962, including identity cards, military service book and property deeds.[14]

The Red Identity cards for those designated as ajanib were issued by the Civil Registrar of the Ministry of Interior (Figure 8.2). They registered the individual as a foreigner inside Syria, and could not be used for travel outside Syria. The Red Card could, however, be used for everyday purposes inside Syria. By contrast, the White Card for the Maktoum could not even be used within Syria, as it was not issued by any government body (Figure 8.3). Rather, it was an informal form of identification issued by the local Mukhtar. Stripping individuals of their rights, and indeed their very identity as Syrians, was a source of anguish for many, as the following quote illustrates:

> I am maktoum. This means my life is worth nothing. If the police sees us talking I will have a big problem. But what can they do? What can they take from me? I have nothing, I am a maktoum. My life can't get worse.[15]

Table 8.2 **Maktum—Ajanib—National Legal Relations**

Wife	Husband	Can their marriage be legally registered?	Can their children be legally registered?
Maktum	National	No	Yes—under father
Maktum	Ajanib	No	Yes—under father
Maktum	Maktum	No	No
Ajanib	National	Yes	Yes
Ajanib	Ajanib	No	Yes—under father
Ajanib	Maktum	No	No
National	National	Yes	Yes
National	Ajanib	No	Yes—under father
National	Maktum	No	No

Sources: Maisel, Sebastian. (2017). Yezidis in Syria: Identity Building among a Double Minority. Lexington Books. page 101

Many of the children born to either maktoum or ajanib Kurds and Yezidis could also not be legally registered as Syrian citizens, even when they (and their parents) were born inside Syria. The discriminatory policies of rendering Syrians as stateless or foreigners in their own country were passed on from one generation to the next (Table 8.2).

The ban on the Kurdish language also impacted the Yezidi minority. Under Ba'athist rule, parents were not allowed to bestow Kurdish names on their children. The Kurdish language was not to be spoken, even at private ceremonies such as weddings.

The discriminatory policies toward stateless Yezidis and Kurds continued until the very end of Assad's rule in the north. On September 17, 2008 the Directorate of Education in Hasakah circulated a letter among the principals of primary and secondary schools in the district requesting them not to issue any grade report or official school documents to maktoum students.

Presidential Decree Number 49 was also passed in September 2008, which expanded the restriction on landownership in the border areas. According to the new law, property registration of land deeds would no longer be allowed, making it illegal to buy, sell, or inherit land property. As discussed in more detail in previous chapters, the population in the borderlands consists of many non-Arab minorities, including Kurds, Yezidis, as well as Armenians and Syriac-Assyrians. The outbreak of the Syrian conflict in 2011 prevented the decree from being fully implemented. Nevertheless, these decrees illustrate that the Arabization

Figure 8.3 White Identity Card for Maktoum Kurds and Yezidis

policies of prior decades that deprived Kurds and Yezidis of their Syrian citizenship, were still being used against these minority communities.

For decades, Yezidi identity had been completely denied and suppressed by the government in Damascus. Sebastian Maisel, who has written one of the very few books in the English language on Yezidis in Syria, summarizes the complete lack of recognition as follows:

> No schools taught Yezidism, no training was provided for the clerics, no authority was appointed or elected to make necessary religious decisions, no directorate was in charge of the religious buildings, shrines, and sanctuaries, no personal status law was codified, no literature was published, and no formal relationship with the government was ever formed.[16]

Attacks on Syrian Yezidis Before the Caliphate

The genocide in 2014 drew the world's attention to the plight of the Yezidis. But even prior to this, Yezidis in Syria had been subjected to brutal attacks, most of which were hardly reported about by the international media. Ilyas from the Yezidi House in the Jazira canton describes below an attack in 2013. He described it as a "Turkish attack," presumably because the various armed groups known at the time as the Free Syrian Army (FSA) would at times stage ambush and hit-and-run operations from across the Turkish border. However, the fighters themselves included people with different nationalities. According to a dossier produced by the Rojava Center for Strategic Studies, when the YPG/YPJ liberated the region around Serêkaniyê, the FSA and al-Nusra fighters withdrew to Turkish territory via the border crossing on September 23, 2013.[17] Ilyas's account of the FSA attack indicates that their intention was not merely to control territory, but that they "destroyed everything Yezidi." At this point, the YPG/YPJ was fighting alone, with no international support.

> The first Turkish attack was in 2013 in the surrounding Yezidi villages like Chafa, Derdara, Esadiya, Xirbet al-Benat. In these places they destroyed everything Yezidi, and because of this they fled their villages. In Esadiya Murad and Ali, two brothers, were martyred there, murdered there, pulled apart between two vehicles, because they refused to leave their homes. Then the YPG/YPJ liberated it, we as the Yezidi House were some of the first ones there. We saw what the terrorists did to their houses, they ruined everything, their houses were completely destroyed, their cabinets were ransacked and thrown everywhere. They even tore the electric cables out of the walls, they didn't leave anything at all. Their kitchens were all burned. They stole everything, down to even the doors and windows. There were some houses that were spared because they [the terrorists] were using them, they left them alone... That was 2013, a large number of the population of Serêkaniyê went to Bakur [Turkey]. We as the Yezidi House told them, "come back, the YPG and YPJ took the villages back, you should come home," but a lot of them didn't return. There were 15 villages surrounding the area, 12 of them Yezidi, like Chafa, Tel Xenzir, Xirbet Benat, Tel Dara, Lizga, Merikis, Can Temr, Sukeriya, Abba, Tel Sekhr, Birno, Tel Beyder, Tileliyeh, Dire'i. In these villages, there were previously Yezidis, but there aren't anymore, they all migrated. For example in Birno, there aren't anymore, in Tel Beyder, there aren't anymore, there's no more in Merikis village. But there are Yezidis in Netef village.[18]

Those few Yezidis who remained in the region around Ras al-Ayn/Serêkaniyê were then displaced by the Turkish intervention in October 2019. At the end of this chapter I include testimonies from four Yezidi families who fled in 2019, who I interviewed in Syria. They described to me how their homes, businesses, and farmlands are now occupied by Turkish-backed militias.

The Islamic State: Slavery and Genocide of the Yezidis

At its height, the Islamic State ruled over some eight million people in Iraq and Syria, controlling a vast territory about the size of Great Britain. While millions of Iraqis and Syrians suffered under the rule of the Islamic State, Yezidis were singled out for the most gruesome crimes. The list of atrocities committed by Islamic State militants included forced religious conversion, mass displacement, kidnapping, torture, destruction of sacred monuments and shrines, and the sexual enslavement of Yezidi women and girls. Islamic State militants swept across Syria, applying the same genocidal policies as in Iraq, as described in more detail in Chapter 4. Former Secretary of State John Kerry said that these "grotesque and targeted acts of violence bear all the warning signs and hallmarks of genocide."[19]

ISIS established and operated slave markets, known in Arabic as *souk sabaya*, in Syria just as in Iraq. These slave markets were set up in numerous cities including: Al Bab, Al Mayadin, Al Shaddadi, Raqqa, and Tadmur (Palmyra). Other holding sites or prisons were created for female captives in Al Shaddadi, Tel Hamis, Al Mayadin, Deir Ezzor, Manbij, Al Bab, Al Tabqah, and Tadmur (Figure 8.4).[20]

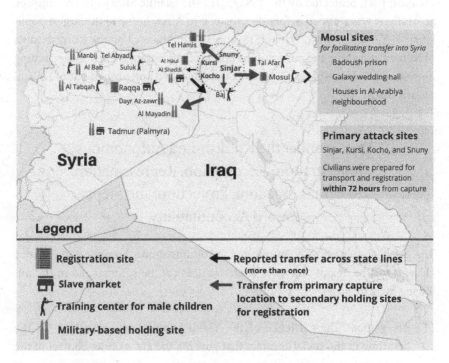

Figure 8.4 ISIS Slave Markets and Holding Sites in Syria and Iraq

A report by the United Nations Human Rights Council describes how
ISIS inflicted different crimes on their victims, depending on their age and
gender:

> Yazidi women and girls are violently and regularly raped, often by dif-
> ferent men, and over a prolonged period of time. They are beaten, sold
> as chattel, insulted and humiliated. The treatment that they endure in
> captivity causes them indescribable physical pain and mental suffering,
> effectively stripping them of their human dignity.[21]
>
> In respect of its abuse of Yazidi boys between the ages of seven
> and 15, ISIS has committed the war crime of using, conscripting, and
> enlisting children.[22]

ISIS was able to operate slave markets for Yezidis across their so-called Caliphate
on both sides of the Syrian-Iraqi border, and ISIS emirs enforced the same fatwas
in both countries. ISIS henchmen conducted beheadings on public squares in
both Syria and Iraq. As the crow flies, there are Yezidi villages in Syria which
are only 63 miles away from Sinjar, where the genocide took place in 2014. And
yet, ISIS was never able to launch the kind of massive assault on a Yezidi community in Syria as they had in Iraq because the Yezidi communities were, for
the most part, protected by the YPG/SDF. The Islamic State's bloody rampage
across Syria was stopped before they made it to Afrin, home to the largest population of Yezidis in Syria. When ISIS launched their attack on the Kurdish town
of Kobani, it was the beginning of the end for the Caliphate. After a siege lasting
more than four months, ISIS militants were defeated and pushed out of Kobani
in early 2015.

Yezidis under the Kurdish-Led Autonomous Administration: Recognition, Representation, Religious Freedom, Protection, and Steps toward Accountability

The establishment of the Autonomous Administration brought about major
changes for the Yezidi minority. These changes can be summarized in the following five categories.

(1) *Recognition*: The existence of the Yezidi people was recognized for the
first time in the social contract that governs the areas under control of the
Autonomous Administration.

(2) *Political Representation*: The Yezidis were represented in the political institutions that were created, and quotas were established to ensure that even tiny minorities were included.

(3) *Religious freedom*: Yezidis were able to openly celebrate their religious holidays and new laws guaranteed the right to religious freedom.

(4) *Protection*: With few exceptions, the YPG and SDF defended Yezidi villages from the Islamic State and ensured that a genocidal assault on the scale of what happened in Sinjar, Iraq, did not take place in Syria.

(5) *Accountability*: By creating local courts to try Syrian ISIS fighters, the Autonomous Administration has arguably done more to achieve justice for the victims of ISIS than the international community.

These are remarkable achievements given that they happened not in peacetime, but during an armed conflict when the beleaguered Self Administration was often struggling for its mere survival. It should also be noted that the cadre who guided the creation of this de facto statelet are for the most part secular or even nonreligious. In all my visits to North and East Syria over many years, I never once saw a cadre or SDF leader praying. And yet the cadre took a conscious decision to protect the right to be religious and to defend religious freedom for all—including the tiny Yezidi minority who had been reviled as devil worshippers by both Islamists and Baath party officials. Furthermore, administration officials dedicated scare resources to protecting and promoting the Yezidis—for the first time in the history of modern Syria.

When the forces of the Assad regime withdrew from northern Syria in the summer of 2012, the Kurdish-led YPG stepped in to fill the vacuum. However, the YPG was not able to establish full control of all the areas from which the regime had withdrawn, but initially only took control of three cantons. These included, from west to east: Afrin, Kobani, and Jazira. The three cantons were noncontiguous and between them other armed groups vied for power.

Virtually all Syrian Yezidis inhabited regions that had fallen under YPG protection since mid 2012. This protection, combined with the geographical isolation, especially of the northwestern canton of Afrin, allowed them to continue to live in their ancestral villages without facing a genocidal onslaught similar to what happened in Sinjar, Iraq in August 2014. The YPG did not only protect the Yezidis from the worst atrocities of Da'esh, the Autonomous Administration that was established allowed Yezidis a degree of religious freedom they had never previously experienced.

Recognition of the Yezidi Existence in Syria

The charter of the Social Contract, published on January 29, 2014, includes three articles that explicitly guarantee freedom of religion and recognize the Yezidi religion. However, the preamble to the 2014 Social Contract does not explicitly mention Yezidis. The new Social Contract from 2016, however, does list Yezidis in addition to the many other ethnic and religious communities in the region (Box 8.1).

Excerpts from the 2014 Social Contract are included in this section, including Articles 31, 32, and 92. It is worth highlighting that the Social Contract of the Autonomous Administration was announced in January of 2014—about eight months prior to the genocide the following August. The commitment to religious freedom and specific recognition of the Yezidi religion took place prior to the atrocities committed by the Islamic State.

Article 31

Everyone has the right to freedom of worship, to practice one's own religion either individually or in association with others. No one shall be subjected to persecution on the grounds of their religious beliefs.

Article 32, Section C

The Yezidi religion is a recognized religion and its adherents' rights to freedom of association and expression is explicitly protected. The protection of Yezidi religious, social and cultural life may be guaranteed through the passage of laws by the Legislative Assembly.

Article 92

a)- The Charter enshrines the principle of separation of religion and State.

b)- Freedom of religion shall be protected. All religions and faiths in the Autonomous Regions shall be respected. The right to exercise religious beliefs shall be guaranteed, insofar as it does not adversely affect the public good.[23]

Religious Freedom

Perhaps the most fundamental change enacted by the Autonomous Administration was the recognition of the Yezidi religion under Article 31 of the original 2014 Social Contract. Instead of hiding their religious beliefs, Yezidis

Box 8.1 The Preamble to the 2014 Social Contract

We, the people of the Democratic Autonomous Regions of Afrin, Jazira and Kobani, a confederation of Kurds, Arabs, Assyrians, Chaldeans, Arameans, Turkmen, Armenians and Chechens, freely and solemnly declare and establish this Charter, which has been drafted according to the principles of Democratic Autonomy.

In pursuit of freedom, justice, dignity and democracy and led by principles of equality and environmental sustainability, the Charter proclaims a new social contract, based upon mutual and peaceful coexistence and understanding between all strands of society. It protects fundamental human rights and liberties and reaffirms the peoples' right to self-determination.

Under the Charter, we, the people of the Autonomous Regions, unite in the spirit of reconciliation, pluralism and democratic participation so that all may express themselves freely in public life. In building a society free from authoritarianism, militarism, centralism and the intervention of religious authority in public affairs, the Charter recognizes Syria's territorial integrity and aspires to maintain domestic and international peace.

In establishing this Charter, we declare a political system and civil administration founded upon a social contract that reconciles the rich mosaic of Syria through a transitional phase from dictatorship, civil war and destruction, to a new democratic society where civic life and social justice are preserved.[a]

The Preamble to the 2016 Social Contract

We, the peoples of Rojava-northern Syria, including Kurds, Arabs, Syriacs, Assyrians, Turkmen, Armenians, Chechens, Circassians, Muslims, Christians, Yezidis, and the different doctrines and sects, recognize that the nation-state has made Kurdistan, Mesopotamia, and Syria a hub for the chaos happening in the Middle East and has brought problems, serious crises, and agonies for our peoples.

The tyrannical nation-state regime, which has been unfair to the different components of Syrian people, has led the country to destruction and fragmentation of the society fabric. To end this chaotic situation, the democratic federal system is an optimal solution to address the national, social, and historical issues in Syria.

The democratic federalism of northern Syria is based on a geographic concept and an administrative and political decentralization; it is part of the united Syrian democratic federalism.[b]

Charter of the Social Contract (2014). https://www.peaceinkurdistancampaign.com/charter-of-the-social-contract/.

Social Contract (2016). https://rojavainformationcenter.com/storage/2021/07/2016-Social-Contract-of-the-Democratic-Federation-of-Northern-Syria.pdf.

were able to identify openly. They could celebrate their religious holidays, they had the freedom to not only practice their religion, but to *choose* their religion. It became possible to convert from one religion to another. Yezidis were promoted to positions within the Autonomous Administration, and a Ministry of Religious Affairs was established in which Yezidis, Christians, and Alevis were represented. A Yezidi Cultural and Social Association was established, with its headquarters in the city of Afrin. Smaller institutions, known as "House of the Yezidis" (Mala Êzîdiyan) were established in areas across North and East Syria (Figure 8.6). When I visited the Mala Êzîdiyan near Amude in the summer of 2019, I met a Yezidi man who told me he had emigrated to Germany some 26 years earlier, and had just returned back to visit his home for the first time. The Caliphate had been defeated in March 2019, and hence it was, he told me, the first time in 26 years that he felt it was safe enough for him to return to his place of birth.[24]

The Autonomous Administration maintains a policy of noninterference in the internal religious affairs of the Yezidi minority. This policy has both advantages and drawbacks, and at times creates contradictions. For example, the Yezidi community is organized in a hierarchy that is sometimes referred to as a caste system, headed by a religious leader known as a Sheikh, and a secular leader known as a Prince. Marriage between men and women of different castes is discouraged. Although the hierarchical caste system of Yezidi culture is at odds with the egalitarian ideology of the Autonomous Administration, which strives to achieve equality between genders and people of various ethnic backgrounds, Administration officials have largely maintained a laissez-faire approach to the Yezidi community.

Maisel's book *Yezidis in Syria: Identity Building among a Double Minority*, was published in 2017, just one year before the Turkish intervention in Afrin. Maisel explains in no uncertain terms the significance of the Autonomous Administration for the Yezidis: "For the first time in history, they [Yezidis] live in an area free from persecution and annihilation and find their beliefs and heritage appreciated by their neighbors. Not by all neighbors and not in every Yezidi village of course, but in those territories controlled by the Syrian Kurds."[25]

The remarkable level of religious freedom has also been recognized by the bipartisan United States Commission on International Religious Freedoms (USCIRF), which was created by Congress in 1998. In their 2020 Annual Report, USCIRF wrote:

> Areas of northeastern Syria under AANES control—under SDF protection but with limited support from the United States and the GCDI [Global Coalition to Defeat ISIS] at year's end—remained a crucial center of positive religious freedom conditions in Syria. As in the prior year, AANES authorities continued to allow Muslims, Christians,

Yazidis, and others to openly practice their faiths and express their religious identities.[26]

Political Representation

Even before the social contract had been published in 2014, Yezidis began to actively take part in the Autonomous Administration. On November 12, 2012, residents of the Yezidi village of Zeydiya voted for their local council. In December 2012 Yezidis from the village of Otelje met to discuss organizing themselves into a council. On February 15, 2013, a local council of eight Yezidi villages in the region of Al Hasakah was created, a decision that was supported by TEV-DEM. The eight villages included Tell Aswad Fawqani, Tell Aswad Tahtani, Gumar Sharqi, Gumar Gharbi, Tell Teyr, Um al-Jafa, Jdeyda, and Antariya.

At times local councils were established by the Autonomous Administration before the central government had even relinquished control of the city. For example, on February 23, 2013, a joint council was formed in the city of Tirbespi. The council included thirty members: ten Kurds, ten Arabs, five Syriac-Assyrians, and five Yezidis. This example also highlights how the new Administration not only included small minority groups, but that some of these minorities may have even been overrepresented, proportionate to their size. Furthermore, every effort was made to ensure equal representation on lower-level committees. For example, the Supervisory Board that was elected on March 13, 2013 consisted of six members, including two Kurds, two Arabs, one Assyrian, and one Yezidi.[27]

On May 14, 2012, a group of Yezidi elders met to discuss ways to revive the practice of their religious and social customs. This meeting was organized by the Yezidi Association in Syria and West Kurdistan. Silêman Cafer, the president of the association, led the discussion. This was still before the regime forces had fully withdrawn from Afrin.[28]

Administration officials strive to maintain good relations with the Yezidi community, attend their holidays, and acknowledge the contribution of Yezidis in defending the homeland and in achieving the larger aims of the Rojava Revolution. According to Maisel, "Syrian Yezidis almost completely adopted the political narrative of the PYD. In contrast, the Sheikhan Yezidis in Iraq consider the PYD and subsequently the PKK a political rival."[29] Other Yezidi survivors from Iraq, however, expressed appreciation for the PKK's rescue efforts during the genocide in 2014. One survivor interviewed in 2014 described the desperation of Yezidis who were stranded atop Mount Sinjar as follows: "If it weren't for the Kurdish fighters, we would have died up there."[30]

Courts in the Autonomous Administration

Yezidis in both Iraq and Syria have called for an international tribunal, similar to the Nuremberg Trials after World War II, in order to seek justice in the aftermath of the genocide.[31] Yet their demands for justice have been largely ignored by the international community.

More than two years after the defeat of the ISIS Caliphate, some 64,000 people were still detained in the Al Hol camp alone. About half of them are Iraqi citizens, 37 percent are Syrians, and 15 percent have another foreign nationality.[32] Many European countries continue to refuse to repatriate their own citizens who joined ISIS, or have even stripped individuals of their citizenship, such as Shamima Begum from Great Britain.[33]

The Autonomous Administration has, however, created their own system of local courts known as "People's Defense Courts" (*Mahkame el Tameez el Istanaf*). These local courts have many shortcomings: they suffer from a lack of resources, lack of biometric data, lack of qualified personnel with prior training as judges, and most importantly a lack of any recognition. They do, however, have the potential to offer a modicum of accountability, and perhaps a sense of justice, to Yezidis and the many other victims of ISIS (Figure 8.5).

Figure 8.5 Social Justice Council, part of the court system created by the Autonomous Administration of North and East Syria

I interviewed the two co-chairs of the People's Defense Courts, who both go by code names due to the sensitive nature of their work. On a warm day in September, I sat down with Amina Hussein and Hassan Suleiman (their code names) in a building that had been converted into a court. They are both Kurds from Afrin, and had studied law at Aleppo University. Because they were both displaced by the Turkish intervention in Afrin in 2018, they were now working and living full time in the Jazira canton.

The first People's Defense Courts were established already in Afrin in 2011. Judge Amina and Judge Hassan were there from the beginning. According to them, units of the FSA had blocked the roads between Afrin and Aleppo, so it was not possible to travel between the two areas, and there were not enough lawyers or judges in Afrin. Some people also started to steal documents from the courts because of the chaotic situation—including important files related to ownership of land and properties. "If we didn't act people would have lost their rights," Judge Amina told me.[34] Furthermore, she explained that after the outbreak of the conflict, many Kurds had moved from Aleppo to Afrin. As the city became overcrowded, problems increased. So, they decided to create their own legal system in areas under YPG control.

The decision to create the People's Defense Courts was born in part out of necessity, but it was also clear they wanted to create a system that was different, and better, from that of the Assad regime. Activist lawyers and judges had started to prepare for the new court system already in 2011, before Assad's forces had even withdrawn from Rojava. It was then formally announced in 2012.

The judicial system of the Assad regime was viewed as unjust for many reasons—not just because Kurds and Yezidis faced discrimination. For example, in the courts in the regime areas, one single judge presides over cases. "He decides based on his bias, his mood," Judge Amina explained. But in the courts of the Autonomous Administration, there are three judges—not just one. The verdict is passed if two of the three judges agree on the decision. The core of the new system is based on the first unit in the community, where they try to resolve problems based on reconciliation rather than the courts. They refer to this as the "Social Justice System" (*Nizam Adela Ichtimaeya*). Only where the village committees are unable to resolve the issue are the cases referred to the courts. Judge Hassan estimated that between 30 and 40 percent of all cases are resolved in the reconciliation committees—which means the case load the courts have to deal with is significantly reduced.

The first Terrorism Courts were announced in 2014. These courts were established to deal with the many ISIS fighters caught by the Syrian Democratic Forces, or those suspected of supporting the Islamic State. Members of other armed groups who have been caught, such as Jebhat Al Nusra or the Turkish-backed Hamza Division or Suleyman Shah Brigade, have also allegedly been put on trial. Between 2014 and 2021, over 8,000 Syrian nationals have been tried in the terrorism courts. Until now, the Autonomous Administration has not tried any Iraqi citizens or other foreign nationals in their custody. Less than 1 percent of those who have been tried until now were women.[35]

While Yezidis and other victims of ISIS have demanded justice, officials in the Autonomous Administration have their own reasons for establishing courts and meting out punishment for crimes. The trials not only provide a sense of justice to the many victims, but are also a way of dealing with the ongoing threat of ISIS sleeper cells, and could potentially deter future attacks. It is key, however, that the trials be conducted in a fair and judicious manner.

A report by the International Center for Counterterrorism (ICCT) in the Hague described the new legal system as follows:

> In developing the Rojava criminal justice system, efforts have been made to implement liberal processes more in line with international law. The AANES has founded a constitution and a legal system of its own which includes a ban on the death penalty, a ban on extradition to death penalty countries like Iraq, inclusion of female judges, and a system of restorative justice. The new justice system also combines accountability with other forms of transitional justice, such as ongoing release under the tribal guaranteed programmes, and amnesties, alongside rehabilitation efforts in detention facilities. Torture is also prohibited in the Rojava justice system, and disciplinary action is supposed to be taken against any guards perceived to be acting in contravention of this ban or humiliating prisoners.[36]

The authors of the ICCT report concur with the International Committee of the Red Cross (ICRC) which stated that the establishment of courts by non-state armed groups such as the SDF raises questions of legitimacy, but that they nevertheless "constitute an alternative to summary justice" and are a way to "maintain law and order" and ensure respect for international humanitarian law.

According to an interview with a prosecutor who works for the Autonomous Administration, their new judicial system strives to be transparent, and inform people when their family members have been arrested. This stands in contrast to the situation in regime-held areas, where enforced disappearances are common.

> During the regime era, we couldn't get a hold of people that had been arrested sometimes for years, as lawyers. They wouldn't say where they were detained. Especially in the case of political prisoners. We wouldn't get any notice or be told in which prisons they were being held. In our system there is nothing like this. Even if it's really difficult, we try to

keep everything transparent for the people. We say, "this person has been arrested," we call the family and say "your son is in our detention facility, facing these and these charges," and we explain the judicial process that they will face.[37]

In addition to problems resulting from the sheer number of cases to be tried and overcrowded facilities, other shortcomings include a lack of biometric data or forensic capabilities. These challenges can at times, however, be offset by the fact that many ISIS supporters were actually proud of their crimes, and were in possession of cell phones with photos and videos that are often incriminating. The new legal system distinguishes between those who supported ISIS as civilians, and those who actually fought in the ranks of ISIS. The table below summarizes the different types of crimes and the length of punishment for each (Table 8.3).

Despite all of the shortcomings of the court system, the authors of the ICCT report came to the conclusion that: "For the AANES, holding trials is the only viable solution—with or without the help of the international community—to contain the threat posed by ISIS and to provide justice including through transitional justice mechanisms."[38]

Having defeated the Caliphate, the Autonomous Administration now has authority over tens of thousands of Syrians and Iraqis, as well as a few thousand European citizens who joined ISIS. Until now, the calls for an international tribunal, akin to the Nuremberg Trials after World War II, have been ignored. The Syrian regime continues to insist that Yezidis have to use Islamic courts. The

Table 8.3 **Crimes and Punishments**

Crime	Length of Punishment
Civilian membership in a terrorist organization	1–2 year prison sentence, according to the role played in the organization
Armed membership	5–10 years minimum
Organized leadership/indirect responsibility for deaths	20 years—life sentence
Rape	15–20 years
Human trafficking (mostly related to Yezidi enslavement)	10–20 years
Fighting against SDF forces	10–20 years
Murder	15 years—life sentence

US position under the Trump and Biden administrations was that each country should repatriate their own citizens who joined ISIS, and that they should be tried in courts in their home countries. However, many European countries have simply refused to do so. France indicated a willingness to repatriate the children, but not the adult fighters. In 2018 the French Foreign Minister Jean Yves Le Drian even indicated that France would not object if the estimated 100 French citizens detained in Northeast Syria as foreign terrorist fighters would be tried by the courts in the Autonomous Administration.[39] This may mean that the Autonomous Administration has no other choice but to put European citizens on trial in their own courts. Whether this could result in de facto legal recognition of their system is too early to tell.

Problems Post-Caliphate: Missing Yezidis and Separation of Yezidi Families

The defeat of the Islamic State Caliphate was a historic turning point in the Syrian conflict—but did not immediately improve the situation for Syrian Yezidis. Many Yezidi women had been forced in captivity to marry ISIS men, and gave birth to children whose fathers were ISIS fighters. While the (male) Yezidi religious leaders made a decision to allow Yezidi women to remain part of the community, their children were not afforded the same welcome.

What this has meant is that Yezidi women who gave birth to children of ISIS fathers are faced with an excruciating decision: to either give up their children and return to their community, or remain with their children but essentially be expelled from Yezidi society.

According to the religion, a child cannot be considered a member of the Yezidi community unless his or her father is Yezidi. Karim Sulaiman, a spokesman for the Yezidi Supreme Spiritual Council justified the decision in this way: "To make special examples in this case would be to whitewash the result of the Yazidi genocide."[40]

Given the stigma associated with rape and the many atrocities to which Yezidis were subjected, it is difficult to know how many children were born to Yezidi mothers and Islamic State fathers. Estimates range from several hundred to more than 1,000.[41]

This has led some Yezidi women to prefer to hide their identity, in order to not risk losing their children. According to one estimate, some 250 Yezidis are in hiding in the Al Hol camp, alongside ISIS detainees.[42] After the Ottoman genocide in 1915, some Armenians hid their identity as a survival strategy. Now, a century later, an estimated 2,800 Yezidis are still missing after the genocide by the Islamic State. At the time of writing, there are no internationally coordinated

Figure 8.6 Mala Ezidiyan

search efforts to find them. With virtually no outside help, the Yezidi House in northern Syria (Figure 8.6) has been trying to locate Yezidis who are in the Al Hol camp and return them to their families.

Yezidis under Turkish Occupation: Destruction of Cultural Heritage and Demographic Change

Despite the lack of international assistance to Yezidi organizations in northern Syria, the Autonomous Administration has managed to improve the situation of the Yezidis and other religious and ethnic minorities in areas they control. However, this bastion of religious freedom in northern Syria is being incrementally destroyed by successive Turkish military interventions. Turkey and Islamist militias on their payroll are now organized in what is known as the Syrian National Army (SNA), also referred to as the Turkish-backed opposition. In January 2018, Turkey launched a major offensive codenamed Operation Olive Branch against the YPG, resulting in the capture of Afrin in March 2018. The entire canton is now occupied by Turkey and a range of militia groups under its support.[43] To what extent Turkey is able to control or influence the actions of these groups is a matter of some disagreement.

What is not in dispute, however, is that the Turkish-led intervention and occupation of Afrin has had a devastating impact on the native population, especially minorities. An estimated 90 percent of the Yezidi population of Afrin have been driven from their homes—either fleeing the area in advance of the oncoming militias, or forcibly evicted by armed gangs once they arrived. All Yezidi villages in Afrin, and those Yezidis who remain, now live under Turkish occupation. This includes the 19 sacred Yezidi shrines in the canton, many of which have been defaced or looted. The Center for the Yezidi Association in Afrin was also attacked and defaced. Yezidi cemeteries in Afrin have been desecrated.

Yezidi Shrines and Cultural Sites in Afrin that Have Been Desecrated or Destroyed since the Turkish "Olive Branch" Operation in 2018

Sheikh Hamid Shrine

Qara Jornah/Huker Shrine

Sheikh Ali Shrine

Sheikh Rukab Shrine

Sheikh Junayd Shrine

Parsa Khatun Shrine

Malak Adi Shrine

Sheikh Barakat Shrine

Sheikh Gharib Shrine

Ezidi Cultural Center

Impact of the Turkish "Peace Spring" Operation on Yezidis

The Turkish intervention in Afrin in Northwest Syria in early 2018 was greenlit by Russia, as the area was protected by Russian aircover since a deconfliction agreement was settled with the United States. US forces had never been stationed in Afrin. For this reason, many residents of the area placed the blame for the ensuing tragedy—including mass displacement of civilians and forced demographic change—on President Putin. However, a similar scenario was then repeated the following year, when the initiation of another Turkish intervention was approved by the United States after a phone call between President Trump and President Erdoğan on October 6, 2019. The so-called Operation Peace Spring led to another wave of mass displacement of civilians and forced demographic change. After Operation Olive Branch launched in January of 2018, virtually all Yezidi villages in Afrin were occupied by Turkey. During Operation Peace Spring, all Yezidi villages in the area of Ras al-Ayn (Serêkaniyê in Kurdish) fell under Turkish occupation as well. By some estimates forced demographic change has happened in more than 10 villages.[44] By other estimates "more than two dozen" Yezidi villages have been deserted.[45]

Operation Peace Spring also had a decimating impact on other religious minorities, especially Assyrians, Armenians, and Syriac Christians. At least 137 Christian families were displaced. Armenian families living in Ras al-Ayn were also evacuated.[46] The Armenian embassy in Damascus provided assistance to between 16 and 30 families. Due to this intervention, the second-deadliest concentration camp of the Armenian genocide in Syria is now under the full control of Turkey and its allied militias. In 1916, an estimated 65,000 Armenians were killed in Ras al-Ayn.

In an effort to end hostilities, Vice President Pence led a delegation to Ankara. The White House statement announcing the October 19 Ceasefire Agreement declared: "Turkey is implementing a Ceasefire. The two governments committed to safeguard religious and ethnic minorities."[47] However, Turkey violated the terms of the Agreement negotiated by Vice President Pence less than one day after it was negotiated.[48] Turkey has continued to violate the Ceasefire Agreement since then, as militias continue to push farther east and west, expanding the areas under its control. There are 33 Assyrian villages in the Khabur region, which are just a few miles away from the area that Turkey and its militias control. Tel Tamer, which is the main population center, is only six miles from the frontlines. Some villages are even closer, however, while others are somewhat farther away.

Box 8.2 **Testimonies of Yezidis Displaced During Turkey's "Peace Spring" Intervention**

Civilians of all ethnic and religious backgrounds were displaced during the Turkish "Peace Spring" intervention in October 2019. Below are testimonies of four Yezidi families I interviewed in Syria in September of 2020.[49] One year after the Turkish invasion, they were still unable to return to their homes (Figure 8.7).

ADEL, YEZIDI FROM THE CITY OF RAS AL-AYN / SERÊKANIYÊ

"On October 9 we fled from Serekaniye. At 3pm we left our house, all our properties behind. I brought my family first to safety then was planning on going back to Serêkaniyê but received a call telling me 'don't go back.' I lost my house, including money I left in my house. I don't have anything."

Figure 8.7 Yezidi family displaced during Turkey's 'Peace Spring' military intervention.

MOTIA, YEZIDI FROM SIKERIYA VILLAGE, EAST OF RAS AL-AYN/SERÊKANIYÊ

"The seeds, the fuel, the generator, all my farm equipment . . . All this was left behind. We had 300 donum (74 acres). We just evacuated. Jeish al Islam is on our land now. We didn't even think to return. Because I am a Kurd and Yezidi. If we return they will kill us. Or they will kidnap us and ask for a ransom. They ask for tens of thousands of dollars. We can't deal with that. As long as one member of the TFSA is there, we can't go back."

YOUSRA, YEZIDI FROM TIL NAIF VILLAGE, WEST OF RAS AL-AYN/SERÊKANIYÊ

"We had a shop in Serêkaniyê (Ras al-Ayn) where we sold sweets and ice cream, and a beautiful house. We fled on October 9, 2019 at 4pm. Now we can't go back because our home is occupied by Hamza Division. We had 700 donum (172 acres), where we grew cotton and wheat. They stole everything: our lands, our cotton, our tractor."

BASIMA, YEZIDI FROM LEZGA VILLAGE, 16KM FROM RAS AL-AYN/SERÊKANIYÊ

"My name is Basima Daoud, I am the wife of Khedr Khabour. We are from the occupied region of Ras al-Ayn. The name of our village is Lezga.

It is a Yezidi village. There are a few other villages around us. Can Tamer, Sikeriya, Tel Saher, all of these are Yezidi villages. And another village is Abba. The Turkish attack took place on October 9, 2019. Wednesday at 4pm in the afternoon the attack started on Tel Khalaf. When we heard the sound of the attack, we were terrified. Two days before that we were in a protest, because we don't want Turkey to attack Ras al-Ayn. We were in the protest tent for three days. I am a housewife. I do not work in the Self Administration. I am a normal wife raising my children. I was going to this protest tent because I don't want Turkey to attack Ras al-Ayn. I don't want them to displace us and our families and destroy our houses, and to take our lands and properties. On Tuesday we were still going to the protest tent. On Wednesday the attack started with planes and airstrikes. It was not an attack with light weapons but with planes. We didn't expect that they would attack our village. Our village is far from Ras al-Ayn, 16km away. We said we would stay in our village and not leave. After six days they arrived to our village, so we had to flee."

Conclusion

Over the past decade, Yezidis in Syria have lived under four different regimes (Table 8.4). When the forces of Bashar al-Assad still controlled the North, Yezidis experienced systemic denial of their identity. In prior decades many Yezidis had been stripped of their Syrian citizenship and had been rendered either as foreigners in their own country (*ajanib*) or entirely stateless (*maktoum*). Those who were allowed to retain their Syrian citizenship were forced to register as Muslims. After Assad's security forces withdrew from northern Syria in mid-2012, Yezidi villages in Afrin and Jazira cantons were protected by the Kurdish-led YPG. When Islamic State militants took over large parts of Syria and established their Caliphate starting in 2014, they were unable to launch a genocidal assault on Yezidi communities as they had done in Sinjar, Iraq, because most Yezidi settlements were guarded by the YPG/SDF. However, ISIS enforced the same extremist policies toward religious minorities. Yezidis who had been captured in Sinjar were bought and sold in slave markets in numerous cities across Syria, just as they were in Iraq.

Once regions of Syria were under YPG/SDF control, the Autonomous Administration passed laws that for the first time recognized the Yezidi religion. No longer required to identify as Muslims, Yezidis could embrace their identity

Table 8.4 **Syrian Yezidis Under Four Regimes**

Regime of Bashar al-Assad	Islamic State	Autonomous Administration of NE Syria	Turkish Occupation
Prior to ~ July 2012 in northern Syria	*ISIS Caliphate controlled ~40% of Syria between 2014 and March 2019*	*The AANES controlled Afrin from July 2012 until January 2018, when Turkey invaded.* *The AANES controlled Ras al-Ayn until October 2019, when Turkey invaded.*	*The Turkish military and their proxies have occupied Afrin since January 2018 and Ras al-Ayn since October 2019.*
Yezidis could not identify as Yezidis on their official ID cards, they were registered as Muslims	ISIS was never able to launch an assault against Yezidis in Syria similar in scale to the genocidal attack on Sinjar, Iraq.	Allowed Yezidis to identify as Yezidis	All 23 Yezidi villages in Afrin are now occupied by Turkey
Could not openly celebrate religious holidays	When ISIS captured Yezidis, they were given two options: convert to Islam or die.	Recognized Yezidi religion as a religion: Article 33 of the Social Contract	All 19 Yezidi shrines in Afrin are under Turkish occupation, many have been looted or defaced
Could not use Yezidi symbols on gravestones	In Syria, ISIS operated slave markets in Al Bab, Al Mayadin, Al Shaddadi, Raqqa, and Tadmur (Palmyra)	Opened a Headquarters of the Yezidi Cultural and Social Association and smaller "Houses of the Yezidis"	All 15 Yezidi villages near Ras al-Ayn are now occupied by Turkey
Could not give Kurdish names to children	Female captives were held at the following military-based holding sites: Al Shaddi, Tel Hamis, Al Mayadin, Dayr Az-zawr, Manbij, Al Bab, Al Tabqah, and Tadmur	Schools could teach about the Yezidi religion	An estimated 90% of the Yezidi population of Afrin has fled since Turkey invaded
Could not name shops with Kurdish names	Female captives were sexually enslaved	Yezidis were promoted to positions within the Self Administration	Yezidis still remaining in Afrin have been frequently kidnapped by Turkish-backed militias. Sometimes militias demand exorbitant sums of money as ransom, and force Yezidis to renounce their religion.
Yezidis were required to take Islamic Studies classes in school, to swear on the Quran in court, and were bound by Islamic Sharia when dealing with marriage, divorce, or inheritance—although they are not Muslims	ISIS atrocities against Yezidis have been recognized as a genocide	Freedom of religion, including freedom to be non-religious and freedom to convert were protected. Between 2015 and April 2019, over 850 Yezidi women were freed from ISIS captivity by the SDF/YPG.	

openly. Yezidis were represented in the Ministry of Religious Affairs and in numerous local councils and committees. For a few years, Yezidis lived free from persecution and annihilation. They experienced recognition and representation, establishing numerous cultural associations. This brief flourishing of Yezidi culture lasted until December 2017 in Afrin and until October 2019 in Ras al-Ayn/ Serêkaniyê, when the Turkish interventions put an end to it.

Virtually all of the gains in religious freedom that were established by the Autonomous Administration have been rolled back in areas now controlled by Turkey. While Turkey claims to only target PKK militants in its interventions in Syria, hundreds of thousands of civilians have also suffered. Furthermore, the cumulative impact of Turkish policies and the actions of Turkish-backed militias has been to change the demography of the areas they control.

Yezidis in Syria who survived the genocide are now subjected to ethnic cleansing. Yezidis living under Turkish occupation have been killed, kidnapped, detained, disappeared, and held for ransom until their families pay exorbitant sums of money to secure their release. Some Yezidis have been subjected to forced religious conversion by militias. They have been forcibly displaced and driven from their homes. Their places of worship have been destroyed, defaced, and looted. Even their cemeteries have been demolished and vandalized. An estimated 90 percent of the Yezidi population of Afrin has fled since the Turkish intervention. Those who remain in Afrin live in a state of fear and are unable to practice their religion openly.

Until now, the government in Damascus has not given any indications that they intend to confer upon Yezidis any of their distinct religious or national rights. It is therefore highly unlikely that restoration of regime control in the area will allow Yezidis to return to their ancestral lands and rebuild their communities. Whether Yezidis will survive as a community in Syria depends to a large extent on conditions in the areas controlled by the Autonomous Administration, and whether Turkey will create conditions in Turkish-held areas that allow Yezidis who fled during their interventions, to return to their homes and live free of persecution.

The Inconclusiveness of Quasi-States

In defiance of the Islamic State, Assad, and Erdoğan, and in a landscape devastated by a decade of war, Kurds and their Arab and Christian allies carved out a statelet to govern their semi-autonomous region. Set up in bombed-out buildings and IDP camps, they embarked upon a radical experiment in self-governance that does more to empower women and minorities than any other region of Syria.

Officials of the statelet claim they are not separatists. In contrast to the Kurdistan Region of Iraq, which held a referendum on independence from Baghdad in 2017, the Autonomous Administration of North and East Syria maintains their commitment to the territorial integrity of Syria. Instead of toppling Bashar al-Assad, they have worked to obtain and then fiercely defend their autonomy from Assad. As the fight against ISIS wore on, and at the behest of the US-led Global Coalition, the SDF expanded far beyond the Kurdish heartland known as Rojava, gaining control of Arab-majority regions. By the time the ISIS Caliphate was defeated in March 2019, they controlled one-third of Syria and two-thirds of its resources.[1]

I trace the genealogy of this social experiment to the Republic of Mount Ararat, where a self-governing entity was proclaimed in 1927 based on solidarity between Kurds and Armenian genocide survivors. Similar to the Republic of Ararat, the Autonomous Administration is founded on the idea of equality between people of different religious and ethnic backgrounds—and on the desire to secure their continued existence, against all odds.

Comparing Mount Ararat 1926–1932 and the Autonomous Administration since 2012

To explain the origins of Syrian Kurdish autonomy proclaimed in three noncontiguous enclaves in 2012, analysts have often begun with the 2004

Statelet of Survivors. Amy Austin Holmes, Oxford University Press. © Oxford University Press 2024.
DOI: 10.1093/oso/9780197621035.003.0009

uprising in Qamishli, or the founding of the PKK in the 1970s. By contrast, I have suggested that a deeper understanding of the experiment in self-rule necessitates a wider historical and geographical lens. In Chapter 2 of this book, I piece together fragments of what we know transpired on the Mountain of Ararat in eastern Anatolia: Kurds and Armenians forged an alliance, fought shoulder-to-shoulder, and formed an organization that boasted a wide array of supporters, including Kurds from all parts of Kurdistan, Yezidis, Assyrians, defected Turkish army officers, and deposed members of the Ottoman dynasty. While both semi-autonomous regions were animated by desires for self-rule, to suggest that either the Mount Ararat revolt or the Rojava Revolution were purely an outgrowth of Kurdish nationalism is to fundamentally misunderstand the historical reality.

Although I have strived to piece together shards of this forgotten history, our knowledge of the Ararat rebellion is still fragmentary. I hope this book will spur on further research, both in the archives and in the field. Despite gaps in our knowledge, I suggest that there are numerous parallels between the Mount Ararat Republic in eastern Turkey and the Autonomous Administration of North and East Syria worth highlighting.

First, many of the Kurdish, Armenian, and Assyrian residents of northern Syria are the actual descendants of those whose ancestors once inhabited the Armenian Highlands and Kurdish regions north of the Syrian-Turkish border. Whether they were forcibly deported or fled persecution, their identities—until today—are fundamentally shaped by their memories of the past. Armenians in Hasakah and Qamishli recited to me how their families had been deported from Diyarbakir, Mardin, Erzurum, Van, and other regions of Turkey a century earlier, as if it was yesterday. They knew the time and place where Kurdish and Arab families took them in, and why their names were changed to hide their identities from Ottoman soldiers. Kurds described how their ancestors who rose up during the Sheikh Said rebellion in 1925, fled across the border into exile. The leaders of the rebellion who did not manage to escape were buried in unmarked graves. Assyrians recounted stories of how their families once lived in an ancient village named Azakh near Midyat, first attested to in the Assyrian Age, and how they took in Armenians fleeing persecution in 1915. For three months, the small village put up a mighty resistance against attacks by Ottoman Turkish soldiers and Kurdish auxiliaries by building fortifications and breaking down the walls between houses. In 1937, the village was renamed by Turkish authorities, from Azakh to İdil. The exodus of the Syriac-speaking population continues until today.

Second, both the Mount Ararat Republic and the Autonomous Administration were created in direct response to mass killings: the Armenian genocide in 1915 and the genocide against Yezidis and Christians in 2014 committed by the Islamic State, as well as the myriad atrocities of the Assad regime that continue until now.

Many of the inhabitants of northern Syria refer to themselves as the descendants of survivors. The creation of the semi-autonomous region in northern Syria has allowed the inhabitants to begin the process of coming to terms with their history and openly commemorate past atrocities in ways that were not possible under the Assad regime. In 2019, on the 104th anniversary of the Armenian-Assyrian genocide, a monument was erected in Qamishli commemorating the Seyfo massacre. The sign is in four languages, Aramaic, Arabic, Kurdish, and English, and says: "The denial of Seyfo is a participation in this crime." Furthermore, many communities across the region have formed local councils as part of their new institutions of self-government. In early 2020, the Armenian Social Council was formed in Al-Hasakah, which provides Armenian language and history classes. The Council is also conducting a census that involves finding and identifying both Christian and Muslim Armenians, or those individuals whose ancestors converted to Islam in the aftermath of the genocide. In so doing, the Council is hoping to document the true size of the Armenian community in Northeast Syria. It is also breaking a significant social taboo by allowing "hidden Armenians" to begin to identify openly as Armenian for the first time.

Third, in contrast to other episodes of rebellion or state-building attempts that were outgrowths of more narrowly defined Kurdish nationalism, both the Mount Ararat Republic and the Autonomous Administration came about due to intraethnic and intrareligious cooperation. The Mount Ararat revolt was the result of an official treaty of cooperation between Kurds and Armenians who formed the Xoybûn-Dashnak alliance—just as Rojava came about due to cooperation between Kurds, Arabs, Armenians, and Syriac-Assyrian Christians. In addition to working to overcome major tensions between Kurds and Armenians in the aftermath of the 1915 genocide, the Xoybûn-Dashnak alliance also had to hold together a large coalition of people from various class backgrounds: urban intellectuals as well as tribal leaders and aghas from rural areas. The Autonomous Administration has faced similar challenges: overcoming distrust between ethnoreligious communities in the wake of atrocities committed by both the Assad regime and the Islamic State, as well as gaping divides between urban and rural areas.

Fourth, from a pan-Kurdish perspective that incorporates all four regions belonging to an imagined Greater Kurdistan, both Ararat and Rojava represent the centers of gravity of movements of their day. And in both cases, these rebellions were launched after a significant ideological shift within the movements. Ararat happened after Kurds abandoned the religious slogans used during the Sheikh Said rebellion in 1925 and turned toward secularism. The Rojava Revolution unfurled after Kurds abandoned the goal of creating a Kurdish state.

Fifth, women played a key role during both periods—and were also subjected to severe repression because of it. Women were executed by a firing squad—even after Turkish officials declared that the revolt on Ararat had been crushed. Besra, the wife of military commander Ferzende Bey, was kept under surveillance in Persia until 1942, for more than a decade after the revolt was crushed and after her husband had died in the Ghasr prison in Tehran. Women in the YPJ have been brutally murdered and their bodies mutilated when they were captured by ISIS. Hevrin Khalaf, a civilian Kurdish politician and important leader in the Autonomous Administration, was brutally assassinated by militias during the Turkish Peace Spring operation in October 2019.

Sixth, precisely because Mount Ararat was the center of gravity at the time, it became a center of liberation not only from the Kemalist authorities in Ankara, but also from the Bolsheviks who had dissolved the First Armenian Republic, and from the authorities in Tehran who allowed the Turkish military to pursue the rebels inside Persia, until they were annihilated. Because the insurgents on Mount Ararat defied all of these states, they united their enemies—and fell victim to their own success. Not unlike Mount Ararat, the Autonomous Administration of North and East Syria is similarly surrounded by hostile entities: Turkey to the north, the Russian and Iranian-backed Assad regime to the south, and Islamic State sleeper cells living in their midst. Will the enemies of the Autonomous Administration unite against them? Will the experiment in self-rule ultimately fail, because it succeeded? Only time will tell.

Finally, in both cases Turkey has engaged in cross-border military operations in order to crush these attempts to create autonomous regions, resulting in an expansion of Turkish territorial control, while also restricting access to the occupied areas. After crushing the rebellion in 1930 on the Turkish side of the border, the Turkish military pursued Kurds inside Persia. The insurgency was only defeated after the governments in Ankara and Tehran agreed to renegotiate their national borders in 1932. After the Turkish military occupied a region inside Persia known as Little Mount Ararat, Reza Shah agreed to cede it to Turkey, in return for receiving a narrow strip of land near Kotur and Bazirgan. Since 2016, the Turkish military and its proxies have launched multiple cross-border operations into Syria, pursuing not only Kurds but also Arab and Christian members of the SDF. As a result, Turkey now occupies almost 10 percent of Syrian territory.

However, there is one critical difference between the two episodes of self-rule. While the insurgents on Mount Ararat actually declared a republic and attempted to separate from Turkey, the Autonomous Administration does not aim for secession, but has remained committed to the territorial integrity of both Turkey and Syria. At times, new nation-states have been formed in the wake of mass atrocities or civil wars: the First Republic of Armenia after the genocide, Israel after the Holocaust, South Sudan after Darfur and the Sudanese civil wars. By contrast, the officials of the Autonomous Administration claim they want to implement their project in all of Syria—not separate from it. This is both due to their ideology inspired by Öcalan, who officially renounced separatism, but also because of the reality that the majority of the inhabitants of North and East Syria under SDF control are now Arabs, in addition to Syriac-Assyrian, Armenian, Turkmen, Circassian, and Yezidi minorities.

As one of the most diverse regions of Syria with an unflinching commitment to gender equality, officials of the Autonomous Administration argue they could act as a democratizing force for the rest of the country. The transformation of Raqqa and Manbij—where women were sold in slave markets a short time ago—would seem to bear out their claims. Under the guidance of the Autonomous Administration, these cities are now co-governed by women. Some residents of Idlib hope their region will be next. The Green Idlib Council was set up by people who were forced to flee from Idlib, and now live as IDPs in Raqqa. Hopeful that they will one day be able to return to Idlib and set up structures similar to the Autonomous Administration, the council functions as a kind of municipal government-in-exile.

Herein lies a contradiction, but also the very secret to their success. In order to survive and manage the territory under SDF control, state-like structures were created—despite their ideology that rejects statehood. Schools run by the Autonomous Administration began to teach a new curriculum while the Baathist propaganda was dropped. The Yezidi religion was recognized as a distinct religion for the first time in the history of modern Syria. New laws were promulgated outlawing polygamy and child marriage, while a gender quota was implemented, dramatically increasing women's participation in local governance. An economic program was launched with the intention of developing the Northeast of Syria, which the Assad regime had kept in a state of perpetual underdevelopment, although the region boasts fertile farmland and oil resources. Revenue was raised in the form of taxes or fees to fund the institutions of the statelet. New security forces were created known as Asayîş in Kurdish and Sutoro in Aramaic that act as local police forces. The YPG and YPJ developed into the multiethnic, multireligious Syrian Democratic Forces, composed of young men and women, who went on to defeat the most horrific terrorist organization in modern history. When the Caliphate was defeated in 2019, the SDF had to immediately transition from fighting ISIS to detaining tens of thousands of ISIS militants and their families. Lacking adequate resources, and perhaps assuming foreign ISIS fighters would only be in their custody temporarily, the SDF set up makeshift camps to house families affiliated with ISIS. Schools and other buildings were requisitioned into detention facilities for Daesh militants. Courts were established to put them on trial.

In January 2022, ISIS detainees in the Al Sina'a prison in Hasakah launched an attack in a brazen attempt to free up to 4,000 prisoners. Fighting lasted for nine days before the SDF regained control of the situation. In addition to underscoring that the Islamic State remained a real threat, the incident also exposed the dire conditions of the detention facilities. Children were among the detainees. CENTCOM released a statement saying that "Daesh affiliates were provided medical treatment for any injuries sustained and they were treated humanely during their transfer to the new detention facility."[2] National Security Adviser Jake Sullivan praised the "bravery and determination" of the SDF. UNICEF Director Henrietta Fore issued a statement calling for the estimated 850 children detained to be evacuated to safety and imploring member states to repatriate their children who are their citizens or born to their nationals.[3] A statement issued by the SDF in response criticized the inaction of the international community:

> Our forces have called on the international community and humanitarian organizations to provide adequate support for the Autonomous Administration of north and eastern Syria to construct and equip rehabilitation centers for Syrian and foreign children until they return home, but these calls fell on deaf ears. [...]
>
> The United Nations and the majority of Member States, primarily those with nationals associated with the terrorist organization of ISIS, ignored the case of their detained nationals in the north and eastern Syria and failed to meet their moral and legal obligations, leaving the Autonomous Administration of north and eastern Syria to bear the burden of the legacy of ISIS terrorism over the years beyond its limited means and capacity."[4]

The prison break happened against the backdrop of the worst drought in 70 years, a Syrian economy in free fall, and the closure of the border to the Kurdistan Region of Iraq for over a month—their only lifeline to the outside world—as tensions between the two semi-autonomous regions stalled the intra-Kurdish dialogue. For about a week, the Hasakah prison break made international headlines, reminding the world of the dire conditions in the detention facilities and the urgent need for countries to repatriate their citizens. There was reason to hope that the international community may pay attention long enough to do something. Then Russia invaded Ukraine, and Northeast Syria dropped out of the headlines again.

The Empowerment of Women—Not Token Inclusion

In Chapter 4, I outlined how the Islamic State governed by creating a war of women against women. The Autonomous Administration governs by reversing this logic: by building solidarity and inclusion. In Chapter 5 I explain how they accomplished this feat. Syrian Kurdish women built off the success of previous internal struggles within the PKK. Beginning in the late 1980s, women such as Sakine Cansiz, who was born in Dersim and whose grandmother was Armenian, played a leading role in the recruitment and education of women in the movement, despite opposition from some of their own male comrades, including initially Öcalan himself. Although Öcalan's decision to support women could have easily been a cynical move to solidify his own power, the result was that the most powerful figure within the PKK became a champion of the autonomous women's movement. His capture in 1999, however, once again led to internecine power struggles that threatened the gains women had made within the PKK. The defection of over a thousand PKK members in the early 2000s, including a faction around Osman Öcalan, signified that the "feminist" wing within the PKK had won.

By the time the Syrian conflict erupted in 2011, Kurdish women in the orbit of the YPJ and PYD were already battle-hardened from these internal struggles against men in their own communities. Ironically, the brutality with which ISIS governed—and their enslavement of women in particular—may have made notions of gender equality all the more appealing to a population with no prior exposure to Öcalanist ideology. Despite a lack of resources and existential security threats, administration officials continue to cling to their ideals of gender equality. The result is a governance system more inclusive than any other region of Syria.

Critics may say that creating a governance system that represents an improvement over the Assad regime is a low bar. But their system also surpasses even the United Nation's benchmarks on gender equality. In October 2000, the UN Security Council adopted Resolution 1325, urging "all actors to increase the participation of women" and set a target of 20 percent female peacekeepers. Yet fifteen years later, only three percent of UN military peacekeepers were women. That same year, an estimated 30 percent of SDF fighters were women. The Autonomous Administration has also promoted women into the highest-ranking positions of their civilian institutions, taken unprecedented steps to protect women from domestic violence, outlawed child marriage and polygamy, and established a women's economy that aims to make women financially independent of men.

All this was possible precisely because they created a statelet.

Skeptics have claimed that these reforms go too far, and risk alienating conservative members of society. In fact, including women in governance and security forces has been shown to benefit entire societies. Empowering women may be one way to escape what scholars refer to as the "conflict trap," or the likelihood that a country will relapse into civil war. An analysis of 58 postconflict states between 1980 and 2003 found that risk of conflict relapse was near zero when women made up at least 35 percent of the legislature.[5] While the Assad regime has no legislated quotas for women, in Northeast Syria, all representational bodies have a quota of at least 40 percent women.

Due to the overwhelming evidence that shows that women's participation in conflict prevention and resolution advances both human security and national security, nearly 90 countries have now adopted National Action Plans (NAP). Syria is not one of them. However, the Autonomous Administration has effectively done more to achieve gender parity—with fewer resources and in less time—than most countries that have adopted NAPs on Women. Northeast Syria should be commended for having surpassed the UN's own benchmarks in its landmark resolution on Women, Peace, and Security. Instead, they are excluded from the UN-led talks over the future of Syria.

Guaranteeing Religious Freedom for Yezidis and All Minorities

Despite the ravages of war and a dire economic crisis, the semi-autonomous region in the Northeast has not only created the most gender-egalitarian local governance system in all of Syria, but also has the best religious freedom conditions. For the first time in the history of modern Syria, the Yezidi faith is recognized as a separate and distinct religion. Ethnic and religious minorities are represented at all levels in the Autonomous Administration. Freedom of religion and nondiscrimination on the basis of religion is guaranteed in the social contract governing North and East Syria.

Chapter 8 provides a historical overview of the Yezidi community, arguably one of Syria's most endangered minorities. In prior decades, hundreds of thousands of Kurds and Yezidis were rendered stateless (*maktoum*) or as foreigners (*ajanib*), although they were born and raised in Syria, due to discriminatory legal decrees. Yezidis were forced to attend courses on Islam in public schools, and to abide by Sharia law in the courts, although they are not Muslims. In Afrin, Ras al-Ayn, and other Turkish-occupied areas of Syria, Yezidis, Christians, and Kurds have experienced mass displacement and the seizure of their properties by Turkish-backed militias.

Yezidis in Syria who survived the genocide continue to face persecution. Yezidis living in Turkish-occupied Afrin have been kidnapped, detained, disappeared, and held for ransom by Turkish-backed Syrian proxies until their families paid exorbitant sums of money to secure their release. Some Yezidis have been subjected to forced religious conversion by militias. They have been forcibly displaced and driven from their homes. Their holy shrines have been destroyed, defaced, and looted. Even their cemeteries have been demolished and vandalized. The UN has warned that these abuses challenge the precarious existence of the Yezidi community.

Until now, the government in Damascus has not given any indications that they intend to confer upon Yezidis any of their distinct religious or national rights. It is therefore highly unlikely that restoration of regime control in the area will allow Yezidis to return to their ancestral lands and rebuild their communities. Whether Yezidis will survive as a community in Syria, concentrated as they are mainly in the north, depends to a large extent on the survival of the Autonomous Administration.

Education

The Autonomous Administration has created their own education system that has introduced Kurdish and Aramaic language instruction, as outlined in Chapter 7. These educational policies are in line with the recommendation by the United Nations that children should receive instruction in their native language. The Social Council of Hasakeh offers Armenian language courses to all Armenians, including Muslims whose ancestors converted to Islam after the genocide. Universities were also established by the AANES. In October 2021, Kobani University graduated its first class of students after a four-year period of study. However, the schools and universities run by the Autonomous Administration suffer from lack of recognition of their degrees. Schools run by the regime still promote pan-Arabism and loyalty to Bashar al-Assad. In schools in Afrin, where Kurdish language instruction was introduced after the regime withdrew, the Kurdish curriculum has been removed. Teachers who previously taught Kurmanci have been arrested.

The Judiciary and Justice after ISIS

The Autonomous Administration has created their own judicial system in which decisions are made by a council of three to five judges, rather than by a single person as in government-controlled Syria. This is intended to prevent arbitrary or politicized decisions. Furthermore, many women trained as lawyers have been promoted as judges, ensuring that women have a say in achieving justice post-ISIS. The death penalty has been abolished, and lawyers say that they strive to be transparent by informing the family members of detainees of their whereabouts. In regime-held areas of Syria, disappearances happen frequently, the death penalty is still enforced, and torture is rampant. The new judicial system suffers, however, from a lack of trained judges. Many of those who are now working as judges previously served as lawyers and underwent a relatively short training to become a judge. By contrast, in regime areas, judges are required to go through a period of lengthy training. The Autonomous Administration, however, faces a huge caseload of tens of thousands of ISIS detainees, in addition to other legal disputes. While the short training period has created a new crop of judges who may lack the depth of legal knowledge of their counterparts, requiring a longer training period would have delayed resolution of these cases even further and exacerbated an already untenable situation.

By the time the Caliphate was defeated in 2019, over 11,000 young women and men in the SDF had been killed in battle. Exhausted from years of war, the SDF were then burdened with another enormous task: responsibility for detaining over 60,000 people suspected of being affiliated with ISIS. The vast majority were women and children of ISIS fighters. Several thousand of the detainees were neither Syrian nor Iraqi citizens, but third-country foreign nationals.

ISIS had a global following. People came from more than 50 different countries around the world to join the Islamic State in Syria. And yet many countries have abdicated responsibility for their own citizens. The slave markets and black sites run by ISIS have been shut down. But the ideology persists. Because countries are refusing to take back their own citizens, a whole generation of children may grow up inside Al Hol and other detention facilities, essentially a mini-Caliphate, where they are exposed to ISIS ideology on a daily basis.

Overwhelmed with the huge burden of feeding and housing so many detainees, and fearful that grievances would emerge, the Autonomous Administration began to release Syrian citizens from Al Hol as part of a reconciliation process beginning in the fall of 2020. However, an estimated 12,000 detainees are from parts of Syria controlled by the regime. Most of them have reportedly refused to leave the camp and return home, either due to fear of retribution or simply because of the dire conditions in government-controlled parts of Syria. Hence they remain in SDF custody.

The AANES has begun programs aimed at the deradicalization and reintegration of ISIS detainees. Because many of the detainees are women, this work is mainly being done by women-run NGOs, such as the Zenobiya Women's Association in Raqqa, Manbij, and Deir Ezzor. However, much of their work is done on a volunteer basis without adequate support. Despite their commitment to women's equality, the AANES is largely relying on the unpaid labor of women to carry out a non-trivial task: the deradicalization of ISIS supporters. At the time of writing, neither the regime nor the Turkish-held areas have programs aimed at deradicalization of former ISIS or Al Qaeda members.

The Syrian Democratic Forces

Originating as an outlawed Kurdish militia, the YPG evolved within the span of just a few years into the second-largest armed force in all of Syria—and the only one that does not discriminate on the basis of gender, religion, or ethnicity. The SDF is now arguably more representative of Syrian society than the Syrian Arab Army of Bashar al-Assad. My survey data highlighted that Arabs from virtually every tribe in Northeast Syria have family members who joined the SDF. I also found numerous Arab men and women who voluntarily—and at great risk to themselves—joined the SDF from areas the SDF had never controlled such as Damascus, Homs, Idlib, Aleppo and other cities. When the SDF's policy of non-discrimination is seen in the context of the transformation of the PYD-aligned movement from one that promoted Kurdish nationalism and separatism to one that promotes co-existence and decentralization within the boundaries of the Syrian state, it should come as no surprise that this project would appeal to non-Kurds, or at least as a better alternative to rule by Assad or extremists.[6]

That said, some residents of Northeast Syria remain critical of conscription, which is currently limited to one year and is not yet implemented in several Arab-majority regions. There is no conscription for women, but women are allowed to enlist and even serve as high-ranking commanders. The liberation of Raqqa was led by female YPJ commanders such as Rojda Felat and Nowruz Ahmed.

The militias that operate in the Turkish-occupied regions of Syria have changed names frequently, and are currently known as the Syrian National Army (SNA). The SNA is characterized by factionalism and frequent in-fighting. One of the Turkish-backed factions, Ahrar al-Sharqiya, was sanctioned by the US Treasury in July 2021 for "abductions, torture, and seizures of private property from civilians" in addition to incorporating former ISIS members into their ranks.[7]

Governance Is Key to the Enduring Defeat of ISIS

The SDF did not just defeat ISIS and protect Yezidis from genocide, they also incorporated Yezidis into their local government. Not content to merely end the practice of enslavement and objectification of women, they catapulted women into the highest positions of power. All of this was possible precisely because they created a statelet. One can hope that this should help ensure that ISIS does not return, because those people who arguably suffered the most under ISIS are now in positions of power. The inclusion of women and underrepresented minorities into the Autonomous Administration also means that their local government is now far more representative of Syrian society than pre-2011, when many officials in the Northeast were Baath Party members appointed from outside the region. In order for the AANES to develop into a truly democratic alternative to the Assad regime, free and fair elections would need to be held at all levels of governance in the semi-autonomous region. At the time of writing, elections have been postponed. The usual democracy promoters have been rather quiet about the need for elections in the AANES. Whether they have given up on the idea of democracy taking root in Syria, or are simply afraid of being seen as supporting a statelet, is too early to tell.

Will Everything Be Lost? Ongoing Threats from Erdoğan and Assad

As this book goes to press, Turkish officials have made renewed threats to launch yet another intervention into Syria targeting the SDF, while the Russian and Iranian-backed Assad regime continues to try and retake SDF-held territory in the northeast. Even if a Turkish ground invasion can be prevented, Ankara's drone campaign could achieve the same goal: the destruction of the Autonomous Administration.

In November 2022, a Turkish drone for the first time hit inside a joint US-SDF base in northern Syria. The Pentagon released a statement saying the drone strike put American troops at risk and called for "immediate de-escalation." While this led to high-level talks between Secretary Blinken and his Turkish counterpart Foreign Minister Çavuşoğlu, and between Defense Secretary Austin and the Turkish Minister of Defense Akar, Turkey's deadly drone campaign continued. Even the devastating earthquakes in Turkey and Syria in February 2023 that killed over 50,000 people did not lead to a pause in Ankara's operations. In the first six weeks of 2023, Turkey carried out over eight drone strikes, killing three civilians, and wounding 26.[8] The aerial bombardment restricts the freedom of movement of General Mazloum and other leaders of the Autonomous Administration. Presumably it's not easy to run a statelet the size of Croatia if the leaders can't leave their bases, for fear of assassination.

Although the conflict has become more dangerous and more of a direct threat to US personnel and interests than ever before, there is no indication that this has led to a rethinking of US policies. If the United States and international community prove unable or unwilling to find a solution, the region may be destroyed by Turkey or retaken by the Assad regime. The statelet—and all the attendant progress it has achieved—may be erased.

Turkey justified its 2018 and 2019 interventions in Syria by claiming the presence of the SDF/YPG along its southern border constituted a grave threat. But my analysis of data from the Armed Conflict Location and Event Data Project (ACLED) indicates the opposite was closer to the truth. Between January 2017 and August 2020, Turkey and Turkish-backed forces carried out 3,319 attacks against the SDF/YPG or civilians. By contrast, the SDF/YPG carried out 22 cross-border attacks into Turkey, the majority of which happened in response to Turkey's 2019 intervention.[9] Turkish officials claim their attacks against the SDF/YPG were tit-for-tat. But that is mathematically impossible.

Statements by two senior American officials, Ambassador Bill Roebuck and National Security Advisor Brett McGurk, have confirmed that the SDF posed no real threat to Turkey. Soon after Operation Peace Spring, Ambassador Roebuck wrote a scathing internal which was leaked to the press and published in *The New York Times*:

> In all the time I was in the northeast, since January 2018, I heard—and sometimes delivered—points that articulated appreciation about Turkey's legitimate security concerns regarding the border with Syria. And yet that border stayed quiet on the Syrian side the entire time—over 20 months—I have been in Syria, until Turkey violated it with its October Peace Spring military operation. When quietly called on this discrepancy, a senior U.S. official explained to me, "well, it's a perceived threat (because of ideological and other affiliations between the PYD and the PKK) that Turkey feels, so we have to take it seriously." But eventually the talking point became reality. We began speaking as if there really were attacks across the border into Turkey, causing real casualties and damage. But these were chimerical—strongly felt perhaps—but palpable only as fears and concerns, not on the ground.[10]

Brett McGurk confirmed in public what Ambassador Roebuck conveyed in private. In an interview with *The New Yorker*, McGurk said "…we have worked on the border to make sure no weapons or fighters crossed that border, and I think we can demonstrate that there were no threats to Turkey across the border."[11]

Turkish officials equate the SDF/YPG in Syria with the PKK in Turkey and Iraq, citing the fact that the SDF grew out of the Kurdish YPG and is headed by General Mazloum, a former PKK cadre. However, my survey data illustrates how the SDF evolved into a multiethnic force, in which Arabs from every tribe are represented, and also includes important units of Syriacs, Assyrians, and Armenians, while the PKK has fought for Kurdish rights, and its fighters are almost exclusively Kurds.

If the SDF does not represent a genuine security threat to Turkey, how can we explain the large-scale Turkish interventions in Syria? For almost a decade, Kurds and their allies in the Autonomous Administration have governed Northeast Syria with far-reaching autonomy from Damascus, and engineered a government with greater rights for women and minorities than the central government offers. The Autonomous Administration represents a political alternative to the Assad regime—and to other authoritarian governments in the region. It is presumably for this reason that the prospect of even limited Kurdish autonomy in Syria is politically threatening to Erdoğan's AKP and his alliance with the far-right MHP, which is in line with their practice of imprisoning elected Kurdish officials inside Turkey and replacing them with government "trustees."

Since the beginning of the conflict in 2011, the leaders of the Autonomous Administration have displayed a willingness to compromise and have on more than one occasion corrected previous wrongdoings. In June 2019, General Mazloum signed a UN Agreement committing to end the use and recruitment of children. In December 2019, Administration officials announced that the opposition Kurdish National Council (ENKS) would be allowed to open offices and carry out political activities without requiring a permit. At the same time, all legal cases against ENKS members were dropped. While the AANES claimed there were no ENKS members detained as political prisoners, the ENKS submitted a list of ten people who they claimed were imprisoned. A committee was created to investigate the matter. And as described earlier, the word "Rojava" was removed from the name of the local government after being criticized by non-Kurds. In other words, the AANES has at least taken steps to accommodate its critics. While still wholly imperfect, Administration officials have displayed a willingness to adapt, to compromise, and to admit when they were wrong. The same cannot really be said for many of the leaders in the international community, who continue to cling to the same policies that have failed to resolve the Syrian conflict.

Despite having state-like structures, the Autonomous Administration is not separatist—for both ideological and practical reasons. Rather, it is the international community that treats them as such. By excluding them from the talks in Geneva over the future of Syria, the international community is treating Northeast Syria as if it was not part of Syria, and hence essentially fueling the very separatist tendencies they renounce. There is the possibility that this will become a self-fulfilling prophecy, and that the region will emerge as semi-independent or a state-within-a-state. Or perhaps everything will be lost. The Assad regime may eventually reassert control over all of the country. Or perhaps Turkey will launch another intervention, destroying the Autonomous Administration and everything they created, just as the Republic of Ararat was crushed. The future is uncertain.

For now, with adversaries on all sides, the Autonomous Administration persists. The peoples of this region descend from genocide, defeated ISIS, and have refused to surrender to the Russian and Iranian-backed Assad regime. They created a statelet of survivors.

Appendix

CAST OF CHARACTERS

Chapter 2

Elizabeth Gawriya: An Assyrian official in the AANES.

Mustafa Kemal Atatürk: The founder and leader of the modern Turkish Republic.

Sharif Pasha: Kurdish representative at the 1919 Paris Peace Conference.

Boghos Nubar Pasha: Armenian representative at the 1919 Paris Peace Conference.

Vahan Papazian: A leader of the Armenian Revolutionary Federation in the 1920s.

Sureyya Bedirkhan: A member of the Executive Committee of Xoybûn.

Jeladet Bedirkhan: A member of the Executive Committee of Xoybûn.

Kamuran Bedirkhan: A member of the Executive Committee of Xoybûn.

Memduh Selim Bey: A member of the Executive Committee of Xoybûn.

Shahin Bey: A member of the Executive Committee of Xoybûn.

Ihsan Nouri: Appointed the General Commander of the Kurdish Forces by Xoybûn during the Ararat Rebellion.

Bro Heski Tello: Appointed the Head of the Civilian Administration by Xoybûn during the Ararat Rebellion.

Ziylan Bey (Ardashes Mouradian): An Armenian rebel leader representing the Armenian Revolutionary Federation during the Ararat Rebellion.

Vali Bey (Vahan Kalusdian): An Armenian rebel leader who had served in the army of the Republic of Armenia who joined the Ararat Rebellion.

Chapter 3

Abdullah Öcalan: The founder and leader of the PKK. He was captured in 1999 and has been imprisoned on Imrali Island in Turkey ever since. His political philosophy of democratic confederalism is the ideological inspiration for the political system of North and East Syria.

Aziz Arab: The PKK's first Arab martyr. He was killed in 1986, two years after the PKK began armed struggle. He has been commemorated by the SDF and AANES across Arab-majority regions of North and East Syria.

Gulay Selmo: A Syrian Kurdish woman from Afrin and a member of Yekitiya Star in Sheikh Maqsoud in Aleppo. She was killed in an attack by Syrian regime forces that resulted in Kurdish forces pushing regime personnel out of Sheikh Maqsoud altogether in March 2012.

Hafez al-Assad: The President of Syria from 1971 until his death in 2000.

Jacob Mirza: A member of the leadership of the Bethnahrain National Council. He has been a part of the Dowronoyo movement since 1994.

Kino Gabriel: Served as official spokesperson for the SDF. A Syriac Christian, he is also a member of the General Command of the Syriac Military Council.

Lorin Efrin: A YPJ commander from Afrin who was active in armed Kurdish efforts in Syria since the establishment of the YXG in 2011.

Mazlum Abdi: The Commander-in-Chief of the Syrian Democratic Forces. A Kurd from Kobani, he joined the PKK in 1990, where he eventually became a high-ranking commander. At the start of the Syrian war in 2011, he returned to his home country to lead the fight against ISIS.

Osman Öcalan: The brother of Abdullah Öcalan and a founding member of the PKK. He left the organization in the early 2000s after disputes over its structure and political goals.

Polat Can: A commander and founding member of the YPG. He was active in the PKK before the Syrian conflict. He has also published several books.

Sanharib Barsoom: The leader of the Syriac Union Party, a left-wing Syriac-Assyrian party which is allied with the PYD and whose members serve in leadership posts in the AANES.

Xebat Derik: A founder of the YPG and a former PKK commander. He was killed in 2012.

Haro Mikhail: The president of the Bethnahrin National Council. He was cited as an ideological inspiration by HSNB fighters.

Bandar al-Humaydi: The leader of the Al-Sanadid Forces, an SDF-aligned Arab tribal militia. He is the son of Sheikh Humaydi Daham al-Hadi.

Humaydi Daham al-Hadi: The leader of the Shammar tribe, a prominent Arab tribal confederation with members across Syria and Iraq.

Nisrine Abdullah: A founding member of the YXG and YPJ who has served as the group's spokesperson.

Meryem Mihemed: A Kurdish woman from Afrin who was the YPJ's first martyr.

Chapter 4

Samantha Sally: An American woman who joined ISIS along with her husband.

Kayla Mueller: An American humanitarian aid worker who was kidnapped and enslaved by ISIS and killed in an airstrike.

Nadia Murad: A Yezidi survivor of ISIS captivity who won the Nobel Peace Prize in 2018 for her advocacy for Yezidi genocide survivors and survivors of conflict-related sexual violence.

Abu Musab al-Zarqawi: The founder of Al Qaeda in Iraq.

Abu Bakr al-Baghdadi: The leader of ISIS from the declaration of the group's caliphate in 2014 to his death in 2019.

Chapter 5

Sakine Cansiz (Sara): One of the two women who participated in the PKK's 1978 founding conference, and perhaps the most prominent woman in the Kurdish freedom movement until her assassination in 2013. Her nom de guerre, Sara, was her Armenian grandmother's name.

Kesire Yildirim: One of the two women who participated in the PKK's 1978 founding conference. She was married to Abdullah Öcalan at the time, but later divorced him and left the movement.

Leyla Zana: The first Kurdish woman to be elected to the Turkish parliament. She entered politics after the imprisonment of her husband, Diyarbakir mayor Mehdi Zana, in the period around the 1980 military coup.

Zeynep Kinaci (Zilan): One of the PKK's early female martyrs. She carried out a suicide bombing targeting a military parade in Tunceli, Turkey in 1996.

Gulnaz Karatas (Beritan): One of the PKK's early female martyrs. She threw herself from the side of a mountain rather than surrender to Turkish and KDP forces in a clash in 1992.

Hediya Yusuf: A founder of Kongra Star who was imprisoned by the regime for her activities in 2010. She went on to become co-chair of Jazira Canton and co-president of the Democratic Federation of Northern Syria.

Evin Sued: A former math teacher who later served as spokeswoman of Kongra Star.

Ilham Ahmed: A Kurdish woman from Afrin who is currently the President of the Executive Committee of the Syrian Democratic Council.

Layla Moustafa: The co-president of the Raqqa Civil Council.

Hevrin Khalaf: The Secretary-General of the Future Syria Party. She was assassinated by Turkish-backed militias in October 2019.

Ilham Amar: A Kurdish activist against gender-based violence who founded, and still administers, the Qamishli Women's House.

Beheya Murad: An administrator at the Qamishli Women's House.

Chapter 6

Ahmed Youssef: An economist from Afrin who became head of the Autonomous Administration's Economic Ministry in 2014 and the Finance Minister of North and East Syria before 2020.

Armanc Mohamed Ahmed: The director of the Women's Economy in North and East Syria.

Abdel Karim Malek: The head of the Jazira Oil Company in North and East Syria.

Chapter 7

Arshek Baravi: One of the founders of the Kurdish-language education system used in North and East Syria.

Bashar al-Assad: The current President of Syria. He inherited power from his father, Hafez al-Assad, in 2000. His government's violent crackdown on mass protests in 2011 led to the Syrian Civil War.

Kamal Moussa: The co-chair of the Autonomous Administration education authority in Deir Ezzor.

Layla Hassan: An Arab woman from Deir Ezzor and the Co-Chair of the Deir Ezzor Civil Council.

Murray Bookchin: An American anarchist thinker whose political theories were based on principles of ecology and libertarian socialism. He was one of many ideological inspirations for Abdullah Öcalan, who read his works while in prison.

Rawa Romy: The co-chair of the Autonomous Administration education authority in Tabqa.

Shirin Hemo: The co-chair of the Education Committee in Jazira Canton.

Chapter 8

Silêman Cafer: A Yezidi official in the AANES from Afrin, Syria.

Mohamed Talab Hilal: A Syrian army lieutenant who conducted a study that laid the basis for the Syrian government's Arabization projects in Kurdish-majority regions in the country's north.

Osman Sabri: The leader of the Kurdish Democratic Party in Syria, who helped to organize resistance to Arab Belt policies among Yezidi communities in Tirbê Spîyê in 1967.

Comparative Governance in Syria

	Central Government in Damascus	Autonomous Administration of North and East Syria	Turkish Occupied Areas
Military Forces Conscription: length of service and age limits	Mandatory conscription for males between 18 and 42. Term is 18–21 months long. Some deferrals and exceptions; legal consequences for those who do not complete their mandatory service. Legislative Decree No. 18 of 2003 governs military service.[1]	Conscription limited to one year for males between the ages of 18 and 30. Conscription not implemented yet in several Arab-majority regions. No conscription for women, but women allowed to enlist and serve as commanders. Law passed to prevent conscription of minors; unevenly enforced.	No conscription in the Syrian National Army. Members join groups for financial incentives.
Judicial System	Death penalty. Systemic torture. About 13% of judges are female.[2]	No death penalty,[3] maximum sentence of 25 years. Female judges.[4]	Widespread torture and sexual violence.[5] Legal system based on Syrian constitution of 1950.[6]
Post-ISIS Programs on Deradicalization and Reconciliation	No deradicalization.	Attempts at deradicalization for ISIS detainees. Tribal Reconciliation Centers.	No deradicalization; ISIS members accused of abuses integrated into SNA groups.[7]
Public Education System	Arabic language only in public schools.[8] 12 years of basic education (primary and secondary) in total. Overseen by Ministry of Education. Curriculum promotes Baathist ideology and Arab identity.	Revised curriculum for public schools omits Baathist ideology. 12 years of basic education (primary and secondary) in total. Introduction of Kurdish and Aramaic language instruction.[9]	Students can take state exams to attend Turkish universities. Education in Arabic and Turkish.

Welfare State: Economic subsidies/ poverty relief	Subsidies for bread in Damascus and Rif-Dimashq.[10] Declining petrol subsidies.[11]	Subsidies for flour, food, and petrol.	Some economic and social services provided by Turkey, but discrimination in service provision by ethnicity.[12]
Women's Rights	Polygamy and child marriage allowed. Mitigating excuses for honor killings were included in legislation until 2020. Prior to that, men who murdered women and justified it with certain excuses got reduced sentences.[13] A man can forbid his wife from working outside of the home.[14] Personal status governed by religious law, which is often unequal.	Quota for women in all governing bodies from local councils to SDC; co-chair system for leadership.[15] Child marriage prohibited Polygamy prohibited (but not yet uniformly implemented). New civil personal status law,[16] equal inheritance for women. Honor killings considered to be murder. Equal economic rights.	Women subjected to "pervasive climate of fear" of discrimination and sexual and gender-based violence perpetrated by SNA groups that confines many to their homes.[17] Polygamy and child marriage not prohibited
Women's Rights	Polygamy and child marriage allowed. Mitigating excuses for honor killings were included in legislation until 2020. Prior to that, men who murdered women and justified it with certain excuses got reduced sentences.[13] A man can forbid his wife from working outside of the home.[14] Personal status governed by religious law, which is often unequal.	Quota for women in all governing bodies from local councils to SDC; co-chair system for leadership.[15] Child marriage prohibited Polygamy prohibited (but not yet uniformly implemented). New civil personal status law,[16] equal inheritance for women. Honor killings considered to be murder. Equal economic rights.	Women subjected to "pervasive climate of fear" of discrimination and sexual and gender-based violence perpetrated by SNA groups that confines many to their homes.[17] Polygamy and child marriage not prohibited

(continued)

Comparative Governance in Syria (Continued)

	Central Government in Damascus	Autonomous Administration of North and East Syria	Turkish Occupied Areas
Minority Rights (Citizenship Rights, Property Rights, Language Rights, and Religious Freedom for Kurds, Yezidis, Alevis, Christians)	Hundreds of thousands of Kurds and Yezidis were rendered stateless (maktoum) or as foreigners (ajanib) under Hafez al-Assad. Aramaic language instruction only for liturgical purposes. Kurdish language instruction banned. Recent law that demands Syrians abroad have to return to Syria or they forfeit their property to the state. No recognition of Yezidi religion.	Kurds and Yezidis recognized as equal citizens, including those declared stateless by the regime. Religious and ethnic minorities represented in AANES. Additional protection of properties belonging to Christians. AANES passed a law that is supposed to protect abandoned property belonging to Christians. Recognition of Yezidis as a distinct ethnic group and religion. Freedom of religion and nondiscrimination on basis of religion in constitution.[18]	Mass displacement of Kurds, Yezidis, and Christians from Afrin and Ras al Ayn.[19] Arabic and Turkish language used officially; Kurdish and Aramaic not formally prohibited but repressed. SNA abuses "challenging the precarious existence of the Yezidi community as a religious minority" according to UN.[20] Systemic and pervasive violations against non-Muslim communities.[21]
Political System	Hereditary authoritarian regime president-for-life. Regulations to register political parties. No measures to increase representation of women or minorities.	Elections at some, but not all, levels of governing bodies. Dominance of PYD party. Regulations to register political parties. Quotas and co-chair system to increase representation of women[22]; constitutional recognition of ethnic and religious minority representation.[23]	Heavy Turkish influence in appointing and electing local officials.[24] Local councils directly supervised by Turkish Ministry of Interior. Turkish governors exercise oversight in occupied Syrian provinces.[25] No measures to increase representation of women or minorities.

Names of Cities and Towns in Syria in Arabic, Kurmanci, and Aramaic

Arabic	Kurmanci	Syriac
Ras al-Ayn	Serê Kaniyê	Rish'Ayno
Ayn al-Arab	Kobanî	
Al-Qahtaniyah	Tirbê Spîyê	Qabre Hewore
Al-Muabbada	Girkê Legê	Arbaen Bokne
Afrin	Efrîn	Cafrin
Al-Malikiyah	Dêrik	Dayrik
Rumaylan	Rimêlan	Rmilan
Tel Abyad	Girê Spî	Talo Hiworo
Tel Tamer	Girê Xurma	Tell Tamr
Al-Yaarubiya	Tel Koçer	
Al-Qamishli	Qamişlo	Beth Zalin

NOTES

Chapter 1

1. Author interview with Sanharib Barsoom, Head of Syriac Union Party, in June 2019 in Qamishli, Syria.
2. Author interview with Nisrine Abdullah, spokeswoman of the YPJ and cofounder of the YXG, on September 12, 2020 in Syria.
3. Cengiz Çandar, *Turkey's Mission Impossible: War and Peace with the Kurds* (Lanham: Lexington Books, 2020), 103.
4. The title of the internal memo reads "Present at the Catastrophe: Standing by as Turks Cleanse Kurds in Northern Syria and De-Stabilize our D-ISIS Platform in the Northeast." The memo was leaked to *The New York Times*. "Read the Memo by a U.S. Diplomat Criticizing Trump Policy on Syria and Turkey," *The New York Times*, November 7, 2019. https://www.nytimes.com/2019/11/07/us/politics/memo-syria-trump-turkey.html.

Chapter 2

1. This phrase is from a Kurdish oral poem about the Republic of Mount Ararat known as "Ferzende Beg." As is common with oral traditions, there are different versions of this poem. The one cited here was performed by the singer Şakiro who was born in Ağrı (Ararat) in 1936, just a few years after the Ararat revolt was crushed. This poem and its significance is analyzed in great detail in Metin Yüksel's article "On the Borders of the Turkish and Iranian Nation-States: The Story of Ferzende and Besra," *Middle Eastern Studies* 52, no. 4 (2016): 656–676. This particular quote is on page 665.
2. Memorandum, Captain P. Paulet King, Special Service Officer RAF at Mosul, to Air Staff Intelligence, Air Headquarters, Hinaidi, and various offices at Mosul, February 26, 1930, No. I/M/42/B. Translation of a letter from an administrator in Mosul, Ismail Beg al Yezidi, to the Administrative Inspector, Mosul Liwa, February 17, 1930, enclosing the Kurdish leaflet he received from the Khoyboun society. In Anita Burdett, *Records of the Kurds: Territory, Revolt and Nationalism*; 1831–1979; British documentary sources. Vol. 7 (Cambridge: Cambridge Archives Ed, 2015), 627.
3. I will use the terms Khoyboun and Xoybûn interchangeably to refer to the Kurdish-Armenian League, and Dashnak as the common abbreviation for Dashnaksutyun to refer to the Armenian Revolutionary Federation (ARF).
4. Benny Morris and Dror Ze'evi, *The Thirty-Year Genocide: Turkey's Destruction of Its Christian Minorities, 1894–1924* (Cambridge, MA: Harvard University Press, 2019).
5. Janet Klein, *The Margins of Empire: Kurdish Militias in the Ottoman Tribal Zone* (Stanford: Stanford University Press, 2011), 52.

6. Cited in Jordi Tejel, "The Last Ottoman Rogues: The Kurdish-Armenian Alliance in Syria and the New State System in the Interwar Middle East," in *Age of Rogues: Rebels, Revolutionaries, and Racketeers at the Frontiers of Empires*, ed. Ramazan Hakkı Öztan and Alp Yenen (Edinburgh: Edinburgh University Press, 2021), 355–382.

7. Lerna Ekmekçioğlu, "Debates over an Armenian National Home at the Lausanne Conference and the Limits of Post-Genocide Co-Existence," in *They All Made Peace. What Is Peace? The 1923 Treaty of Lausanne and the New Imperial Order*, ed. Ozavci Ozan and Jonathan Conlin (London: Gingko Library, 2023) 118–140.

8. Seda Altuğ, "Sectarianism in the Syrian Jazira: Community, land and violence in the memories of World War I and the French mandate (1915–1939)," unpublished dissertation thesis, June 2011.

9. Göçek, *Denial of Violence*.

10. Cited in Raymond H. Kevorkian, *The Armenian Genocide: A Complete History* (London: I.B. Tauris, 2011), 650.

11. Cited in Kevorkian, *The Armenian Genocide*, 650.

12. Kevorkian, *The Armenian Genocide*, 651.

13. Kevorkian, *The Armenian Genocide*, 652.

14. Cited in Altuğ, "Sectarianism in the Syrian Jazira," 159.

15. Ayşe Gül Altınay and Fethiye Çetin, *The Grandchildren: The Hidden Legacy of "Lost" Armenians in Turkey* (New Brunswick, NJ: Transaction Publishers, 2014).

16. Joseph Yacoub, *Year of the Sword* (Oxford: Oxford University Press, 2016), 2.

17. Kamal Soleimani, "The Kurdish Image in Statist Historiography: The Case of Simko," *Middle Eastern Studies* 53, no. 6 (2017): 1–17.

18. Cited in Yacoub, *Year of the Sword*, 10.

19. British defense review of Iraq "Military Report on Iraq" issued by the Air Ministry, August 1929. Surma Khanum is described as the aunt of Mar Shimon in the section of the report on Personalities. In Burdett, *Records of the Kurds*, 405.

20. President Joe Biden issued a statement on April 24, 2021 that said: "We remember the lives of all those who died in the Ottoman-era Armenian genocide and recommit ourselves to preventing such an atrocity from ever again occurring." https://www.whitehouse.gov/brief ing-room/statements-releases/2021/04/24/statement-by-president-joe-biden-on-armen ian-remembrance-day/.

21. Yacoub, *Year of the Sword*.

22. Although signed between Britain and France, there was a copy of the secret Sykes Picot Agreement in the Russian archives, which the Bolsheviks later discovered and leaked to the public.

23. Burdett, *Records of the Kurds*.

24. Arshak Safrastian, *Kurds and Kurdistan* (London: The Harvill Press, 1948), 77.

25. Robert Olsen, "The Rebellions of Sheikh Said (1925), Mt. Ararat (1930), and Dersim (1937–38): Their Impact on the Development of the Turkish Air Force and on Kurdish and Turkish Nationalism," *Die Welt des Islams* 40, no. 1 (March 2000): 67–94.

26. "Decision of the President of the United States of America respecting the Frontier between Turkey and Armenia, Access for Armenia to the Sea, and the Demilitarization of Turkish Territory Adjacent to the Armenian Frontier." November 22, 1920. See also Ara Papian, "The Arbitral Award on Turkish-Armenian Boundary by Woodrow Wilson (Historical Background, Legal Aspects, and International Dimensions)," *Iran & the Caucasus* 11, no. 2 (2007): 255–294.

27. Safrastian, *Kurds and Kurdistan*, 78.

28. Tejel, "The Last Ottoman Rogues," 363.

29. Garabet K. Moumdjian, "Armenian Involvement in the 1925 (Ararat) and 1937 (Dersim) Kurdish Rebellions in Republican Turkey: Mapping the Origins of 'Hidden Armenians,'" *Uluslararası Suçlar ve Tarih / International Crimes and History Journal* 19 (2018): 177–242.

30. Yüksel, "On the Borders of the Turkish and Iranian Nation-States."

31. Wadie Jwaideh, *The Kurdish National Movement: Its Origins and Development* (Syracuse: Syracuse University Press 2006), 210.

32. British defense review of Iraq "Military Report on Iraq" issued by the Air Ministry, August 1929. The preface of the report states, "Since the outbreak of the Great War very few Europeans have been permitted to visit any part of Turkish Central Kurdistan, and they are still prevented from doing so." In Burdett, *Records of the Kurds*, 313.

33. Point one of the official proclamation of the Republic of Mount Ararat, from CADN, Fonds Beyrouth, Cabinet Politique 1055. "Proclamation de l'occupation effective et de l'institution du gouvernement." Services civils du Délégué no. 1982. Alep, le 23 mai 1933.

34. For a detailed history of the role of Kurdish militias in the late Ottoman period, see Klein (2011), *The Margins of Empire*.

35. According to an article from the *Los Angeles Times* published in 1930: "Turkish officials admit the rebellion was more serious than the revolt by Sheikh Said in 1925 and that Turkish officers who deserted are leading the Kurds still holding out in the fastnesses of Mt Ararat." In "Turks Will Begin Final Drive Today: Rebel Kurds Intrenched at Base of Mt. Ararat to be Exterminated," *Los Angeles Times*, July 16, 1930.

36. Yüksel, "On the Borders of the Turkish and Iranian Nation-States."

37. David McDowall, *A Modern History of the Kurds* (London: I.B. Tauris, 2007) and Olsen, "The Rebellions of Sheikh Said (1925), Mt. Ararat (1930), and Dersim (1937–38)," *Die Welt des Islams* (2000): 67–94.

38. Moumdjian, "Armenian Involvement in the 1925 (Ararat) and 1937 (Dersim) Kurdish Rebellions in Republican Turkey," 185–186.

39. Ekmekçioğlu, "Debates over an Armenian National Home," 2023.

40. Jwaideh, *The Kurdish National Movement*, 211.

41. Dispatch, Sir George Clerk to Sir Austen Chamberlain, Foreign Secretary, August 9, 1927, No. 417, reviewing Turkish Government's policy of forced migration of Kurds.

42. Jwaideh, *The Kurdish National Movement*, 211.

43. Jordi Tejel, *La Ligue Nationale Kurde Khoyboun: Mythes Et Réalités De La Première Organisation Nationaliste Kurde* (Paris: L'Harmattan 2007). See the section "Le Khoyboun et la révolte de l'Ararat (1927–1931)," 18ff. https://bnk.institutkurde.org/images/pdf/GBQLXFW TP7.pdf.

44. Extracts from Intelligence Reports, November 12 and December 3, 1927, regarding Kurdish activities in Syria-Iraq, In Burdett, *Records of the Kurds*, 82–83.

45. Aram S. Sayiyam, "The Symbol of Armenian-Kurdish Alliance: Newfound Documents about the Life and Activity of Ardashes Mouradian," *VEM Pan-Armenian Journal* (2021).

46. Garabet Moumdjian, "Armenian Involvement in the 1925 (Ararat) and 1937 (Dersim) Kurdish Rebellions in Republican Turkey: Mapping the Origins of 'Hidden Armenians'," *Uluslararası Suçlar ve Tarih / International Crimes and History* 19 (2018): 177–242. The quote is from footnote 13 on page 188.

47. Sayiyan, "The Symbol of Armenian-Kurdish Alliance: Newfound Documents about the Life and Activity of Artashes Muradyan," *VEM Pan-Armenian Journal*, 276. https://vemjournal. org/en/archive/the-symbol-of-armenian-kurdish-alliance-2021-4/?lang=en.

48. Bozarslan, 182–186.

49. "Form of Oath: Khoyboun Society" reprinted in Memorandum, Special Service Officer at Mosul to Air Staff Intelligence, Air Headquarters, Hinaidi, and various offices at Mosul, February 26, 1930. In Burdett, *Records of the Kurds*, 627.

50. McDowall, *A Modern History of the Kurds*, 197–198.

51. Jwaideh, *The Kurdish National Movement*, 211.

52. Yüksel, "On the Borders of the Turkish and Iranian Nation-States," 658.

53. "Kurdish Rebels Use New Machine Guns: Turkish Exiles Believed to Be in Command of Tribesmen Around Mount Ararat," *New York Times*, July 13, 1930.

54. McDowall, *A Modern History of the Kurds*, 199.

55. According to Sir Telford Waugh, the Turkish officers who were caught by the Kurds were subjected to "Kieur Kanuni" (blind man's code) a "sort of drumhead court-martial"—they inflicted punishments and mutilations. Waugh cited in Jwaideh, *The Kurdish Nationalist Movement*, footnote 59, 361.

56. Tejel, "The Last Ottoman Rogues," 366.

57. Jwaideh, *The Kurdish National Movement*, 208.
58. Celîlê Celil, "Bitlis Ayaklanması—Tarihi Araştırma," April 1, 2018. http://www.bitlisname.com/2018/04/01/bitlis-ayaklanmasi-arastirma/.
59. Cited in Yüksel, "On the Borders of the Turkish and Iranian Nation-States," 666.
60. Cited in Yüksel, "On the Borders of the Turkish and Iranian Nation-States," 666.
61. Dispatch, Sir G. H. Clerk, British Ambassador to Turkey, to Sir Austen Chamberlain, Foreign Secretary, October 4, 1927. In Burdett, *Records of the Kurds*, 41.
62. "Turk Soldiers Kill Five Kurdish Chiefs," *New York Times*, July 8, 1930.
63. Minutes of a meeting between Hoyboun and the ARF Central Committee in Paris, May 28, 1931, pages 1–10. Unpublished archival document from the Archives of the Armenian Revolutionary Federation (ARF) in Watertown, MA. Original title in French "*Proces verbal.*" I am very grateful to Khatchig Mouradian for sharing this document with me.
64. Unpublished minutes of a meeting between Hoyboun and the ARF Central Committee in Paris, May 28, 1931. ARF Archives in Watertown, MA.
65. Unpublished letter from the ARF Central Committee in Paris to Sureya Bedrkhan, dated July 20, 1931. No 3037/2561. ARF Archives in Watertown, MA.
66. Yüksel, "On the Borders of the Turkish and Iranian Nation-States," 659.
67. The cartoon is included in the memoirs of Ihsan Nouri Pasha, General Ihsan Nouri Pasha, *La Révolte De L'Agri Dagh: "Ararat" (1927–1930)*. (Genève: Editions Kurdes Genève, 1986), 170.
68. This statement appeared originally in the Milliyet newspaper on September 19, 1930, quoted in Olson, "The Kurdish Rebellions of Sheikh Said," 93, 103.
69. McDowall, *A Modern History of the Kurds*, 198.
70. Data from the Organization for Economic Co-operation and Development (OECD) from 2018. https://stats.oecd.org/.
71. Jordi Tejel Gorgas, "Les territoires de marge de la Syrie mandataire: le mouvement autonomiste de la Haute Jazîra, paradoxes et ambiguïtés d'une intégration 'nationale inachevée (1936–1939)." "The territory margins of the Mandatory Syria: the autonomist movement in Upper Jazîra, paradoxs and ambiguities of an uncompleted 'national' integration (1936–1939)," *Revue des mondes musulmans et de la Méditerranée*, November 2009; and Altuğ, "Sectarianism in the Syrian Jazira," 201.

Chapter 3

1. Author interview with Polat Can, founding member of the YPG, on March 22, 2019 in Syria.
2. Hassan M. Fattah, "Kurds, Emboldened by Lebanon, Rise Up in Tense Syria," *The New York Times*, July 2, 2005. https://www.nytimes.com/2005/07/02/world/middleeast/kurds-emboldened-by-lebanon-rise-up-in-tense-syria.html.
3. Author interviews with numerous Syrian Kurds who lived in Qamishli and Kobani at the time of the 2004 uprising.
4. Joseph Daher, *Syria after the Uprisings: The Political Economy of State Resilience* (Chicago: Haymarket Books, 2019), 151.
5. Sam Dagher, *Assad or We Burn the Country: How One Family's Lust for Power Destroyed Syria* (New York: Back Bay Books, 2019), 15.
6. Daher, *Syria after the Uprisings*, 151.
7. According to Polat Can, they tried to set up an armed group, but had no weapons or even ammunition. "So we went to Murat Karayilan and Jalal Talabani, and also to the Barzani family to ask for help. Mam Jalal agreed to help, but since he had good relations with the Assad family, he did not give us ammunition. But they did create training camps." The name of the training camp was Arbat, which years later was turned into a refugee camp. Author interview with Polat Can on March 2019.
8. The PYD, PJAK, and KDSP were all created between 2002 and 2004. Due to the presence of KDP and PUK Peshmerga in the Kurdistan Region of Iraq, the KDSP did not have an armed wing, while PJAK and PYD both had armed wings. See "The PKK's Fateful Choice in Northern Syria." International Crisis Group, May 4, 2017. https://www.crisisgroup.org/middle-east-north-africa/eastern-mediterranean/syria/176-pkk-s-fateful-choice-northern-syria.

9. Hozan Afrini was born in the northwestern part of Syria in the canton of Afrin in 1970, and became active in the Kurdish movement in 1990. After leaving the PKK, he was unable to return to Syria for many years because he was on the Assad regime's Most Wanted List. He later returned to Syria and became head of the Rojava Journalist Syndicate Bureau of Relations, as well as head of the Hawar Syrian Refugees Rights Organization. His bio is on the website of the Washington Kurdish Institute from February 9, 2016. https://dckurd.org/2016/02/09/hozan-afrini/.

10. Interview with Nisrine Abdullah, Spokeswoman of the YPJ and Co-Founder of the YXG, on March 12, 2018 in Syria.

11. Author interview with Nisrine Abdullah, Spokeswoman of the YPJ and Co-Founder of the YXG, on September 12, 2020 in Syria.

12. Author interview with Polat Can, founding member of the YPG, on March 22, 2019 in Syria.

13. Lorin Efrin, "A Revolutionary First in Rojava: YPJ." Interview by Deniz Yesilyurt, March 8, 2017. https://anfenglish.com/women/a-revolutionary-first-in-rojava-ypj-18897.

14. A YouTube video from March 10, 2012, shows youth in the Kurdish Sheikh Maqsood neighborhood of Aleppo setting up barricades and chanting "Yaskot Bashar Al-Assad" (Down with Bashar Al-Assad.) تنسيقية التآخي: الحواجز في الأحياء الكوردية

15. ANF News. "لجان الحماية الشعبية تصدّ هجوماً للشبيحة على منازل المواطنين الكرد في حلب", March 10, 2012. https://anfarabic.com/akhr-l-khbr/ljn-lhmy-lsh-by-tsdw-hjwman-llshbyh-l-mnzl-lmwtnyn-lkrd-fy-hlb-2457.

16. Michael Knapp, Anja Flach, Ercan Ayboğa, David Graeber, and Asya Abdullah, *Revolution in Rojava: Democratic Autonomy and Women's Liberation in Syrian Kurdistan*, trans. Janet Biehl (London: Pluto Press, 2016), 150.

17. A 2017 International Crisis Group report speculates that the PKK ordered its Iranian offshoot (PJAK) to implement a unilateral ceasefire with Iran in September 2011 in order to begin to realign with the Syrian regime, and thereby Iran, against Turkey. This may have helped pave the way for the withdrawal of Syrian regime forces from northern Syria in July 2012. However, the authors of the report concede that "no hard evidence has surfaced of a deal." "The PKK's Fateful Choice in Northern Syria." *International Crisis Group*, May 4, 2017, 3. https://www.crisisgroup.org/middle-east-north-africa/eastern-mediterranean/syria/176-pkk-s-fateful-choice-northern-syria.

18. The PDKS was led by Jamal Sheikh Baki, and not to be confused with the PDK-S which was led by Abdulhakim Bashar, and which was a sister party of Barzani's KDP. While the PDKS works with the Autonomous Administration, the PDK-S is part of the Kurdish National Council.

19. Author interview with Idris Nassan, former member of the Syrian Kurdish Democratic Party, in March 2019 in Syria.

20. Author interview with Polat Can, founding member of the YPG, on March 22, 2019 in Syria.

21. "YPG'ê li Rojava bi fermî avabûna xwe ragihand," *ANF News*, July 20, 2012. https://anfkurdishmobile.com/kurdistan/ypg-e-li-rojava-bi-fermi-avabuna-xwe-ragihand-3921.

22. Daher, *Syria after the Uprisings*, 162–163.

23. Anja Flach, Ercan Ayboğa, and Michael Knapp, *Revolution in Rojava: Frauenbewegung und Kommunalismus zwischen Krieg und Embargo* (Hamburg: VSA Verlag, 2015), 198.

24. See the YouTube video of the women's battalion in Afrin: "Li Efrîn Yekemîn Tabura Jinan ya 'YPG' Hat Avakirin" (The First Women's Battalion of the YPG was established in Afrin). https://www.youtube.com/watch?v=wX1BeAmtU6s.

25. Joost Jongerden, "Gender Equality and Radical Democracy: Contractions and conflicts in Relation to the 'New Paradigm' within the Kurdistan Workers' Party (PKK)," *Anatoli* 8 (2017). https://journals.openedition.org/anatoli/618#tocto1n4.

26. "First Martyrs of YPJ Remembered: Silava and Bêrîvan Fell during the Foundation Process of the YPJ," *ANF News*, May 28, 2020. https://anfenglish.com/news/first-martyrs-of-ypj-remembered-44089.

27. Beritan Sarya, "'Uluslararası güçlere değil, örgütlülüğümüze güvenmeliyiz'" ("We Should Trust Our Organization, Not International Powers"), *ANF News*, June 15, 2020. https://anfturkce.com/rojava-surIye/uluslararasi-gueclere-degil-oerguetluelueguemueze-guevenmeliyiz-142119.

28. Amy Austin Holmes, "What Are the Kurdish Women's Units Fighting for in Syria?" *The Washington Post*, December 23, 2015. https://www.washingtonpost.com/news/monkey-cage/wp/2015/12/23/what-are-the-kurdish-womens-units-fighting-for-in-syria/.

29. Dilar Dirik, *The Kurdish Women's Movement: History, Theory, Practice* (London: Pluto Press, 2022).

30. "The Constitution of the Rojava Cantons," archived on the personal blog of Mutlu Civiroglu. https://civiroglu.net/the-constitution-of-the-rojava-cantons/.

31. "Rojava," *Capitalism, Nature, Socialism,* February 3, 2015. https://www.tandfonline.com/doi/abs/10.1080/10455752.2015.1006948#.VmwTGdDhafQ.

32. Michael Knights and Wladimir van Wilgenburg, *Accidental Allies: The US-Syrian Democratic Forces Partnership Against the Islamic State* (London: I.B. Tauris, 2021), 36.

33. Amy Austin Holmes (@AmyAustinHolmes), "July 19 is the day #Kurds celebrate the liberation of Kobani from the Baathist regime. The semi-autonomous region has grown & been defended for 8 years—in defiance of Assad, ISIS, and Erdoğan. Odd that such a significant day is largely ignored by #Syria analysts." Twitter post, July 19, 2020. https://twitter.com/AmyAustinHolmes/status/1285004141375500288?s=20

34. "Operation Inherent Resolve," Lead Inspector General Report to the US Congress, 2019, 29–30. https://www.dodig.mil/Reports/Lead-Inspector-General-Reports/Article/1926689/lead-inspector-general-for-operation-inherent-resolve-quarterly-report-to-the-u/.

35. Aziz Arab was the first Arab martyr of the PKK. He was killed in 1986. In 2018, there were commemoration ceremonies held for him in North and East Syria. The Sports Union of the Jazira region opened a stadium in Al-Shaddadi that was named in honor of Aziz Arab. See "Commemorating Martyr Aziz Arab, Opening Stadium under His Name," *Hawar News Agency*, April 17, 2018. http://hawarnews.com/en/haber/commemorating-martyr-aziz-arab-opening-stadium-under-his-name-h795.html.

36. Amy Austin Holmes, "SDF's Arab Majority Rank Turkey as the Biggest Threat to NE Syria: Survey Data on America's Partner Forces," *The Woodrow Wilson International Center for Scholars,* 2019. https://www.wilsoncenter.org/publication/sdfs-arab-majority-rank-turkey-the-biggest-threat-to-ne-syria-survey-data-americas.

37. Author interview with General Mazloum Abdi, September 22, 2020, in Al-Hasakah, Syria.

38. Carl Drott, "The Revolutionaries of Bethnahrin," *Warscapes*, May 25, 2015. http://www.warscapes.com/reportage/revolutionaries-bethnahrin.

39. Syriac Military Council/Mawetbo Fulhoyo Suryoyo, January 27, 2013. https://www.youtube.com/watch?v=tnv706gPCEY.

40. Author interview with Abjar Dawud, Spokesperson for the MFS, in Syria, March 2019.

41. The MUB is the supreme body of the Dowronoyo movement that replaced the GHB in 2005. See Drott, "The Revolutionaries of Bethnahrin."

42. Author Interview with Kino Gabriel, July 26, 2019, in Derik, Syria.

43. Minority Rights Group International, "World Directory of Minorities and Indigenous Peoples—Syria: Christians, Armenians and Assyrians," *Refworld*, March 2018. https://www.refworld.org/docid/49749ca133.html.

44. Author Interview with Ashurina (code name has been changed), Assyrian-Syriac commander of the HSNB, March 5, 2019 in Syria.

45. Ibid.

46. Ibid.

47. Ibid.

48. Ibid.

49. Ibid.

50. Ibid.

51. Holmes, "SDF's Arab Majority Rank Turkey as the Biggest Threat to NE Syria: Survey Data on America's Partner Forces," 15–16.

52. Author interview with Sheikh Humaydi Daham al-Hadi, head of the Shammar tribe in eastern Syria, July 22, 2019.

53. Ibid.

54. "YPG Kills 103 IS Fighters and Enters Tal Hamis after Taking over 103 Villages," *The Syrian Observatory For Human Rights*, February 27, 2015. https://www.syriahr.com/en/13724/.

55. "YPG, Backed by al- Khabour Guards Forces, al- Sanadid Army and the Syriac Military Council, Expels IS out of More than 230 Towns, Villages and Farmlands," *The Syrian Observatory For Human Rights*, May 28, 2015. https://www.syriahr.com/en/18733/.

56. Author interview with Bandar al-Humaydi, Commander of the Sanadid Forces, July 22, 2019 in Tal Alo, Syria.

57. Ibid.

58. Author interview with Sheiko, Turkman member of Manbij Military Council, February 2019, in Manbij, Syria.

59. Yasser Munif, "Syria's Revolution Behind the Lines," *Socialist Review*, October 2013. http://socialistreview.org.uk/384/syrias-revolution-behind-lines.

60. Author interviews with the two Co-Presidents of the Executive Council: an Arab man by the name of Mohammed Kheir and a Kurdish woman named Nazifa Hillo; and with the two Co-Presidents of the Legislative Council: a Circassian man by the name of Satea Kabr and Suzanne Hussein, a Kurdish woman. Manbij, Syria, February 2019.

61. Author interview with Mohammed Kheir, Co-President of the Executive Council in Manbij, in Manbij, Syria, February 2019.

62. Hadeel Al-Saidawi, "The Meaning of Manbij," *Carnegie Middle East Center*, October 5, 2018. https://carnegie-mec.org/diwan/77417.

63. Nicholas Heras, "The Manbij Conundrum: Evicting SDF May Threaten the US Syria Mission," *The Defense Post*, February 13, 2018. https://www.thedefensepost.com/2018/02/13/opinion-syria-manbij-conundrum/.

64. Harriet Allsopp and Wladimir van Wilgenburg, *The Kurds of Northern Syria: Governance, Diversity, and Conflicts* (London: I.B. Tauris, 2019), 99.

65. Gayle Tzemmach Lemmon, *The Daughters of Kobani* (New York: Penguin Press, 2021), 132.

66. Maria Abi Habib, "U.S. Compromises Won Turkey's Backing for Kurdish-Led Offensive," *Wall Street Journal*, July 14, 2016. https://www.wsj.com/articles/u-s-compromises-won-turkeys-backing-for-kurdish-led-offensive-1468539313.

67. Aaron Stein, "The Roadmap to Nowhere: Manbij, Turkey, and America's Dilemma in Syria," *War on the Rocks*, June 29, 2018. https://warontherocks.com/2018/06/the-roadmap-to-nowhere-manbij-turkey-and-americas-dilemma-in-syria/.

68. Heras, "The Manbij Conundrum: Evicting SDF May Threaten the US Syria Mission."

69. Author interview with Kurdish member of the Manbij Military Council in Ain Issa, March 2019.

70. Author Interview with members of the Manbij Civil Council in February 2019 in Manbij, Syria.

71. Ibid.

72. Author interview with Shervan Derwish, Abu Adel, and Abu Ali, commanders of the Manbij Military Council, in Manbij, February 2019.

73. Ibid.

74. Ibid.

75. Fermun Çırak had a checkered life and appears to have been radicalized at a young age. He fled Turkey after the 1980 military coup, first moving to France where he worked as the bodyguard of Yılmaz Güney. He later joined the military wing of the Communist Party of Turkey (TKP/ML) and trained in Lebanon's Beqaa Valley. From 1991 to 1992 he fought in the First Nagorno-Karabakh War against Azerbaijan. In July 2015, he became a commander of the International Freedom Battalion (IFB) that organized international volunteers to support the YPG in their fight against the Islamic State.

76. "Nubar Ozanyan Armenian Brigade declared," ANF News, April 24, 2019. https://anfenglish.com/rojava-northern-syria/nubar-ozanyan-armenian-brigade-declared-34506.

77. Author interview with General Mazloum Abdi, September 22, 2020, in Al-Hasakah, Syria.

78. Ibid.

79. Ibid.

80. Ibid.

81. Oren Lieberman, "US Military Says American Troops Were at Risk from Turkish Strike on Base in Syria This Week," *CNN*, November 23, 2022. https://www.cnn.com/2022/11/23/politics/us-military-turkey-drone-strike/index.html.

82. "Turkiye Will Not Stop Military Activity in Syria or Iraq: Cavusoglu," *The Cradle*, April 14, 2023. https://thecradle.co/article-view/23649/turkiye-will-not-stop-military-activity-in-syria-or-iraq-cavusoglu.

83. "Mazloum Abdi Playing the Saz after the Incident in Slemani," Twitter post by Wladimir van Wilgenburg, April 8, 2023. It is unclear when the video of Mazloum Abdi playing the traditional guitar was recorded, but it was shared on social media one day after the drone strike in Sulaymaniyah. https://twitter.com/vvanwilgenburg/status/1644630617718415360?s=20.

Chapter 4

1. This document and others that follow can be found in the Archive of Islamic State Documents, on the website of Aymenn Jawad al-Tamimi: http://www.aymennjawad.org/2015/01/archive-of-islamic-state-administrative-documents.

2. Edith Lederer, "Amal Clooney Requests Extradition of ISIS Wife Who Prepped Victims with Makeup," *The National Post*, April 23, 2019.

3. United States Attorney's Office, "Former Elkhart, Indiana Resident Sentenced to over Six Years in Prison," November 9, 2020, https://www.justice.gov/usao-ndin/pr/former-elkhart-indiana-resident-sentenced-over-six-years-prison.

4. "Lawyers Seek Testimony for US Woman Charged with Aiding IS," *AP News*, September 15, 2019, https://apnews.com/article/b068011fea7945ddb64fef98999dcaea.

5. For a discussion of the US response to the crimes committed by ISIS against the Yezidi community, see: "By Any Other Name: How, When, and Why the United States Has Made Genocide Determinations" by Todd Buchwald and Adam Keith, published by the United States Holocaust Memorial Museum, March 8, 2019.

6. Nelly Lahoud, "Empowerment or Subjugation: An Analysis of ISIL's Gendered Messaging," *UN Women*, June 2018.

7. Author interview with a judge in the courts of the Autonomous Administration, Qamishli, October 2021.

8. Nadia Murad, *The Last Girl: My Story of Captivity, and My Fight against the Islamic State* (New York: Penguin Random House, 2018).

9. Kongra Star Women's Movement Rojava (@starrcongress). "Our activists in Baghouz interviewed a foreign Daesh woman." *Twitter*, March 9, 2019.

10. After living in Syria for several years, Ms. Abdi decided to return to Germany, and made her way to Turkey where she reported herself to the German embassy in August 2016. She feigned innocence and claimed to have been tricked by her husband who was an ISIS commander. She and her children were allowed to return to Germany and escape prosecution—until two investigative journalists, Jenan Moussa and Harold Doornbos, found her cell phone in Syria and then tracked her down in Germany. See also: Amy Austin Holmes, "How Journalists and NGOs Help Track Down ISIS Criminals: Lessons from Iraqi Kurdistan," *Wilson Center*, March 19, 2020.

11. Ms. Sally later pled guilty to concealing her financial support to the Islamic State. And Ms. Abdi showed her allegiance to ISIS, even as she was being arrested from her home, by flashing the one finger salute. A video of her arrest can be viewed here: https://twitter.com/Free_Yezidi/status/1171518617642393602?s=20.

12. Although their book *Civil War in Syria* is focused on Syria, their chapter analyzing "The Caliphate" explains the rise of ISIS almost entirely with reference to these conditions specific to Iraq, not Syria. Adam Baczko, Giles Dorronsoro, and Arthur Quesnay, *Civil War in Syria: Mobilization and Competing Social Orders* (Cambridge: Cambridge University Press, 2018).

13. Fawaz A. Gerges, "ISIS and the Third Wave of Jihadism," *Current History* 113, no. 767 (December 2014): 8.

14. Vera Miranova, "Is the Future of ISIS Female?" *The New York Times*, February 20, 2019, https://www.nytimes.com/2019/02/20/opinion/islamic-state-female-fighters.html.

15. "Women of the Islamic State: A Manifesto on Women by the Al Khanssaa Brigade," *Quilliam*, January 2015, 17.

16. Ibid.

17. Ibid., 18. In this passage, which I have italicized for emphasis, it becomes clear that the Islamic State seemed to believe that men's domination over women was the natural order of things all over the world, not just in the Middle East or among pious Muslims.

18. Lahoud, "Empowerment or Subjugation," 2.

19. Aymenn Jawad al-Tamimi, Archive of Islamic State Documents. https://justpaste.it/fatwa40.

20. James Messerschmidt and Achim Rohde, "Osama Bin Laden and his Jihadist Global Hegemonic Masculinity," Gender & Society 32, no. 3 (May 2018).

21. "Women of the Islamic State: A Manifesto on Women by the Al Khanssaa Brigade," 22.

22. Jonathan Landay, Warren Strobel, and Phil Stewart, "Exclusive: Seized documents reveal Islamic State's Department of 'War Spoils,'" Reuters, December 28, 2015.

23. Translation by Aymenn Jawad Al-Tamimi, "Unseen Islamic State Pamphlet on Slavery," aymennjawad.org, December 29, 2015. In this blog entry, Mr. Al-Tamimi says that he had actually obtained the pamphlet from a contact in Syria earlier in the year, but does not specify an exact date.

24. Ibid.

25. Mia Bloom, Bombshell: Women and Terrorism (Philadelphia: University of Pennsylvania Press, 2012); also talk at the Doha Forum on the panel "How ISIS wins women, how women win the war against ISIS," December 14–15, 2019, available here: https://www.womenforwardin ternational.org/isiswomen-dohaforum.

26. "ISI Confirms That Jabhat Al-Nusra Is Its Extension In Syria, Declares 'Islamic State Of Iraq And Al-Sham' As New Name Of Merged Group," The Middle East Research Institute, April 8, 2013, https://web.archive.org/web/20141006085808/http://www.memri.org/report/en/0/0/0/0/0/0/7119.htm; Rania Abouzeid, "The Jihad Next Door: The Syrian Roots of Iraq's Newest War," Politico. June 23, 2014, https://www.politico.com/magazine/story/2014/06/al-qaeda-iraq-syria-108214.

27. This document and others that follow can be found in the Archive of Islamic State Documents, on the website of Aymenn Jawad al-Tamimi: http://www.aymennjawad.org/2015/01/arch ive-of-islamic-state-administrative-documents.

28. Baczko, Dorronsoro, and Quesnay, Civil War in Syria, 195.

29. Lucy Kafanoy, "How All-Female ISIS Morality Police 'Khansaa Brigade' Terrorized Mosul," NBC News, November 20, 2016.

30. Azadeh Moaveni, "ISIS Women and Enforcers in Syria Recount Collaboration, Anguish and Escape," The New York Times, November 21, 2015.

31. Aymenn Jawad al-Tamimi, Archive of Islamic State Documents, https://justpaste.it/isistela byaddec2013.

32. Kashmira Gander, "Iraq Crisis: ISIS Orders Shop Keepers to Cover Mannequins," The Independent, July 24, 2014.

33. The following passage justifies allowing women to travel without a mahram to join the Islamic State: "Here I want to say with the loudest voice to the sick-hearted who have slandered the honor of the chaste sisters, a woman's hijrah from dārulkufr [infidel lands] is obligatory whether or not she has a mahram [male chaperone], if she is able to find a relatively safe way and fears Allah regarding herself. She should not wait for anyone but should escape with her religion and reach the land where Islam and its people are honored." Quoted in: Louisa Tarras-Wahlberg, "Seven Promises of ISIS to its female recruits," January 9, 2017. Original: Al-Muhajirāh, U.S. (2015a). "The Twin Halves of the Muhājirīn," Dabiq 8; Sharia alone will rule Africa, al-Hayat Media Center, 32–37.

34. Aymenn Jawad al-Tamimi, Archive of Islamic State Documents. https://justpaste.it/hasa kaheidadha1.

35. Lizzie Dearden, "ISIS Calls on Women to Fight and Launch Terror Attacks for First Time," The Independent, October 6, 2017. https://www.independent.co.uk/news/world/middle-east/isis-war-syria-iraq-women-call-to-arms-islamic-state-terror-attacks-propaganda-cha nge-ban-frontline-a7986986.html.

36. Norma Costello, "Dramatic ISIS Video Shows Burqa-Clad Women Fighting for First Time as Cowardly Jihadi Leaders Flee Crumbling Caliphate," The Sun, February 9, 2018. https://www.thesun.co.uk/news/5535728/isis-caliphate-jihadi-brides-fight/.

37. Ibid.

38. Rachel Bryson, "Female Fighters Show ISIS Changing Nature," *Institute for Global Change*, February 13, 2018. https://institute.global/insight/co-existence/female-fighters-show-isiss-changing-nature.

39. Nelly Lahoud, *The Jihadis' Path to Self-Destruction* (London: Hurst, 2010).

Chapter 5

1. Author interview with Ilham Amar, Co-Founder of the Women's House in Qamishli, March 2018.

2. Erica Chenoweth and Maria J. Stephan, *Why Civil Resistance Works: The Strategic Logic of Nonviolent Conflict* (New York: Columbia University Press 2011), 35.

3. Danièle Djamila Amrane-Minne, *Des femmes dans la guerre d'Algérie* (Paris: Éditions Karthala, 1994).

4. Landmark Resolution on Women, Peace, and Security, Office of the Special Adviser on Gender Issues and Advancement of Women (OSAGI) at the United Nations, October 2000. https://www.un.org/womenwatch/osagi/wps/.

5. Jamille Bigio and Rachel B. Vogelstein, "How Women's Participation in Conflict Prevention and Resolution Advances U.S. Interests," Council on Foreign Relations, October 2016. https://www.cfr.org/report/how-womens-participation-conflict-prevention-and-resolut ion-advances-us-interests.

6. Paul White, *The PKK: Coming Down from the Mountains* (London: Zed Books, 2015), 132.

7. Amy Austin Holmes, *Social Unrest and American Military Bases in Turkey and Germany since 1945* (Cambridge: Cambridge University Press, 2014).

8. Author interview with PKK defector, Erbil, September 2016.

9. Hamit Bozarslan, "Les revoltes Kurdes en Turquie Kemaliste (quelques aspects)," *Guerres Mondiales et Conflits Contemporains* 38, no. 151 (1988): 121.

10. Robert Olson, "The Rebellions of Sheikh Said (1925), Mt. Ararat (1930), and Dersim (1937–38): Their Impact on the Development of the Turkish Air Force and on Kurdish and Turkish Nationalism," *Die Welt des Islams* 40, no. 1 (March 2000): 67–94.

11. Metin Yüksel, "The Encounter of Kurdish Women with Nationalism in Turkey," *Middle Eastern Studies* 42, no. 5 (September 2006): 777–802.

12. Ibid., 796.

13. "Ex-Military Intel Chief Signals Turkey Was Behind Paris Murders of Kurds," *Kurd Press*, February 19, 2021. https://kurdpress.com/en/news/525/Ex-military-intel-chief-signals-Turkey-was-behind-Paris-murders-of-Kurds/.

14. One report suggested Cansiz was known for her opposition to "the alleged head of the PKK's armed-wing, Syrian citizen Ferman Hussein" and that she was also in disagreement with "the PKK's alleged financial head, Zübeyir Yılmaz." See "Three PKK Members Killed in Paris Attack," *Hurriyet Daily News*, January 10, 2013. https://www.hurriyetdailynews.com/three-pkk-members-killed-in-paris-attack-38748.

15. "Recent German Actions Against the PKK: Raids and Arrests," April 27, 2007. https://wikile aks.org/plusd/cables/07BERLIN855_a.html.

16. Khatchig Mouradian, "The Road from Diyarbakir: A Call to Deepen Kurdish Commitment to Genocide Justice," *Armenian Weekly*, May 13, 2014. https://armenianweekly.com/2014/05/13/the-road-from-diyarbakir/.

17. Sakine Cansiz, *Sara: My Whole Life Was a Struggle*, Janet Biehl, trans. (London: Pluto Press, 2018).

18. "Saralardan Nalînlere büyüyen kadın ordulaşması özgür ve demokratik toplumun garantisidir," *Serxwebun* no. 428 (August 2017). A historical archive of *Serxwebun* can be found at this link: https://archive.org/details/serxwebunpkk?&sort=-week&page=5.

19. "Duran Kalkan, Eruh ve Şemdinli eylemlerini anlatıyor," *ANF News*, August 14, 2018. https://anfturkce.com/kurdistan/duran-kalkan-eruh-ve-Semdinli-eylemlerini-anlatiyor-112015.

20. Constanze Letsch, "Sakine Cansiz 'A Legend among PKK Members,'" *The Guardian*, January 10, 2013. https://www.theguardian.com/world/2013/jan/10/sakine-cansiz-pkk-kurdish-activist.

21. Author interview in Erbil, July 2016.

22. Aliza Marcus, *Blood and Belief: The PKK and the Kurdish Fight for Independence* (New York: New York University Press, 2007), 172.

23. Ibid.

24. Marcus, *Blood and Belief,* 174.

25. Handan Çağlayan, *Women in the Kurdish Movement: Mothers, Comrades, Goddesses* (Cham: Palgrave Macmillan, 2020), 60.

26. Anja Flach, *Frauen in der kurdischen Guerilla: Motivation, Identität, und Geschlechterverhältnis in der Frauenarmee der PKK,* 2007, 117.

27. "Neden Kadın Ordulaşması." https://pajk.org/tr/neden-kad-n-ordulasmas/.

28. Yüksel Genç, *PKK'de Kadının Dönüşüm Anatomisi* (Sweden: Weşanen Jina Serbilind, 2002).

29. Karen Kempwirth, *Feminism and the Legacy of Revolution: Nicaragua, El Salvador, Chiapas* (Athens: Ohio University Press, 2004).

30. Çağlayan, *Women in the Kurdish Movement,* 2020, 69.

31. Cited in Joost Jongerden,"Gender Equality and Radical Democracy: Contractions and Conflicts in Relation to the "New Paradigm" within the Kurdistan Workers' Party (PKK)," *Anatoli,* no. 8 (2017): 237. https://journals.openedition.org/anatoli/618?lang=fr#quotation.

32. White, *The PKK,* xiii.

33. Michael M. Gunter, *Historical Dictionary of the Kurds* (Lanham: Rowman & Littlefield, 2018), 239.

34. Author interview with Osman Öcalan, July 2016.

35. Ibid.

36. Author interview with member of the women's movement in Iraqi Kurdistan, September 2016.

37. Ibid.

38. "Women of Rojava Building a Free Society," *Hawar News,* March 10, 2013. http://web.archive.org/web/20140922083209/http://www.hawarnews.com/english/index.php?option=com_content&view=article&id=14:women-of-rojava-building-a-free-society&catid=2:women&Itemid=3.

39. Mariana Miggiolaro Chaguri and Flavia Paniz, "Women's War: Gender Activism in the Vietnam War and in the Wars for Kurdish Autonomy," *Sociologia & Antropologia* 9, no. 3 (December 2019). https://www.scielo.br/j/sant/a/3B5HbL46RJx4TySvqprMc9d/?format=pdf&lang=en.

40. Jongerden, "Gender Equality and Radical Democracy," 2017.

41. Zilan Diyar, "Kurdistan Woman's Revolution: How to Write Our Struggle," November 9, 2018. https://web.archive.org/web/20210613131810/ and https://komun-academy.com/.

42. "Kurdistan Women's Liberation Struggle, *Jineoloji,* January 2, 2021 https://jineoloji.org/en/2020/04/22/kurdistan-womens-liberation-struggle/

43. Andrea Novellis, "The Rise of Feminism in the PKK: Ideology or Strategy," *Zanj: The Journal of Critical Global South Studies.* https://air.unimi.it/retrieve/handle/2434/817740/1726883/zanjglobsoutstud.2.1.0115.pdf.

44. Author interview in Gaziantep, June 2015.

45. Cited in Jongerden, "Gender Equality and Radical Democracy," 2017.

46. Flach, *Frauen in der kurdischen Guerilla,* 119.

47. Marcus, *Blood and Belief,* 291.

48. Chris Kutschera, "Kurdistan Turkey: PKK Dissidents Accuse Abdullah Öcalan," August 9, 2017. http://chris-kutschera.com/A/pkk_dissidents.htm.

49. Author interview with Osman Öcalanin Erbil, July 2016.

50. Author interview with Kongra Star activist in Qamishli, March 2018.

51. "Explainer: Kongra Star, the Women's Congress," Rojava Information Center, June 4, 2020. https://rojavainformationcenter.com/2020/06/explainer-kongra-star-the-womens-congress/.

52. "سلطات سجن عدرا المركزي تمنع لجنة المراقبين العرب من اللقاء بالسياسيات الكرد." *ANF News,* January 18, 2012. https://anfarabic.com/akhr-l-khbr/sltt-sjn-dr-lmrkzy-tmn-ljn-lmrqbyn-l-rb-mn-llq-blsysyt-lkrd-2100.

53. Author interview with Kongra Star activist in Qamishli, March 2018.

54. Anja Flach, Ercan Ayboğa, and Michael Knapp, *Revolution in Rojava: Democratic Autonomy and Women's Liberation in Syrian Kurdistan* (London: Pluto Press, 2016), 128.

55. Author interview with Fauzia Youssef, former Co-Chair of the Autonomous Administration, in Amude, September 8, 2020.
56. Lemmon, *Daughters of Kobani*, 164.
57. On the fifth anniversary of the founding of the Bethnahrin Women Protection Forces, Colonel Myles Caggins, the Spokesperson of the Global Coalition at the time, tweeted "The Coalition congratulates the courageous @HSNB for 5 years of success against ISIS. Kashirotho. #WomenPeaceSecurity." OIR Spokesperson (@OIRSpox), Twitter post, August 30, 2020. https://twitter.com/OIRSpox/status/1300144603379773440?s=20.
58. Amy Austin Holmes, "Interview with Lelwy Abdullah, Co-Chair of the Deir Ezzor Military Council." *The Wilson Center*, September 24, 2020. https://www.wilsoncenter.org/blog-post/special-edition-interview-lelwy-abdullah-co-chair-deir-ezzor-military-council-syria.
59. Amy Austin Holmes, "The Future (and Present) of Northeast Syria Is Female." *The Hill*, March 8, 2019. https://thehill.com/opinion/international/433177-the-future-and-present-of-northeast-syria-is-female.
60. Holmes, "Interview with Lelwy Abdullah."
61. Author Interview, Zenobiya Association, Manbij Syria, September 30, 2021.
62. Amberin Zaman (@amberinzaman), "A 'polygamy' bureau has been opened in the Turkish controlled northern Syrian town of Azaz. In the Kurdish controlled northeast polygamy is banned and gender equality aggressively promoted," Twitter post, October 23, 2021. https://twitter.com/amberinzaman/status/1451927726676488198?s=20.
63. Wladimir van Wilgenburg, "Top UK General Praises Leadership of Layla Mustafa on Raqqa Council," *Kurdistan 24*, March 5, 2019. https://www.kurdistan24.net/en/news/6f9324e7-0ea4-4de8-a508-06ede4e0ed01.
64. According to reporting by Matthew Petti, "State Department officials attempted to condemn the brutal murder of Kurdish-Syrian politician Hevrin Khalaf only to have their efforts waylayed by Ambassador James Jeffrey, who oversees anti-ISIS efforts. Jeffrey blocked the statement, they said." In "Exclusive: Inside the State Department's Meltdown with the Kurds," *The National Interest*, October 22, 2019. https://nationalinterest.org/blog/middle-east-watch/exclusive-inside-state-departments-meltdown-kurds-90241.
65. "Mexico Adopts Feminist Foreign Policy," Press Release 15, January 9, 2020. https://www.gob.mx/sre/prensa/mexico-adopts-feminist-foreign-policy?idiom=en.
66. "Rojava Information Center, "Building Peace: North and East Syria's Women's House," *Sur International Journal on Human Rights* 17, no. 30 (August 2020), 52. https://sur.conectas.org/wp-content/uploads/2020/08/sur-30-ingles-rojava-information-center.pdf.
67. Amy Austin Holmes, "Biden-Harris Should Lead on Women's Rights and Help End Syrian Conflict," *CFR Blog*, March 26, 2021. https://www.cfr.org/blog/biden-harris-should-lead-womens-rights-and-help-end-syrian-conflict.
68. Meghan Bodette, "The United States Can't Ignore Turkey's War on Syrian Women," *The National Interest*, October 1, 2020. https://nationalinterest.org/blog/middle-east-watch/united-states-cant-ignore-turkeys-war-syrian-women-169886.

Chapter 6

1. Author interview with Finance Minister of North and East Syria, in Qamishli, Syria, September 12, 2020.
2. Eva Garzouzi, "Land Reform in Syria," *Middle East Journal* 17, no. 1–2 (Winter–Spring 1963): 83–90.
3. Myriam Ababsa, "Agrarian Counter-Reform in Syria (2000–2010)," in *Agriculture and Reform in Syria*, ed. Raymond Hinnebusch, Atieh El Hindi, Munzur Khaddam, and Myriam Ababsa (Boulder: Lynne Rienner Publishers, 2011), 83–107. 85.
4. Raymond Hinnebusch, "The Baath's Agrarian Revolution (1963–2000)," in *Agriculture and Reform in Syria, edited by Raymond Hinnebusch, Atieh El Hindi, Munzur Khaddam, and Myriam Ababsa* (Boulder: Lynne Rienner Publishers, 2011), 3.
5. Ibid., 14.

6. Hannes Baumann, ed., *Reclaiming Home: The Struggle for Socially Just Housing, Land, and Property Rights in Syria, Iraq, and Libya* (For Socially Just Development in MENA, 2019). http://library.fes.de/pdf-files/bueros/tunesien/15664.pdf.

7. Maxim Lebsky, "The Economy of Rojava," *Liva Internet Journal*, March 17, 2016. https://liva.com.ua/obzor-ekonomiki-rozhavyi.html.

8. Sinan Hatahet, "The Political Economy of the Autonomous Administration of North and East Syria," *European University Institute 17* (November 29, 2019): 83–90.

9. UNESCO data on the Syrian Arab Republic. http://uis.unesco.org/en/country/sy.

10. Joost Jongerden, "Kurdish Autonomy between Dream and Reality," *ROAR Magazine*, June 4, 2015. https://roarmag.org/essays/kurdish-autonomy-jongerden-interview/.

11. Sirwan Kajjo and Zana Omar, "Iraqi Refugees in Syria Refuse to Return Home," *VOA News*, November 1, 2018. https://www.voanews.com/extremism-watch/iraqi-refugees-syria-refuse-return-home.

12. These claims about economic growth in Afrin should be treated with caution, however, given the paucity of reliable economic data during the conflict. At the same time, it is also true that the relative stability of Afrin prior to the Turkish intervention would have allowed for a better business environment than other parts of Syria ravaged by the war. See "Can Afrin Resume Its Economic Growth," *Enab Baladi*, July 12, 2018. https://english.enabbaladi.net/archives/2018/07/can-afrin-resume-its-economic-growth/.

13. Amy Austin Holmes, "Biden-Harris Should Lead on Women's Rights and Help End Syrian Conflict," *Council on Foreign Relations*, March 26, 2021. https://www.cfr.org/blog/biden-harris-should-lead-womens-rights-and-help-end-syrian-conflict.

14. Dr. Ahmed Youssef, "The Experience of Rojava in the Social Economy," *International Seminar on Solidarity Economy*, November 17, 2014. https://sange.fi/kvsolidaarisuustyo/wp-content/uploads/Dr.-Ahmad-Yousef-Social-economy-in-Rojava.pdf.

15. Can Cemgil and Clemens Hoffman, "The 'Rojava Revolution' in Syrian Kurdistan: A Model of Development for the Middle East?" *IDS Bulletin 47*, no. 3 (2016): 53–75.

16. Author interview with Dr. Ahmed Youssef, Finance Minister of North and East Syria, in Qamishli, Syria, September 12, 2020.

17. See Aysegul Aydin and Cem Emrence, *Zones of Rebellion: Kurdish Insurgents and the Turkish State* (Ithaca, NY: Cornell University Press, 2015).

18. Anja Flach, Michael Knapp, and Ercan Ayboga, *Revolution in Rojava: Democratic Autonomy and Women's Liberation* (London: Pluto Press, 2016); and Cemgil and Hoffman, "The 'Rojava Revolution' in Syrian Kurdistan: A Model of Development for the Middle East?", 53–75.

19. "Revolution and Cooperatives: Thoughts about My Time with the Economic Committee in Rojava," *Internationalist Commune of Rojava*, September 2020. https://internationalistcommune.com/revolution-and-cooperatives-thoughts-about-my-time-with-the-economic-committee-in-rojava/.

20. Himberyan Kousa, "The 'Arab Belt': The Story of the Largest Demographic Change in Syria," *Raseef22*, August 20, 2019. https://raseef22.net/article/1074813-the-arab-belt-the-story-of-the-largest-demographic-change-in-syria.

21. Independent International Commission of Inquiry on the Syrian Arab Republic, "Human Rights Abuses and International Humanitarian Law Violations in the Syrian Arab Republic 21 July 2016–28 February 2017," *ReliefWeb*, March 10, 2017. https://reliefweb.int/sites/reliefweb.int/files/resources/A_HRC_34_CRP.3_E.pdf.

22. Hatahet, "The Political Economy of the Autonomous Administration of North and East Syria."

23. Joseph Daher, *Syria after the Uprisings: The Political Economy of State Resilience* (Chicago: Haymarket Books, 2019); Hatahet, "The Political Economy of the Autonomous Administration of North and East Syria."

24. Thomas Schmidinger, *The Battle for the Mountain of the Kurds: Self-Determination and Ethnic Cleansing in the Afrin Region of Rojava*, PM Press, 2019.

25. Author interview with Dr. Ahmed Youssef, Finance Minister of North and East Syria, in Qamishli, Syria, September 12, 2020.

26. Sardar Mullah Darwish, "Will Syria's Kurds Succeed at Economic Self-Sufficiency?" April 28, 2016. https://www.al-monitor.com/originals/2016/04/kurdish-areas-norther-syria-econ omy-self-sufficiency.html.

27. Ibid.

28. Thomas McGee, " 'Nothing Is Ours Anymore'—HLP Rights Violations in Afrin, Syria," in *Reclaiming Home: The Struggle for Socially Just Housing, Land, and Property Rights in Syria, Iraq, and Libya*, ed. Hannes Baumann (For Socially Just Development in MENA, 2019). http:// library.fes.de/pdf-files/bueros/tunesien/15664.pdf.

29. "Revolution and Cooperatives."

30. Author interview with Armanc Mohamed Ahmed, Head of the Women's Economy in North and East Syria, in Qamishli, Syria, September 13, 2020.

31. Ibid.

32. Ibid.

33. "First Women Economy Conference Started in North Syria," *ANHA*, June 15, 2017. https:// en.hawarnews.org/1st-women-economy-conference-started-in-north-syria/#prettyPhoto.

34. Ruba Eli, "Komîteya Jinan a Reqayê Derfetên Kar Ji Jinan Re Peyda Kir," *ANHA*, October 1, 2020. https://hawarnews.com/kr/haber/komteya-jinan-a-reqay-derfetn-kar-ji-jinan-re-peyda-kir-h36799.html.

35. A video produced by ANHA in September 2017 that announced the opening of the Beit Al Baraka in Manbij shows women cleaning and preparing molokheya. https://www.youtube.com/watch?v=GsWhtGoJt6U&feature=emb_logo.

36. Meghan Bodette, "An Overview of AANES Women's Institutions in Manbij," *Cooperation in Mesopotamia*, August 16, 2020. https://mesopotamia.coop/an-overview-of-aanes-womens-institutions-in-manbij/.

37. "Revolution and Cooperatives."

38. Ibid.

39. Author interview with Armanc Mohamed Ahmed in Qamishli, Syria, September 13, 2020.

40. Ibid.

41. Rachel Hagan, "Kurdish Women Are Working the Land to Achieve Financial Independence," *VICE News*, September 18, 2020.

42. "Revolution and Cooperatives."

43. Charles Tilly, "War Making and State Making as Organized Crime," in *Bringing the State Back, edited by Peter B. Evans et al.* (Cambridge: Cambridge University Press, 1985), 169–191, 181.

44. Lebsky, "The Economy of Rojava."

45. Jeff Carter, Michael Bernhard, and Glenn Palmer, "Social Revolution, the State, and War: How Revolutions affect War-Making Capacity and Interstate War Outcomes," *Journal of Conflict Resolution 56*, no. 3 (2012): 439–466.

46. Hatahet, "The Political Economy of the Autonomous Administration of North and East Syria," 12.

47. Author interview with Ra'ed Sheikhan, Co-Chair of the Taxation Directorate of the Jazira Canton, in Qamishli, March 29, 2023.

48. Quy-Toan Do et al., "*How Much Oil Is the Islamic State Group Producing?: Evidence from Remote Sensing*," Policy Research Working Paper (Washington, DC: World Bank, October 2017). https://openknowledge.worldbank.org/handle/10986/28617.

49. Wladimir Van Wilgenburg and Harriet Allsopp, *The Kurds of Northern Syria: Governance, Diversity and Conflicts* (London: I.B. Tauris, 2019), 103.

50. "Interview with the Prime Minister of Jazeera: A Federal Way out for Syria?" *The Maghreb and Orient Courier*, May 2015. http://lecourrierdumaghrebetdelorient.info/syria/syria-interv iew-with-the-prime-minister-of-jazeera-a-federal-way-out-for-syria/.

51. "Oil Exports into Iraqi Kurdistan Give Syrian Kurds a Financial Lifeline." *Iraq Oil Report*, April 2020. https://www.iraqoilreport.com/wp-content/uploads/ior-pe-mar2020.pdf.

52. Ibid.

53. David Brown, "Trump Says U.S. Left Troops in Syria 'Only for the Oil,' Appearing to Contradict Pentagon," *Politico*, November 13, 2019.

54. Scott Horsley, "Fact Check: President Trump's Plan for Syrian Oil," *NPR*, October 28, 2019. https://www.npr.org/2019/10/28/774053444/fact-check-president-trumps-plans-for-syr ian-oil.

55. Matthew Petti, "Trump administration helped GOP donors get Syria oil deal," *Responsible Statecraft,* December 9, 2020. https://responsiblestatecraft.org/2020/12/09/trump-adminis tration-helped-gop-donors-get-syria-oil-deal/.
56. Author interview with Abdel Karim Malek, Head of the Jazira Oil Company in Rumaylan, Syria, September 12, 2020.
57. Ibid.
58. Hatahet, "The Political Economy of the Autonomous Administration of North and East Syria," 11.
59. Amberin Zaman, "Intel: Syrian Kurds court Moscow to avert potential Turkish attack," *Al Monitor,* September 2, 2020. https://www.al-monitor.com/originals/2020/09/syria-kurds-sdf-court-moscow-turkey-attack-russia-regime.html#ixzz75WtrPkU0.
60. Shawn Snow, "Bradleys and Army Infantry Roll into Syria to Help Secure Oil Wells," *Military Times,* October 31, 2019. https://www.militarytimes.com/flashpoints/2019/10/31/bradl eys-and-army-infantry-roll-into-syria-to-help-secure-oil-wells/.
61. "PKK Confirms Death of Senior Commander during Turkish Airstrike," *Bas News,* September 6, 2020. https://www.basnews.com/en/babat/631885.
62. Author interview with Abdel Karim Malek, September 12, 2020.
63. Aaron Lund, "The Factory: A Glimpse into Syria's War Economy," *The Century Foundation,* February 21, 2018. https://tcf.org/content/report/factory-glimpse-syrias-war-economy/?agreed=1.
64. Gayle Tzemach Lemmon, *The Daughters of Kobani: A Story of Rebellion Courage and Justice* (New York: Penguin Press, 2021).
65. "Global Gender Gap Report 2020," *World Economic Forum,* December 16, 2019. http://www3.weforum.org/docs/WEF_GGGR_2020.pdf.
66. "Facts and Figures: Women, Peace and Security," *UN Women.* https://www.unwomen.org/en/what-we-do/peace-and-security/facts-and-figures#_ednref32.

Chapter 7

1. Interview with Shirin Hemo, Co-Chair of the Education Committee in the Jazira canton of Northeast Syria, March 24, 2020. A trip I had planned to Northeast Syria in March 2020 had to be postponed due to travel restrictions during the Coronavirus pandemic. Instead, answers to my questions were provided by email with the help of a local assistant who worked for the Rojava Information Center.
2. In her book, *We Crossed a Bridge and It Trembled: Voices from Syria,* Wendy Pearlman includes a quote from an accountant from Aleppo who describes the Baathist education system as follows: "We weren't educated about the different people in the country, so there wasn't real integration. Arabs didn't know about Kurdish culture. Arabs and Kurds knew nothing about Turkmens. We'd hear that there were people called Syriacs and Assyrians, but who are they and how do they live? We didn't know. The Druze? You know that they live in Syria, but what is their culture and what do they want? We were all just groups of strangers. A country of closed communities, held together by force." Wendy Pearlman, *We Crossed a Bridge and It Trembled: Voices from Syria* (New York: Custom House, 2017), 7.
3. Michael M. Gunter, *Out of Nowhere: The Kurds of Syria in Peace and War* (London: Hurst & Company, 2014).
4. Patrick Haenni and Arthur Quesnay, "Surviving the Aftermath of the Islamic State: The Syrian Kurdish Movement's Resilience Strategy", *EUI,* Research Project Report, February 17, 2020.
5. US Department of State, Bilateral Relations Fact Sheet, Bureau of Near Eastern Affairs, May 6, 2020. https://www.state.gov/u-s-relations-with-syria/.
6. See Office of Inspector General Report, "Department of State Stabilization Programs in Syria Funded Under the Further Continuing Security Assistance Appropriations Act 2017." See table 1, "Syria Stabilization Assistance Appropriated Under the Further Continuing and Security Assistance Appropriations Act, 2017" (as of September 7, 2018), 6.
7. Abid Kar, "A Refugee Camp's Self-Organized Education System," *Komun Academy,* November 25, 2018. https://komun-academy.com/2018/11/25/a-refugee-camps-self-organized-educat ion-system/.

8. For a discussion of Jineology, see Nadje Al-Ali and Isabel Käser, "Beyond Feminism? Jineolojî and the Kurdish Women's Freedom Movement," *Politics & Gender* 18, no. 1 (March 2022): 212–243. For a critical response to their article, see "Open Letter to the Public about the article 'Beyond Feminism? Jineolojî and the Kurdish Women's Freedom Movement' published by the Jineology Committee Europe in *Jadaliyya*," May 24, 2021. https://www.jadaliyya.com/Details/42819/Open-letter-to-the-public-About-the-article-%E2%80%98Beyond-Feminism-Jineoloj%C3%AE-and-the-Kurdish-Women%E2%80%99s-Freedom-Movement%E2%80%99.

9. World Bank data on adult literacy in Syria in 2004 can be found at https://data.worldbank.org/indicator/SE.ADT.LITR.FE.ZS?locations=SY&most_recent_value_desc=false.

10. The Makhmour refugee camp consisted largely of Kurds who had fled from persecution in Turkey, some of whom had fought in the PKK.

11. Delil Souleiman, "Syriacs Protest Kurdish Authorities over Syria School Curriculum," *AFP*, September 12, 2018. https://www.yahoo.com/news/kurds-christians-split-over-syria-school-curriculum-041427147.html?guccounter=1.

12. Author interview with Jalinos, in Qamishli in February 2019.

13. Author interview with Arif Qesebiyan, Co-Chair of the Armenian Social Council in Al-Hasakah in October 2021.

14. Wladimir van Wilgenburg, "Young Female Mayor Breaks Boundaries in Syrian Town Freed from Islamic State," *Middle East Eye*, August 3, 2016. https://www.middleeasteye.net/features/young-female-mayor-breaks-boundaries-syrian-town-freed-islamic-state.

15. Cited in Pinar Dinç, "The Content of School Textbooks in (Nation) States and 'Stateless Autonomies': A Comparison of Turkey and the Autonomous Administration of North and East Syria (Rojava)," *Nations and Nationalism* 26 (2020): 994–1014, 997.

16. "Group Denial: Repression of Kurdish Political and Cultural Rights in Syria," *Human Rights Watch Report*, 2009, 11.

17. "From Afrin to Jarablus: A Small Replica of Turkey in the North," *Enab Baladi*, August 28, 2018. https://english.enabbaladi.net/archives/2018/08/from-afrin-to-jarabulus-a-small-replica-of-turkey-in-the-north/.

18. "Displacement as Challenge and Opportunity: Urban Profile of Refugees, Internally Displaced Persons, and Host Community," *UNHCR*, August 2016. See page 66 for a description of the language barriers.

19. Author interview with Mariam in Manbij, in northern Syria. February 2019.

20. Author interview with Rawa Romy, Co-Head of Education Committee in Tabqa, March 3, 2019.

21. Author interview with Layla Hassan, Co-Head of the Deir Ezzor Civil Council, in Deir Ezzor in eastern Syria, March 2019.

22. Author interview with Kamal Moussa, Co-Chair of Education in Deir Ezzor, in Deir Ezzor in eastern Syria, March 2019.

23. Oliver Holmes and Suleiman Al-Khalidi, "Islamic State Executed 700 People from Syrian Tribe: Monitoring Group," *Reuters*, August 16, 2014. https://www.reuters.com/article/us-syria-crisis-execution/islamic-state-executed-700-people-from-syrian-tribe-monitoring-group-idUSKBN0GG0H120140817.

24. Interview with Kawthar Duko, Co-President of Autonomous Administration Education Commission. Answers provided by email, March 30, 2020.

25. Haenni and Quesnay, "Surviving the Aftermath of the Islamic State."

26. Dinç, "The Content of School Textbooks in (Nation) States and 'Stateless Autonomies,'" 1003–1004.

27. Ibid., 1007.

28. Survey of the Syrian Democratic Forces (SDF) including its components parts (YPG/YPJ, Manbij Military Council, and Al Sanadeed Forces) conducted by the author in all six governorates of North and East Syria between 2015 and 2020. For more information on the SDF survey, see Chapter 3.

29. Author interview with Esraa in Qamishli in northern Syria, in March 2019.

30. Harriet Allsopp and Wladimir van Wilgenburg, *The Kurds of Northern Syria: Governance, Diversity, and Conflicts* (London: I.B. Tauris, 2019), 110.

31. Allsopp and van Wilgenburg, *The Kurds of Northern Syria*, 113.

Chapter 8

1. Cira Mancusco, "Where Are the Nuremberg Trials for the Yazidis?" Interview with Pari Ibrahim, Georgetown Institute for Women, Peace, and Security, May 30, 2019. https://giwps.georgetown.edu/where-are-the-nuremberg-trials-for-the-yazidis/.

2. Amy Austin Holmes, "Syrian Yezidis under Four Regimes: Assad, Erdoğan, ISIS and the YPG," *The Wilson Center*, Occasional Paper Series, No. 37, July 2020. https://www.wilsoncenter.org/sites/default/files/media/uploads/documents/MEP_200710_OCC%2037_FINAL.pdf.

3. Sebastian Maisel, *Yezidis in Syria: Identity Building among a Double Minority* (Lanham: Lexington Books, 2017), 78.

4. The reason for the range in number of villages is because some count only those that are inhabited solely by Yezidis (estimated 23 in Afrin) while others include mixed villages (estimated 33 in Afrin). Thomas Schmidinger, *The Battle for the Mountain of the Kurds: Self-Determination and Ethnic Cleansing in the Afrin Region of Rojava* (Oakland: PM Press, 2019), 118.

5. Alternative spellings include Yazîdî, Izadî, Êzidî, Azîdî, Zedî, Izadî, and Yazdani, but "Yezidi" has become commonplace in English publications and will be used here.

6. U.S. Department of State, "Report on International Religious Freedom: Syria," 2017. https://www.state.gov/reports/2016-report-on-international-religious-freedom/syria/.

7. David Meseguer, "Stranded between Syria's Frontlines, Afrin's Yazidis Yearn for Lost Homelands," *Middle East Eye*, October 31, 2018. https://www.middleeasteye.net/news/stranded-between-syrias-frontlines-afrins-yazidis-yearn-lost-homelands.

8. Maisel, *Yezidis in Syria*, 17.

9. Majid Hassan Ali and Seyedeh Behnaz Hosseini, "Between Rights, Political Participation, and Opposition: The Case of Yezidis in Syrian Kurdistan (Rojava)," *Syrian Studies Association Bulletin* 23, no. 1 (2018): 1–6.

10. Excerpt from Lieutenant Hilal's Study taken from "The Kurds in Syria and Lebanon" by Ismet Cheriff Vanly, in *The Kurds: A Contemporary Overview*, ed. Philip Kreyenbroek and Stefan Sperl (London: Routledge, 2005), 4–5

11. Excerpt from Lieutenant Hilal's Study taken from "The Kurds in Syria and Lebanon."

12. Excerpt from Lieutenant Hilal's Study taken from "The Kurds in Syria and Lebanon,"

13. Maisel, *Yezidis in Syria*, 29.

14. "Syrian Citizenship Disappeared: How the 1962 Census Destroyed Stateless Kurds' Lives and Identities," *Syrians for Truth and Justice*, 2018. https://stj-sy.org/uploads/pdf_files/Syrian%20Citizenship%20Disappeared%20-%20How%20the%201962%20Census%20destroyed%20stateless%20Kurds'%20lives%20and%20identities.pdf.

15. "Consequences of Statelessness: Ajanib and Maktoum in Syria" (MA thesis, *Amsterdam Free University*, 2011), 56. Cited in Thomas McGee, "The Stateless Kurds of Syria," *Tilburg Law Review* 9 (2014): 171–181.

16. Maisel, *Yezidis in Syria,*120.

17. "The role of the YPG, YPJ, and SDF in the war against ISIS," Dossier for the International Forum on ISIS: Dimensions, Challenges and Strategies of Confrontation, *Rojava Center for Strategic Studies*, 2019.

18. Author interview with Ilyas from the Yezidi House in northern Syria. Communication via WhatsApp on July 3, 2020.

19. For a discussion of the US response to the crimes committed by ISIS against the Yezidi community, see: "By Any Other Name: How, When, and Why the United States Has Made Genocide Determinations" by Todd Buchwald and Adam Keith, published by the *United States Holocaust Memorial Museum*, 2019. https://www.ushmm.org/m/pdfs/Todd_Buchwald_Report_031819.pdf.

20. Nadia Al-Dayel and Andrew Mumford, "ISIS and Their Use of Slavery," *International Centre for Counter-Terrorism*, January 27, 2020. https://icct.nl/publication/isis-and-their-use-of-slavery/.

21. Commission of Inquiry on the Syrian Arab Republic, "They Came to Destroy: ISIS Crimes against the Yazidis" (Geneva: United Nations Human Rights Council, 2016), 32.

22. Ibid.

23. Charter of the Social Contract (2014).

24. Author Interview with a Yezidi originally from a village near Amude who emigrated to Germany in the 1990s. When I met him, it was his first time to return to Syria in 26 years; July 2019 in Syria.
25. Maisel, *Yezidis in Syria*, 1.
26. "Annual Report: 2020." *United States Commission on International Religious Freedom* (USCIRF) 41 (2020).
27. Maisel, *Yezidis in Syria*, 147.
28. Maisel, *Yezidis in Syria*, 148.
29. Maisel, *Yezidis in Syria*, 150
30. Tracey Shelton, "If It Wasn't for the Kurdish fighters, We Would Have Died Up There," *GlobalPost*, August 29, 2014. https://www.pri.org/stories/2014-08-29/if-it-wasn-t-kurdish-fighters-we-would-have-died-there.
31. Mancusco, "Where Are the Nuremberg Trials for the Yezidis?"
32. Tanya Mehra and Matthew Wentworth, "New Kid on the Block: Prosecution of ISIS Fighters by the Autonomous Administration of North and East Syria," *International Centre for Counter-Terrorism*, March 16, 2021. https://icct.nl/publication/prosecution-of-isis-fighters-by-autonomous-administration-of-north-east-syria/.
33. "Who Is Shamima Begum and How Do You Lose Your UK Citizenship?" *BBC News*, March 2, 2021. https://www.bbc.com/news/explainers-5342819.
34. Author Interview with Judge Amina and Judge Hassan, in Syria, September 2020.
35. "The Anti-Terror Trial System in NES," *Rojava Information Center*. March 13, 2021. https://rojavainformationcenter.com/2021/03/the-anti-terror-trial-system-in-nes/.
36. Mehra and Wentworth, "New Kid on the Block," *International Centre for Counter-Terrorism*.
37. Quote from an interview with prosecutor whose name was withheld for security reasons. Interview conducted by the Rojava Information Center, "The Anti-Terror Trial System in NES." https://rojavainformationcenter.com/2021/03/the-anti-terror-trial-system-in-nes/.
38. Mehra and Wentworth, "New Kid on the Block," *International Centre for Counter-Terrorism*.
39. "Une centaine de jihadistes français sont détenus en Syrie, selon Le Drian," *France 24*, July 2, 2018. https://www.france24.com/fr/20180207-jihadistes-francais-centaine-detenus-syrie-le-drian-irak-familles-rapatriement-justice.
40. Louisa Loveluck and Mustafa Salim, "Yazidi Women Raped as ISIS Slaves Face Brutal Homecoming Choice: Give Up Their Child or Stay Away," *Washington Post*, July 30, 2019. https://www.washingtonpost.com/world/middle_east/yazidi-women-raped-as-isis-slaves-face-brutal-homecoming-choice-give-up-their-child-or-stay-away/2019/07/30/f753c1be-a490-11e9-b7b4-95e30869bd15_story.html.
41. Ibid.
42. Zana Omer and Namo Abdulla, "The Yazidi Women Who Do Not Want to Be Known," *VOA News*, February 25, 2021. https://www.voanews.com/extremism-watch/yazidi-women-who-do-not-want-be-known.
43. In addition to Turkish soldiers, the following are the armed groups known to be operating in Afrin: Hamza Division, Ahrar al-Sham, Jaysh al-Islam, Faylaq al-Sham, National Front for Liberation, Sultan Murad, Mu'tasim Billah Brigade, Faylaq al-Majd, Firka Shimal, Rijal al-Harb, and others.
44. "Demographic Change in Rural Ras al-Ain: Yazidi Community Face Systematic Violations by Turkish-Backed Factions in More Than Ten Villages," *Syrian Observatory for Human Rights*, April 20, 2020. https://www.syriahr.com/en/160922/.
45. Elizabeth Hagedorn, "Now We Await Our Fate: Displaced Yezidis Fear Loss of Land in Syria," *The New Arab*, November 1, 2019. https://english.alaraby.co.uk/english/indepth/2019/11/1/displaced-yazidis-fear-loss-of-land-in-syria.
46. Amy Austin Holmes and Lerna Ekmekçioğlu, "Armenian Genocide Descendants Face Another Turkish Onslaught, One Century Later," *Belfer Center for Science and International Affairs*, November 25, 2019. https://www.belfercenter.org/publication/armenian-genocide-descendants-face-another-turkish-onslaught-one-century-later.
47. See the official White House statement announcing the ceasefire on October 17: "The United States and Turkey Agree to Ceasefire in Northeast Syria," October 17, 2019. https://www.whitehouse.gov/briefings-statements/united-states-turkey-agree-ceasefire-northeast-syria/.

48. Alex Ward, "The Syrian Ceasefire the US Brokered Is Already Falling Apart," *Vox*, October 18, 2019. https://www.vox.com/world/2019/10/18/20920806/syria-turkey-ceasefire-trump-kurds-pence.

49. These four testimonies were published originally in my report, "Threats Perceived and Real: New Data and the Need for a New Approach to the Conflict," Wilson Center, Occasional Paper Series No. 39, May 2021. https://www.wilsoncenter.org/publication/threats-perceived-and-real-new-data-and-need-new-approach-turkish-sdf-border-conflict.

Chapter 9

1. In this concluding chapter, I summarize the main arguments laid out in the book. Bibliographic references are included in the previous chapters.

2. "Regarding the situation in Hasakah, Syria," US Central Command, Special Operations Joint Task Force—Levant / Public Affairs Office, January 30, 2022. https://www.centcom.mil/MEDIA/NEWS-ARTICLES/News-Article-View/Article/2917023/regarding-the-situation-in-hasakah-syria/.

3. Statement by UNICEF Executive Director Henrietta Fore, "Children Caught Up in al Hasakah Prison Violence Must Be Evacuated to Safety," January 25, 2022. https://www.unicef.org/press-releases/children-caught-al-hasakah-prison-violence-must-be-evacuated-safety.

4. Statement by The SDF Media Centre Regarding The So-Called "Caliphate Cubs," January 27, 2022. https://sdf-press.com/en/2022/01/statement-by-the-sdf-media-centre-regarding-the-so-called-caliphate-cubs/.

5. Jacqueline H.R. Demeritt, Angela D. Nichols, and Eliza G. Kelly, "Female Participation and Civil War Relapse," *Civil Wars* 16, no. 3 (2014): 346–368.

6. Amy Austin Holmes, "Arabs across Syria Join the Kurdish-Led Syrian Democratic Forces," *Middle East Report Online*, July 28, 2020.

7. U.S. Department of the Treasury, "Treasury Sanctions Syrian Regime Prisons, Officials, and Syrian Armed Group," July 28, 2021. https://home.treasury.gov/news/press-releases/jy0292.

8. Rebecca Anne Proctor, "Drone Attacks Mount in Syria as SDF Anticipates Turkish Attack Amid Quake Crisis," *The Defense Post*, February 16, 2023. https://www.thedefensepost.com/2023/02/16/turkey-drone-attacks-syria/.

9. Amy Austin Holmes, "Threats Perceived and Real: New Data and the Need for a New Approach to the Turkish-SDF Border Conflict," *Wilson Center Occasional Paper Series*, No. 39, May 2021.

10. "Read the Memo by a U.S. Diplomat Criticizing Trump Policy on Syria and Turkey," *The New York Times*, November 7, 2019. https://www.nytimes.com/2019/11/07/us/politics/memo-syria-trump-turkey.html.

11. Isaac Chotiner, "Q.&A. The Former U.S. ISIS Envoy on Trump and the Crisis in Syria," *The New Yorker*, October 19, 2019. https://www.newyorker.com/news/q-and-a/theformer-us-isis-envoy-on-trump-and-the-crisis-in-syria.

Appendix

1. The law in Arabic is available at http://www.parliament.gov.sy/arabic/index.php?node=5571&cat=16006.

2. Sarah Williamson, "Syrian Women in Crisis: Obstacles and Opportunities," in *Occasional Paper Series: Women's Economic Participation in Conflict Afflicted and Fragile Settings*, Georgetown Institute for Women, Peace and Security, January 2016. https://giwps.georgetown.edu/wp-content/uploads/2017/08/Occasional-Paper-Series-Womens-Economic-Participation.pdf.

3. Matthew Krause, "Northeastern Syria: Complex Criminal Law in a Complicated Battlespace," *Just Security*, October 28, 2019. https://www.justsecurity.org/66725/northeastern-syria-complex-criminal-law-in-a-complicated-battlespace/.

4. Krause, "Northeastern Syria."

5. United Nations, General Assembly, *Report of the Independent International Commission of Inquiry on the Syrian Arab Republic,* A/HRC/45/31. September 15, 2020. https://undocs.org/A/HRC/45/31.

6. Khaled al-Khateb, "Northern Syria Takes Step toward New Judicial System," *Al Monitor,* October 5, 2018. https://www.al-monitor.com/originals/2018/10/syria-euphrates-shield-area-turkey-justice-palace-courts.html#ixzz764rmzSIr.

7. Syrians for Truth and Justice, "Ongoing Violations Without Accountability: Islamic State Members in the Syrian National Army," June 28, 2021. https://stj-sy.org/en/ongoing-violations-without-accountability-islamic-state-members-in-the-syrian-national-army/.

8. World Education News and Reviews, "The Education System in Syria," April 4, 2016. https://wenr.wes.org/2016/04/education-in-syria.

9. The Kurdish, Arabic and Aramaic-language textbooks used by the AANES can be viewed here: https://minhac.info/.

10. "Syria to Face First Severe Bread Shortages Since Start of War," *VOA News,* July 9, 2020. https://www.voanews.com/middle-east/syria-face-first-severe-bread-shortages-start-war.

11. David Butter, "Syria's Economy Picking up the Pieces," Chatham House, June 2015, 3. https://pdfs.semanticscholar.org/c1d9/209388a6864030e0fc258693bcc0c9223518.pdf.

12. Khayrallah al-Hilu, "The Turkish Intervention in Northern Syria: One Strategy, Discrepant Policies," *European University Institute,* 2021. https://web.archive.org/web/20210204031148/https://cadmus.eui.eu/bitstream/handle/1814/69657/Khayrallah%20al-Hilu%20-%20The%20Turkish%20Intervention%20in%20Northern%20Syria%20One%20Strategy%20Discrepant%20Policies.pdf?sequence=1&isAllowed=y.

13. Saleh Malass, "How Have Provisions of "Honor Killings" Evolved in Syrian Law," *Enab Baladi,* March 19, 2020. https://english.enabbaladi.net/archives/2020/03/how-have-provisions-of-honor-killings-evolved-in-syrian-law/.

14. Williamson, "Syrian Women in Crisis." https://giwps.georgetown.edu/wp-content/uploads/2017/08/Occasional-Paper-Series-Womens-Economic-Participation.pdf.

15. Meghan Bodette, "Syrian Women's Leadership in a Fractured State," *Wilson Center Middle East Program,* April 1, 2020. https://www.wilsoncenter.org/article/syrian-womens-leadership-fractured-state.

16. See the text of the Women's Laws as passed in 2014 on the website of Kongra Star at https://eng.kongra-star.org/2019/04/06/womens-laws-in-rojava-northern-syria/.

17. United Nations, General Assembly, *Report of the Independent International Commission of Inquiry on the Syrian Arab Republic,* A/HRC/45/31. September 15, 2020. https://undocs.org/A/HRC/45/31.

18. See the 2017 Social Contract of the Democratic Federation of Northern Syria at https://internationalistcommune.com/social-contract/.

19. Amy Austin Holmes and Wladimir van Wilgenburg, "The International Community Must Stop Turkey's Ethnic Cleansing Plans in Northern Syria," *Washington Post,* October 11, 2019. https://www.washingtonpost.com/opinions/2019/10/11/international-community-must-stop-turkeys-ethnic-cleansing-plans-northern-syria/.

20. Cited in "Syria 2020 International Religious Freedom Report," https://www.justice.gov/eoir/page/file/1397631/download.

21. United States Commission on International Religious Freedom, *Annual Report 2021,* 44–46. https://www.uscirf.gov/sites/default/files/2021-04/2021%20Annual%20Report.pdf.

22. Bodette, "Syrian Women's Leadership in a Fractured State. https://www.wilsoncenter.org/article/syrian-womens-leadership-fractured-state.

23. See the 2017 Social Contract of the Democratic Federation of Northern Syria at https://internationalistcommune.com/social-contract/.

24. Khayrallah al-Hilu, "Afrin Under Turkish Control: Political, Economic and Social Transformations," *European University Institute,* 2019. https://web.archive.org/web/20201005132525/https://cadmus.eui.eu/bitstream/handle/1814/63745/MED_2019_10.pdf?sequence=3&isAllowed=y.

25. Al-Hilu, "The Turkish Intervention in Northern Syria."

INDEX

For the benefit of digital users, indexed terms that span two pages (e.g., 52–53) may, on occasion, appear on only one of those pages.

Tables, figures, and boxes are indicated by *t*, *f*, and *b* following the page number